W9-DIW-172

WITHDRAWN

CULTURE, THOUGHT, AND DEVELOPMENT

The Jean Piaget Symposium Series
Available from LEA

OVERTON, W. F. (Ed.) • The Relationship Between Social and Cognitive Development

LIBEN, L. S. (Ed.) • Piaget and the Foundations of Knowledge

SCHOLNICK, E. K. (Ed.) • New Trends in Conceptual Representation: Challenges to Piaget's Theory?

NEIMARK, E. D., DeLISI, R., & NEWMAN, J. L., (Eds.) • Moderators of Competence

BEARISON, D. J., & ZIMILES, H. (Eds.) • Thought and Emotion: Developmental Perspectives

LIBEN, L. S. (Ed.) • Development and Learning: Conflict or Congruence?

FORMAN, G., & PUFALL, P. B. (Eds.) • Constructivism in the Computer Age

OVERTON, W. F., (Ed.) • Reasoning, Necessity, and Logic: Developmental Perspectives

KEATING, D. P. & ROSEN, H. (Eds.) • Constructivist Perspectives on Developmental Psychopathology and Atypical Development

CAREY, S., & GELMAN, R. (Eds.) • The Epigenesis of Mind: Essays on Biology

BEILIN, H., & PUFALL, P. (Eds.) • Piaget's Theory: Prospects and Possibilities

WOZNIAK, R. H., & FISCHER, K. W. (Eds.) • Development in Context: Acting and Thinking in Specific Environments

OVERTON, W. F., & PALERMO, D. S. (Eds.) • The Nature and Ontogenesis of Meaning

NOAM, G. G., & FISCHER, K. W. (Eds.) • Development and Vulnerability in Close Relationships

REED, E. S., TURIEL, E., & BROWN, T. (Eds.) • Values and Knowledge

AMSEL, E., & RENNINGER, K. A. (Eds.) • Change and Development: Issues of Theory, Method, and Application

LANGER, J., & KILLEN, M. (Eds.) • Piaget, Evolution, and Development

SCHOLNICK, E., NELSON, K., GELMAN, S. A., & MILLER, P. H. (Eds.) • Conceptual Development: Piaget's Legacy

NUCCI, L. P., SAXE, G. B., & TURIEL, E. (Eds.) • Culture, Thought, and Development

CULTURE, THOUGHT, AND DEVELOPMENT

Edited by

Larry P. Nucci
The University of Illinois at Chicago

Geoffrey B. Saxe
Elliot Turiel
University of California, Berkeley

LAWRENCE ERLBAUM ASSOCIATES, PUBLISHERS

2000   Mahwah, New Jersey   London

Lawrence Erlbaum Associates, Inc., Publishers
10 Industrial Avenue
Mahwah, New Jersey 07430

Cover design by Kathryn Houghtaling Lacey

Library of Congress Cataloging-in-Publication Data

Culture, thought, and development / edited by Larry P. Nucci, Geoffrey B. Saxe, Elliot Turiel.
    p. cm. – (The Jean Piaget Symposium Series)
    Includes bibliographical references and indexes.
    ISBN 0-8058-3009-X (cloth : alk. Paper)
    1.   Culture. 2. Social evolution. 3. Developmental psychology. I. Nucci, Larry P. II.
Saxe, Geoffrey B. III. Turiel, Elliot. IV. Series.

HM626 .C85 2000
306—dc21

          00-042207

Printed in the United States of America
10   9   8   7   6   5   4   3   2   1

Contents

Preface

Efforts to understand relations between culture and human development are longstanding in the social and behavioral sciences. It is infrequent, however, that scholars pursuing varied questions related to the topic have the opportunity for sustained interaction. The 1997 meetings of the Jean Piaget Society in Santa Monica, California, were planned to support just this kind of protracted cross-disciplinary exchange. This volume consists principally of invited contributions to the meeting. In addition, we are grateful to contributors who were not able to attend, including Penelope Brown and Stephen Levinson, as well as Martha Nussbaum.

The collection of chapters is unusual. All depart in significant ways from the "received" accounts of relations between culture and human development. In what we take as the received view, culture and the individual are understood as separate entities, and the crux of scholarly questions concern whether or in what way one factor—culture of the individual—affects change in the other.

Such received accounts vary widely. Some argue that culture and individual are autonomous, neither affecting the other in any fundamental way. For instance, one might argue that the development of the individual is controlled principally by self-regulative processes (e.g., biological) and that culture change is controlled principally by social or economic forces. Other accounts argue for causal relations—typically that the development of the individual is a product of cultural life. Such latter accounts vary with the kind of development that is to be explained. For instance, childrearing practices may be studied as a factor that affects the moral or affective development of children, or language may be studied as a factor that affects children's classifications.

This volume contains a host of fresh perspectives. Often, authors seek to reconceptualize problems, offering new frames for understanding relations between culture and human development. Accounts often span disciplinary boundaries. Indeed, contributors to this volume include scholars from the disciplines of philosophy (Margolis); philosophy, law, and theology (Nussbaum); anthropology (Levinson, Strauss); developmental psychology (Brown, Greenfield, Nucci, Turiel); neuro- and evolutionary psychology (Donald); linguistics (Bowerman); and cognitive science and physics (diSessa). To help organize the discussion, we have partitioned the volume into three parts. Each part reflects an arena of scholarly activity related to the analysis of culture, cognition, and development.

EPISTEMOLOGICAL ISSUES

Two chapters address epistemological issues in the study and analysis of human development from a cultural perspective. Margolis, from the perspective of a philosopher, presents an extended argument about methods. Donald, from the perspective of a neuro- and evolutionary psychologist, offers a perspective on hominid evolution focusing on the emergence of both culture and higher cognitive functions.

Margolis' argument is an extended cautionary note on methods—what we can know and how we can know it in analyses of infant cognition. He points to what he sees as a key constraint on efforts to understand cognition in the preverbal (or "precultural") infant. Margolis argues that the analyst is always in the unfortunate posture of anthropomorphizing the psychology of infant cognition, attributing what come to be cultural constructions of mind involving intention and purpose. This is an unfortunate but intrinsic condition of the analytic enterprise.

Donald offers a very different epistemological argument. With a broad stroke, Donald frames the problem of understanding relations between culture and development in evolutionary terms, exploring a symbiosis between the origins of our species, the emergence of culture, and the dawn of human thought. He seeks to understand the "ecological" relations between these evolving systems as well as pointing to continuities and discontinuities in the nature of the transformations in each during the past 5 million years.

PERSONAL, SOCIAL, AND AFFECTIVE DEVELOPMENT

Four chapters address issues related to culture and personal and social development. Cultural treatments of personal and social development have often been regarded as problems of social reproduction—how individuals' identities, characters, and social understandings are molded by the communities in which they are reared and function. Each of the chapters in the volume, from individuals working in quite different disciplines, departs from this tack in interesting ways.

In her chapter on emotions and social norms, Nussbaum offers a framework to understand emotional development. She points out that taxonomies for emotions vary across societies. She argues that even what might be considered "generic emotions"—love, fear, grief, anger, jealousy, envy, and compassion—have varying manifestations across cultures, and points out that there is some but by no means complete correspondence across emotional categories. She also argues that, although the variant cultural constitutions of emotion afford particular paths of human affective development, that development is also crafted by individuals themselves, reflecting "intelligent pieces of human normative activity." The interplay between social categories of emotion and individual variation and choice in emotional expression and development presents for Nussbaum an important vehicle for personal growth and social change.

In their chapter titled "Continuities of Selfhood in the Face of Radical Developmental and Cultural Change," Chandler, Lalonde, and Sokol explore an area that has received increasing attention by individuals working in a range of social science disciplines—personal identity. Whereas in prior work positions were polarized as arguing for universal developmental processes that occur insulated from culture or for a culture-oriented situationalism in which culture molds individuals into particular identities, these authors argue that what is needed is a fresh approach that incorporates multiple levels of analysis. In their view, all accounts of the development of personal identity must allow for construction of a sense of self-continuity in which situational or age-related changes in the person still result in a sense that these changes belong to the same individual. Culture interacts with this transcultural element of selfhood to provide the particular operational strategy for maintaining self-continuity.

Strauss, in "The Culture Concept of the Individualism-Collectivism Debate: Dominant and Alternative Attributions for Class in the United States," presents a distinction that is common in discourse on cultural and social development—individualism and collectivism. Strauss points out that in the 1990s literature, cultures are conceptualized as points on a linear dimension. At one pole, collectivist societies are characterized as composed of individuals with interdependent self-definitions, who give to group goals, who focus on social norms and duties, and who value the maintenance of interpersonal relationships. In contrast, individualist societies are characterized as composed of individuals who have independent self-definitions, who value personal goals, needs and rights, and who value personal relationships to the extent that they are personally advantageous. Strauss argues that the characterization of societies along this dimension is at best only partially useful. Based on interview data with working- and middle-class U.S. residents, Strauss points out that one cannot move from findings of predominance of orientation to conclusions that such predominance measures "cultural syndromes." This is because expressions of a predominant orientation, such as individualism, cover broad and often opposite meanings. In addition, these modes of individualism may vary across social classes although appearing on the surface to express the same dominant ideology.

In chapter 6, Nucci and Turiel argue for the necessity of attending to heterogeneity in analyses of development, thought, and culture. Our analyses focus on interactive, reciprocal processes of culture and thought at all levels of development. We maintain that starting in childhood, the interplay of moral and personal judgments produce both acceptance of and conflict over social norms and practices. Adolescence entails further development of moral judgments along with increased assertions of a personal sphere of activities. We show that the personal and moral domains, in conjunction with elements of social hierarchies, produce conflicts and contested understandings within cultures. Furthermore, we argue that current efforts to dichotomize cultures into one or another set of properties (such constructs as individualistic vs. collectivistic cultures) obscure contradictions and the seeds of change in human activity, social arrangements, and social cognition.

THE DEVELOPMENT OF PHYSICAL AND SPATIAL KNOWLEDGE

The volume's final part is concerned with how children come to make sense of their physical and social worlds as they grow in a complex matrix of social practices. In his chapter, diSessa explores relations between the development of physical and social cognition in developing children. The two subsequent chapters, one by Brown and Levinson and the other by Bowerman, focus on relations between language and spatial cognition. In the last chapter, Greenfield provides an analysis of weaving in a Mayan community, using her case as a forum for a general treatment of relations between historical change and children's cognitive development.

DiSessa, a physicist by training, explores the extension of his framework on physical knowledge to the social world. Key to diSessa's discussion is whether the construct of "phenomenological-primitives"—low-level abstractions of regularities children abstract from their physical experience—might also be used by children to organize social phenomena. DiSessa covers much ground, critiquing positions on modularity and situationalism. He argues that physical and social knowledge—at least key structural dimensions of each—are organized by the same constructivist processes. Furthermore, over development, the transformations in physical and social knowledge inform one another, development and learning involving an interaction across domains.

Brown and Levinson report on research conducted with Mayan children speaking Tzeltal and describe a linguistic system that differs fundamentally in its structuring of space from most of today's languages. Through developmental analyses, Brown and Levinson find that children acquire the Euclidean-Absolute system (one in which space is defined by lines and specific angles) prior to a topological-intrinsic system (one that groups all figures on the basis of whether they share global features such as containment and surface support), a finding that reverses the order of Piagetian findings in children's conceptual development. Brown and Levinson argue that these findings alone do not in themselves discount a Piagetian view of conceptual development. However, they argue that conceptual development may not be particularly important for the acquisition of spatial terms and that the acquisition of a particular linguistic system may frame children's interactions with their spatial world in system-specific ways that have implications for the developing child's subsequent intellectual constructions.

Like Brown and Levinson, Bowerman considers relations between language and spatial cognition. Instead of focusing on a single case, Bowerman widens her lens and surveys different language communities. She shows that languages differ remarkably in how they structure spatial categories. Furthermore, she shows that very early in their production and comprehension of language, children are sensitive to the particular ways in which languages partition space. Bowerman clearly acknowledges that the development of spatial cognition does not begin with the onset of language and presents a case for an important interplay between children's linguistic and conceptual activities over the course of development.

Greenfield's chapter ends the collection with an integrative analysis of the interplay between maturational, sociocultural, historical, and ecological processes in development. Greenfield's analytic frame unfolds as she describes research on weaving, a practice that has been alive since pre-Columbian times, in Nabenchauk, a Mayan community in Chiapas, Mexico. She offers a model for a conceptualization of development as constituted by age-dependent periods for cultural learning, arguing that similar stages in development will take different forms across cultures linked to the historically driven practices with which individuals are engaged.

We cast a wide but carefully crafted net in assembling contributions to this volume. Although the contributors span a wide range of disciplines, features common to the work include both clear departures from the polemics of nature-nurture debates and clear focus on interacting systems in individuals' activities, leading to novel developmental processes. All accounts are efforts to mark new and productive paths for exploring intrinsic relations between culture and development.

The 1997 meetings of the Jean Piaget Society were a critical success. We hope that the interested reader will come away with some sense of the enormity of the contributors' analytic task, the importance of the contributions, and a sense of the synergy generated by the collected efforts.

—*Larry P. Nucci*
—*Geoffrey B. Saxe*
—*Elliot Turiel*

Part I

EPISTEMOLOGICAL ISSUES

Would You Say Developmental Psychology Was a Science? The Cultural Paradigm of Mind

Joseph Margolis
Temple University

ANTHROPOMORPHIZING PRELINGUISITIC THOUGHT

We are, I think, at an extraordinary place in our theorizing about the human mind—a fortiori, about any mind, no matter how different it may be from ours. Piaget is the great initiator of our best contemporary efforts to understand the development of intelligence in children from the earliest prelinguistic and "preoperational" stages (which are not the same, as Piaget makes clear) to the dawning of linguistic competence and the maturation, within its terms, of the fullest forms of rational and logical order that we know. About that continuum, I have a great many qualifications to insist on, most of which, I daresay, Piaget would have opposed; although it is my honest belief—if you do not mind the impertinence—that he would have been well advised to come to terms with most of them. There! I cannot displease you more by the details of my own theory than by this frontal confession: I feel sure you will allow me to continue as a self-acknowledged deviationist without portfolio; there cannot be much harm in it because it is hardly meant to misrepresent Piaget's own doctrine.

What I think is extraordinary about our theorizing about the mind's development, working at the end of the 20th century, is that we are poised rather uncertainly between the poles of Piaget's original inquiries about its earliest stages and the recent flowering of new inquiries into artificial intelligence and the machine simulation of intelligence. Now, it is at that

3

precise point that I intrude a suggestion for the largest possible departure—
the largest I can imagine—from Piaget's very sane and sensible observations
about prelinguistic children. Here, I claim, the description of prelinguistic
thought in children, not at all unlike the description of the minds of sublinguistic animals, machines, and even the biology of the brain and body
thought to be implicated in what we are pleased to call the development
of the mind, is always anthropomorphized and cannot but be anthropomorphized, in the sense that such descriptions are modeled on the paradigm of mental life—the reflexive, selfconscious, linguistically apt capacity of encultured human selves (ourselves) in the way of reporting what
they are conscious or aware of.

I do not mean by this that there is no nonlinguistic thinking or consciousness; or that there is none among the linguistically apt; or that the
prelinguistic cannot intelligibly be said to exhibit processes very different
from what obtain among linguistically apt adults or in the stages of early
language acquisition; or that there are no significant idiosyncratic variations at both the prelinguistic and linguistic stages; or that there are no
important species-specific differences between prelinguistic human and
sublinguistic animal intelligence; or that the successful machine simulation of the human mind rightly counts as an accurate description of
human mental processes. No. I mean only that, in observing and describing the intelligence of prelinguistic children (and the rest), we cannot
escape the endogenous constraint of having to subtract from, deform, or
qualify, what, reflexively, we theorize obtains at the languaged and "operational" level at which we describe ourselves—when we describe the minds
of children or other creatures or machines or, indeed, the biology or sub-
conscious processes of the mind.

In a word, psychology rightly proceeds top down, although most of the
prevailing models—neurocomputational or simply materialist—favor bottom up strategies. (See Sellars, 1963; Churchland, 1989.) I do not say psychology is necessarily top down, only that every known bottom-up exemplar fails to make its case. Top-down conceptions win faute de mieux. At
any rate, that is the essential focus of dispute in the whole of psychology
at the end of the 20th century. Piaget, I should say, was a top-down theorist who, however, reversed the priorities between children and adults: his
principal work does not concede that the development of the child's intelligence must be seen, top down, from the reporting vantage of our reflexive description of ourselves. That is the nerve of Piaget's structuralism (see
Piaget, 1971a).

To be sure, this is not an innocent or modest adjustment; it is not meant
to be. There are enormous, wide-ranging consequences that follow from
this single confession. For instance, with this argument, a modular theory
of mind proves impossible: I mean one such as the innatist doctrine

Chomsky (1980a) and Fodor (1983) proposed (in somewhat different ways). I should say that Chomsky's notion of a universal grammar cannot rightly be modular, can only be "homuncular" (or modular in the homuncular way); although saying that hardly disallows some forms of innatism. I may as well say that I have the gravest doubts about Chomsky's universal grammar—which, of course, cannot be what it is said to be if strict modularism fails. Cognitive intelligence cannot be completely modular in any one creature; that would be a contradiction in terms. On the anthropomorphizing thesis, it cannot but fail, because the posit of a modular grammar will require positing a whole series of associated modules, from the conjoint functioning of which the seemingly molar functioning of an integrated human subject would first emerge or be derived. By *homuncular*, by contrast, I mean precisely the subfunctioning of any would-be module (or nonmodular process) as a relationally defined part of some molar functioning, without reference to which it (the subfunctional function) designates nothing. I believe it to be a very strong intuition of Piaget's that we cannot map the development of the child's intelligence except by internalizing in constructivist terms the mental import of the child's overt bodily activity. (See Piaget & Inhelder, 1969.)

With that much I wholly agree. I go on to insist, however, that the modeling of the child's molar intelligence is itself anthropomorphized in terms of the paradigm of "self-conscious" mind: our reflexive reporting capacity. Even at the adult level, of course, it is clear (in the reporting sense) that the human mind is not a mere language machine. Beyond that, I permit myself two inferences against certain fairly well-known views in the philosophical literature regarding the nature of mind. Nagel (1979), for one, is very well known for having raised the question, "What is it like to be a bat?" (that is, seen from the "inside"). Nagel intended to draw attention to the puzzle implicit in admitting minds in the first place (which, he believed, could not be adequately characterized in physical terms) and the impossibility of characterizing the mind of the bat conformably (because we are not bats). Nagel, I should say, was mistaken in his second claim: bats do not know what it is like to be a bat; only humans do! That is the lesson "anthropomorphizing" affords. Only human adults know what it is like to be a prelinguistic child. Piaget (I think) ultimately agrees, although this seems much clearer in his later than in his earlier work. It is certainly not compatible with his structuralism, strictly construed.

Again, if this picture be correct, then, as far as we understand machine intelligence, it must be the case that human intelligence cannot be adequately simulated by an intelligent machine because, of course, machine intelligence is thoroughly modular and human intelligence cannot be. If that is so, then computational models of the mind as different as those advanced by Dennett and Churchland (familiar, I am supposing, to developmental psychologists) must be utterly mistaken, although that is not to say that we cannot admit modular subfunctions keyed to parts of our neurophysiology (parts of the cerebellum, for instance) within the homuncular model that I have already acknowledged may be needed. It goes without saying that, apart from simulation, the human mind cannot be modeled neurocomputationally. (See Dennett, 1969; Churchland, 1989; Edelman, 1987).

You may, of course, contest this strong verdict—to the effect that the human mind cannot be adequately simulated or analyzed in machine terms. I defer to some extent to your objection. I do believe, however, that the verdict is the correct one, but it would take us too far afield to draw out the necessary argument. The matter depends on what we make of the molar powers of encultured selves (or encultured minds). I myself make a great deal of that, too much in fact for any mere intelligent machine to acquire, unless it already begins to be an android of some sort—capable of being encultured in the way human infants are.

Let me mention, then, two insuperable difficulties to fix our ideas against the reductive and eliminative strategies: for one, the well-known "frame" problem; for another, the problem of explaining reference and predication in mental terms. As I see matters, these are very closely related problems. I shall touch on the second only, in order to make matters clearer—but not yet. In any case, there is no algorithmic solution to either problem, which is precisely why machine simulation and analysis are limited in the way they are. If machines functioned in a molar way akin to the human mode of functioning, then (on the argument) they could not function computationally. If their functioning were completely modular and computational, they could not but be subaltern (homuncular) modes of functioning, and they could never adequately model human functioning. If that be so, then strong nativisms, such as Chomsky's and Fodor's, must fail because they too are modular, which is to say, modeled on the structure of machine simulation. The only possible way to turn the tables would be to provide a completely modular—hence, a computationally conceivable—analysis of the cognitive powers of the human mind. But if no (psychological or cognitive) module were cognitively penetrable from another would-be module internal to the same creature, the model proposed would instantly fail to capture what was most characteristic of human cognition functioning at the molar level. You see the heroic difficulty the bottom-up theorists embrace.

Part of my argument, I must concede, is directed against Piaget. Although Piaget rightly opposes Chomsky's innatism, chiefly (as I understand it) because Chomsky does not distinguish with sufficient care between the prelinguistic and preoperational aspects of the child's development (about which I thoroughly agree), Piaget himself is not altogether convincing in his efforts to explain and justify the necessary concatenation of the constructed stages of prelinguistic intelligence. If you permit the observation, I fear you will also have to concede that Chomsky will have very cleverly caught Piaget, in their well-known debate, when Chomsky (1980b) questioned Piaget about the invariant sequence of the structured stages of childhood development. The weakness of Piaget's argument is partly due to conceptual difficulties in his account of genetic structuralism, particularly with respect to the relationship between observational findings and structuralist interpretations (see Piaget, 1970), and partly due to the fact that there is no empirical way to construe the structuralist (the necessary) sequence of mental development except in innatist terms (that is, where environmental factors merely trigger the interior evolution of innate modules).

If Piaget had held to something like the homuncular model, he would have been obliged to concede an ampler and more variable development of the self's conceptual powers; conceding that, he would have drawn back from a strict structuralism and admitted the nonmodular (hence, significantly interactive) powers of molar selves within their environing worlds. I think this cannot be very far from Bruner's objection to Piaget (Bruner, 1983, ch. 8), for instance. Certainly it bears on whether, and when, a child can escape "egocentrism."(See Boden, 1979, ch. 3; Bruner, 1975; Vygotsky, 1962.)

My own objection is a little simpler. The very effort to map the developmental intelligence of the child proceeds in the reverse direction from that development; that is, it must be anthropomorphized, described, top down, in terms of the child's gradual "transformation" into a linguistically apt "self" (the functional "site," let us say, of such reflexively apt functioning). This is not to urge the exclusive importance of the purely linguistic, but emphasizes, instead, the peculiarity of developmental psychology viewed as a science.

If it is possible to begin to grasp the viewpoint of another, even at the sensorimotor level, as Bruner supposes, then Piaget must be seriously mistaken in his treatment of the relationship between structuralist and empirical work. It is just such a consideration that supports my remarks on modular and homuncular explanations and on the ubiquity of anthropomorphizing. What I am saying is this. First, it may, contrary to what Piaget supposes, be possible for children at the sensorimotor stage to begin to understand the viewpoint of another—which makes sense only if the modularist orientation is mistaken. Second, even the egocentric development of the child is, to some extent, an artifact of our anthropomorphizing, which goes against the strict autonomy of the structuralist method, particularly the reading of the evolution of intelligence. Third, the very formation (or "construction") or "morphogenesis" of the child's intelligence entails forms of collective enculturation, whether linguistic or prelinguistic, whether sensorimotor or more advanced, that require a less tendentious methodology than Piaget allows. In short, Piaget's strict structuralist analyses of intelligence determine what we may admit, empirically, in the study of the child; whereas the anthropomorphizing model concedes, quite frankly, that there is no empirical access to the child's cognitive development save through the anticipatory descriptions uniquely accessible to a society of already competent selves.

If one calls the modular model into question, one calls into question as well the evolutionary autonomy of the sequence of interactional processes between organism and environment—at least as far as intelligence goes—extending even to the pertinent developmental stages of the embryo. Piaget's strenuous interest in bringing his research to bear on the resolution of the Lamarckian/Darwinian quarrel may have obscured for him the ultimate disanalogy between the development of mind and the development of body. (See Piaget, 1971c; Waddington, 1957.) For, if one admits the sui generis nature of cultural formation, the would-be "ontogenetic" variations of the would-be "phylogenetic" evolution of the mind may mask the entirely different historical and culturally constructive processes by which a biologically gifted child is transformed into a linguistically and socially apt self.

THE PARADIGM OF THE MENTAL

Certainly, Piaget's paramount contribution (which I cannot pretend to assess with authority) is centered in the interplay between biological and cultural processes of "structuring" the intelligence of the prelinguistic and pre-operational child. There can be no question that Piaget's bias in favor of the self-regulating processes of epigenesis has alerted him in an unusually astute way to certain essential features of the earliest (sensorimotor) intelligence of the pre-encultured child. (I use the term *bias* deliberately here, but not with malice or derogatory intent.) Nevertheless, there are at least two fundamental objections to be lodged against Piaget's general treatment of the development of intelligence. One I have already explored: namely, the inescapably anthropomorphizing control of the description and explanation of the prelinguistic child's development. The other answers to the complexities of how we should understand cognition itself and why it is that the paradigm of the mental and the intelligent cannot but be formulated in terms of the paradigm of cognitive states.

The model of consciousness, I should say, is self-consciousness; and self-consciousness is, paradigmatically, the competence of human selves to report (linguistically) what they are conscious or aware of. Actually, it is the second theme that drives the first; that is, it is the epistemic paradigm of the mental that ensures the inevitability of anthropomorphizing the description of the intelligence of prelinguistic children. For, if you feature the cognitive side of the mental, you realize that you cannot address the mental life of children, animals, or machines except in terms of a linguistic model. Only if the cognitive could be reduced behaviorally, neurophysiologically, or computationally, could the irreducibility (hence the anthropomorphizing) of the cognitive be retired. Piaget obviously does not believe that that is possible—and, if I may say so, neither do I.

But it is one thing to admit irreducibility; it is quite another to insist on the necessary—structuralist—ingredients of knowledge itself (for instance, the alleged necessities of logic). Piaget (1971a, 1971b) makes a great deal of the inherent inadequacy of the contingent, descriptive, or empirical features of cognition as opposed to the underlying, necessary and necessarily linked, structuralist order of cognitive development. But if you feature the culturally constructed nature of the self, formed by the child's internalizing the language and collective practices of its environing society, then the import of treating the mental in terms of what is paradigmatically cognitive (which I take to be well-nigh ineluctable and which Piaget plainly favors) is at once that there cannot be a principled disjunction between the empirically descriptive and the supposedly necessary structuralist dimensions of cognition itself. If what is paradigmatic of the "minds of selves" is culturally constructed and if the description of the mental is anthropomorphized in terms of that paradigm (wherever the mental is itself other than encultured or enlanguaged), then (a) there are no strict necessities of the mental (in the epistemologist's sense); (b) the enculturing and cultural features of the mental cannot be captured by any extension of the biological or biologically grounded evolution of organisms or minds; and (c) whatever we posit as the sensorimotor, prelinguistic, and "intermediary" or "intuitive" stages of a child' s cognitive development cannot fail to be an artifact of our anthropomorphizing *tertia*.

I do not deny that Piaget makes concessions in this general direction, and I have no interest in entering the turf quarrels between the Piagetians and the non-Piagetians. But there is a decisive weakness in Piaget's account of the social life of the child, which, rightly understood, leads in the direction of correcting (if I may say so) his general theory. You will find a tactful sense of Piaget's tendency to scant the social—in friendly efforts toward rehabilitating his doctrine, in the face of a long history of objections. For example, in an effort to counter the often unfavorable reading of Piaget's reference to the social dimension of learning, particularly after he formulated a full picture of sensorimotor development, Lourenço and Machado (1996, p. 150) emphasized that, according to Piaget, "cognitive structures and operations come from the subject's own coordination and self-regulation"; and that, in spite of that, Piaget characteristically insists that, were it not for the social milieu of learning, "the individual would never achieve complete conservation and reversibility."

Now, I think there cannot be any doubt that when he speaks of the social context in which the child develops, prior to acquiring language and in originally acquiring language and operational competences "egocentrically," Piaget believes the child's development may well be facilitated ("triggered") socially, although the learning process is not itself (for that reason) essentially social—in the distinct sense of being inherently socialized, encultured, or characterizable as the mastery of competences that are collective or consensual and not reducible to any "compound" of prelinguistic competences. (See Piaget, 1950.) That, as I say, is what Chomsky astutely noticed.

My own theory insists on the primacy of the cultural—in epistemic terms. The paradigm of the mental (I argue) is and must be reflexively specified and hence is characterized in terms of our reporting—our cognitive—competence. But that same competence (what, minimally, we mean by *self-consciousness*) is an artifact of enculturation, the acquisition, in infancy, of a natural language and the emergence of a "self." A *self*, then, is simply (as matters now stand, because we know no extra-terrestrials) any member of *Homo sapiens* transformed or "second-natured" by the acquisition of a collectively shared language and culture—that is, a language and culture already mastered by an aggregate of apt adult selves. (See Margolis, 1997.) But in saying that, I do not deny at all that prelinguistic infants and nonlinguistic animals exhibit distinctive forms of intelligence and learning. I say only that what they exhibit is attributable under the reflexive paradigm.

What this shows is that Piaget has no clear way to demonstrate or dispute whether or to what extent the incipient enculturation of the human infant—quite apart from social facilitation—is an essential ingredient in any and every stage in the process of cognitive development. The argument is not (or not simply) that Piaget scants the social, but rather that he has no operative basis on which to confirm that the epigenetic development of the child is autonomous and evolutionary under favorable (social) conditions. As a structuralist, he does not agree that the child's development is inherently keyed to internalizing the sui generis features of cultural life.

I do not deny that the prelinguistic child begins to acquire a language by exercising its biologically grounded competences. But, I claim, the child (the member of *Homo sapiens*) is being transformed into a functioning self (becomes encultured) by acquiring linguistic competence; and the mark of that developing achievement is the very dawning of the child's reflexive, linguistic, reportorial, self-conscious, consensually focused, and cognizing powers.

The point is this. If the linguistic and the cultural cannot be constructed, bottom up, from the child's biologically grounded competence (triggered by its interaction with its environment—including its social environment), then structuralism fails. We should then have to fall back to the cognitive paradigm; and then, all other mental powers—genuine enough—will be anthropomorphized, under that model. Their description and analysis would be conceptually dependent on the model of reflexive reporting; although, within its terms, their own alien precultural quality may still be reasonably ascribed. There is no other way to proceed.

It is perfectly clear that we can never fix the point at which the prelinguistic yields to the linguistic or the egocentric to what is culturally shared. We infer, rather, that it must have been present after a certain threshold competence is posited. The very idea of that continuum is an artifact of our anthropomorphizing model: there is no independent, punctuated, developmental sequence from the precultural to the cultural, apart from how, from the vantage of our already encultured powers, we posit, retrospectively, something like Piaget's developmental scheme. But it cannot (although it remains objective) have the methodological standing of the precise structuralist sort Piaget supposes, that is, the verdict is a direct consequence of admitting (what I am calling) anthropomorphizing and the role of the model we invoke in anthropomorphized description and explanation.

TOP-DOWN AND BOTTOM-UP ANALYSES
OF DEVELOPMENTAL PSYCHOLOGY

There is something extremely bland about the argument I have been sketching. And yet, if the truth be known, it harbors some extraordinarily radical notions about the mind. First of all, I must say that I agree with Piaget in insisting that the mind and its development cannot be rightly described or explained in precisely the same way in which any randomly selected (noncognitional) natural phenomenon may be. For, if the mind is modeled cognitively ("epistemologically," as Piaget often says), then there is a uniquely close conceptual connection between mental states (which need not, of course, be forms of cognition) and cognitive states, on which (on the argument) validly affirming whatever we do affirm may be judged to be objectively correct. That is to say, in the paradigm (but not otherwise), mental and cognitive states cannot be segregated, and, there, cognitive states cannot be described as no more than a particular "first-order" natural phenomenon. Cognitive states—a fortiori, mental states as paradigmatically reported—implicate higher order legitimative concerns in virtue of which (sine qua non) we concede certain first-order mental states to count as states of knowledge. But, of course, the grounds for doing so cannot (so at least it seems) be captured by any mere biological, neurophysiological, behavioral, or computational process or state. The cognitive, you see, is both sui generis and second-order. That, on my argument, is why it cannot be *naturalized*, described and explained in terms of the causal order confined to the biological or the physical.

Now, if that is so (trivially so), then the analysis of the development of a child's intelligence cannot be straightforwardly mapped in any indisputably objective, observational way. It will have to be hostage, qua objective, to disputed second-order theories of what children can know and what, within our anthropomorphizing practice, we posit as the child's competence. For example, whether children at sensorimotor levels can or cannot, or do, however incipiently, grasp the viewpoint of another will substantively affect (a) the validity of Piaget's theory of the child's model of development, (b) the validity of any structuralist account of such development, and (c) what we should regard as the conditions of any objective account of a child's development. These are matters that are often ignored in disputes within and about the precincts of developmental psychology. I think they cannot be ignored.

There is a second puzzle that I should like to draw from another relatively bland concession—well, from the concession, perhaps not quite so bland as the first—that collects my anthropomorphizing thesis and the artifactual nature of the languaged mind that is the paradigm on which anthropomorphizing depends. What is mind, after all; or, what is the mind, in the paradigm? The answer is open to considerable dispute, just as the answer to the first puzzle was; whatever answer we give will skew the possibilities of responsive debate. Roughly speaking, two lines of thought may be pursued: one holds that the mind, whatever its accomplishments, is, in some as yet unfathomed way, a competence of the living brain or organism. The other holds that, whatever may be true of the first, the paradigmatic mind is a sui generis, historied artifact that incorporates, by enculturation, the native powers of a biologically gifted mind (and, of course, its brain) but transforms it, under the conditions of acquiring a natural language, so that it comes to exhibit a form of self-consciousness that is at once the sharing of a collective, distinctly cultural competence and an idiosyncratic variant of same. Once again, that signifies that self-consciousness is natural, but not naturalizable. (See Quine, 1969.)

The mystery of the second puzzle is an important one. For what it confirms is that the explanation of how a child develops epigenetically, so as to acquire language and the operational abilities Piaget dotes on, cannot possibly be provided in any way but top down, that is, from the vantage of our having already acquired language and the abilities that language makes possible. Any bottom-up attempt to resolve the matter would signify the adequacy of a broadly biological account of human intelligence at the paradigmatic level: in effect, the would-be benefit of the first line of thinking. But if I have caught the puzzle correctly, then there is very good reason to believe the first line—which is, or is very close to, Piaget's preference—cannot possibly work. I shall come to the reason directly. But, before I do, I must insist that how the puzzle is finally resolved will decide the fate of what can be achieved through the usual resources of developmental psychology. That is what I was suggesting in exploring the first puzzle. I should say that we are gambling here with plausible prejudices and that whatever we may claim to mean by *objectivity* in describing a child's development cannot be entirely free of such prior gambles.

I am afraid I must insist, here, on a specific philosophical difficulty that bears further on the second puzzle. Piaget (1965) was on to it—at least tangentially—in his discussions of the child's powers of seriation. The point is that putting items in a serial order—for example, dolls by size—requires a grasp (in some sense) of (a) the relevant kind of ordering that is wanted, (b) what actually is instantiated as common to the items thus ordered (in virtue of which, that is, there is a right order to be assigned), and (c) a grasp of the general respect in which the different features of the items ordered may be concretely compared for the purpose of correct placement. Piaget does not come to grips directly with the problem of general predicables, which the seriation question broaches and entails, but solves it largely in terms of what he takes for granted in terms of the consensus of apt adults. That is not enough, I should say.

You may confirm the general way in which Piaget addresses predication from his well-known paper, "Science and Philosophy" (1971b). The difficulty is this. There is and can be no criterial or algorithmic solution to the problem of predication—at any level of human intelligence—except by way of one or another version of Platonism. Platonism is held to be any cognitive or criterial grasp of ideal Forms, or natural essences, or constructed concepts, such that the correct application of a predicate, whether linguistically specified or not, whether well-formed enough to be rightly called conceptual, or whether at least, even if more primitive or more inchoate, is objectively confirmed by the same means. But there is no known version of Platonism that is operative in this sense! You will look in vain among Plato's Dialogues to find a single place where Plato himself actually tells us (through his spokesman) how to detect a Form in predicating anything of anything. Fodor and Chomsky are indeed Platonists in this sense—and fail for that reason. Piaget, I fear, needs to hold to something very much like Platonism if he is to remain consistent with his views on epigenesis.

My own thesis is that the ancient quarrel between the realists and the nominalists is a complete dead end, utterly unproductive. There cannot be a criterial or algorithmic (or Platonist) solution to the problem of predication—nor, for that reason, to the problem of seriation, nor to any form of the problem of developmental intelligence. Paradigmatically, the problem is solved only and adequately in terms of the predicative practices of an already languaged society, that is, in terms of its consensual (not criterial) tolerance of what it judges to be suitably similar to given exemplars—as in the seriation cases. The solution lies with the sharing of a cultural history, a "form of life" (in Wittgenstein's well-known phrase). It has no epistemologically explicit form. (See Margolis, 1996.) Cognitive success rests on such a sharing: it does not direct it in any executive way. That is as close to a settled philosophical finding as any we are likely to propose.

What all this means is this. The entire sequence of the developmental stages of a child's intelligence—which cannot avoid predication—cannot fail to be anthropormophized in terms of some contingently encultured solution of the predicative problem. But, of course, no such solution can be characterized operationally. That is, unless mastering the consensual practices of a languaged society counts as operational in spite of lacking determinate criteria. To concede all that—or at least to concede the difficulty of escaping its challenge and lesson—is to concede the captive standing of Piaget's entire doctrine. Not that any other investigative strategy could possibly elude the difficulty. Only that, admitting the fact, we should find ourselves drawn to reconsider what to understand by a *human science*, a science specifically addressed to the human condition—a fortiori, what to understand by any science, because every science will be a human science as far as the objectivity of predicative claims is concerned. You see the radical possibilities.

This begins to explain the unique connection between mental states and cognitive states—the common ground between philosophers and developmental psychologists. If you grant the point, or at least if you grant the need to address its challenge, you begin to see the sense in which, paradigmatically (but not otherwise), *mind* (the mature human mind) is nothing but the cognitional aptitude of biologically incarnate minds (precultural minds) transformed by sharing the consensual practices of an encultured, or second-natured, aggregate of artifactual (or emergent) selves. The paradigm of the mind is located, then, in cultural space, not in any local part of the biology of the human species (not in the brain, for instance). Of course, whatever is first located in cultural space cannot violate the biological limits that make our second nature possible (whatever those limits may prove to be) and cannot ensure that the cognitional competence of every society will be demonstrably the same.

Let me offer, in passing, two intriguing illustrations that bear obliquely on the issue. (I shall not pursue them, however.) Consider, first, that Siamese fighting fish fail to discern predicative similarities (of size, shape, and color spot) in decoy fish beyond a certain range, which we would be willing to admit as similar for one purpose or another. (See Tinbergen, 1969.) How should this affect our sense of an animal's perception of similarity? Do dogs perceive a continuum of dogginess, for instance? Secondly, in the study of the universality of human color discrimination—discerning different "reds" as "red," say—it appears that investigators frequently disallow a priori, as data bearing on color discrimination proper, perceptual responses that, however salient, even dominant, in target societies, mingle in some unusual or culturally complex way what we isolate as hue within distinctions that we do not treat as color distinctions at all or treat only as marginally concerned with color. But that, of course, actually entrenches the color scheme we happen to favor, which may well go contrary to the classificatory distinctions favored in very different societies. (See Rosch, 1981.)

Biologically gifted minds, the minds of children for instance, are, on the account being offered, ineluctably anthropomorphized in terms of the paradigm of a languaged or self-conscious mind. Nevertheless, there is no distortion there, for the very notion of distorting the objective description of the mind is internal to the reflexive competence of our own second-natured powers. Alternatively put, objectivity is itself an artifact of our paradigm. (There are no other witnesses, you see.)

I confess this is a picture of mind and science that not very many will be entirely willing to accept. I have no illusions about that. I reserve for myself no more than the right to question the theorizing credentials of any developmental account that would proceed along different lines. Piaget's is the boldest and most ramified such effort that I know. I see no reason to think its best research cannot be reclaimed (with whatever adjustments of detail are required) within the space of a conception of the sort I offer. We would not be driven—I assure you—by that concession to abandon any fruitful line of inquiry at all; but we would have to call into question any supposed exceptionless or necessary rules of reasoning or incontrovertible structures of thinking or the like. I judge every such conjecture—Chomsky's or Piaget's, it makes no difference—to be a conceptual mistake, albeit a recoverable one. If you find that uncongenial, then I must ask you how you mean to escape; and if you find it congenial, then I must warn you of its conceptual price.

SUMMARY

Permit me, then, to summarize my own brief. I can do no better. Developmental psychology focuses on our cognitive powers. But cognitive competence can only be modeled linguistically or by way of linguistic reporting; all else regarding the mind must be anthropomorphized. The upshot is that the paradigm of the mental or the conscious is the self-conscious.

It follows at once that, although culturally or linguistically apt mental processing must depend on prelinguistic powers, the mapping of that process must be an artifact of our paradigm. Furthermore, the cognitive proves to be sui generis, to be such that it cannot be described or explained in terms that reduce or eliminate what is distinctive of cognitional achievement. The denial of that constraint is what is generally called *naturalism* in contemporary philosophy. (See Quine, 1969.) It appears in such protean forms as reductionism, eliminativism, nativism, supervenientism, and computationalism. On the argument opposing naturalism, our cognitive competences are, uniquely, second order, meaning by that that they cannot be merely described in neurophysiological terms or in functional or normative terms that are themselves naturalizable.

I feature one insuperable difficulty for all the forms of naturalism, namely, that of natural-language predication, which I take to be ineliminable in any adequate model of cognitive intelligence. If Platonism fails, then, I argue, there is no way to model human intelligence—the paradigm of intelligence—except in terms of the molar, encultured, linguistic, collectively consensual competences of human selves. But then, two consequences fall out: for one, naturalism fails; for the other, naturalistic models of science fail. Put another way, what a science is is every bit as much an artifact of our cognitional paradigm as are our cognitive powers themselves. Piaget, of course, is a naturalizing theorist of sorts, although an ingenious one. Insisting on the epistemological import of developmental psychology, he easily grasped the inadequacy of any canon close to the positivist theory of science, and, hence, his structuralist proclivities. But if you admit the artifactual standing of cognition, you must abandon both naturalism and any claims of structuralist necessity—for the same reasons. There are no demonstrable necessities in nature, and those we admit are artifacts of our contingent history. If you concede that much, you see that you have abandoned all the familiar canons of what a science is.

Developmental psychology is, preeminently, a top-down discipline. My sense is that it is, for that reason, the exemplar of the entire range of scientific psychology. Ultimately, what I claim is nothing less than this: that, at the human level, it is impossible to disjoin psychology from cognition; that the paradigm of consciousness cannot be anything but our unique self-conscious ability to report mental states; that that ability is artifactually acquired by acquiring, in infancy, living among competent adults, the same competences by which, as a result, humans (the members of *Homo sapiens*) come to function as a society of selves, whose own self-conscious powers cannot be naturalized; and, finally, that all other forms of consciousness and mental life are, from the human point of view, described only by anthropomorphizing such descriptions (by casting them heuristically, not fictively) in terms of the human paradigm.

To admit all that is to challenge, as far as psychology goes, the canonical picture of science. That is where we find ourselves today.[1]

REFERENCES

Boden, M. A. (1979). *Jean Piaget*. New York: Viking.

Bruner, J. S. (1975). The ontogenesis of speech acts. *Journal of Child Language, 2*, 1–19.

Bruner, J. S. (1983). *In Search of mind: Essays in autobiography*. New York: Harper.

Chomsky, N. (1980a). *Rules and representation*. New York: Columbia University Press.

Chomsky, N. (1980b). On cognitive structures and their development: A reply to Piaget. In M. Piattelli-Palmarini (Ed.), *Language and learning: The debate between Jean Piaget and Noam Chomsky* (pp. 35–66). Cambridge, MA: Harvard University Press.

Churchland, P. M. (1989). *A neurocomputational perspective: The nature of mind and the structure of science*. Cambridge, MA: MIT Press.

Dennett, D. C. (1969). *Content and consciousness*. London: Routledge & Kegan Paul.

Edelman, G. M. (1987). *Neural Darwinism: The theory of neuronal group selection*. New York: Basic Books.

Fodor, J. A. (1983). *The Modularity of Mind*. Cambridge, MA: MIT Press.

Lourenço, O., & Machado, A. (1996). In defense of Piaget's theory: A reply to 10 common criticisms. *Psychological Review, 103*, 143–164.

Margolis, J. (1996). The "politics" of predication. *Philosophical Forum, 27*, 198–219.

Margolis, J. (1997). The meaning of "social." In J. D. Greenwood (Ed.), *The mark of the social: Discovery or invention?* (pp. 183–198). Lanham, MD: Rowman & Littlefield.

Nagel, T. (1979). What is it like to be a bat? *Moral questions* (pp. 165–180). Cambridge, England: Cambridge University Press.

Piaget, J. (1950). *Psychology of intelligence* (M. Piercy & D. E. Berlyne, Trans.). New York: Harcourt Brace.

Piaget, J. (1965). *The child's conception of number* (C. Gattegno & E. M. Hodgson, Trans.). New York: W. W. Norton.

Piaget, J. (1970). *Structuralism* (C. Maschler, Trans.). New York: Basic Books.

Piaget, J. (1971a). *Genetic Epistemology* (E. Duckworth, Trans.). New York: Norton.

Piaget, J. (1971b). *Insights and illusions of philosophy* (W. Mays, Trans.). New York: World Publishing.

Piaget, J. (1971c). *Biology and knowledge*. Chicago: University of Chicago Press.

Piaget, J., & Inhelder, B. (1969). *The psychology of the child*. New York: Basic Books.

Quine, W. V. (1969). Epistemology naturalized. *Ontological Relativity and Other Essays* (pp. 69–90). New York: Columbia University Press.

Rosch, E. (1981). Prototype classification and logical classification: The two systems. In E. Scholnick (Ed.), *New trends in cognitive representation: Challenges to Piaget's theory* (pp. 73–86). Hillsdale, NJ: Lawrence Erlbaum Associates.

Sellars, W. (1963). Philosophy and the scientific image of man. *Science, perception and reality* (pp. 1–40). London: Routledge & Kegan Paul.

Tinbergen, N. (1969). *The study of instinct*. New York: Oxford University Press.

Vygotsky, L. S. (1962). *Thought and Language* (E. Hanfman & G. Vakar, Trans.). Cambridge, MA: MIT Press.

Waddington, C. H. (1957). *The strategy of the genes*. London: Allen & Unwin.

---

[1] I must thank Professor Willis Overton (Department of Psychology, Temple University) for drawing my attention to the current state of Piaget studies and for his expert advice.

Chapter 2

The Central Role of Culture in Cognitive Evolution: A Reflection on the Myth of the "Isolated Mind"

Merlin Donald
Queen's University, Ontario

Human symbolic culture constitutes a distinctive, species-universal trait, usually thought to be the result of our having evolved special cognitive capacities, such as language. Seen from this vantage point, the flow of influence runs from cognition to culture, in that order, and the task of evolutionary psychology should be to decide how and when the basic cognitive foundations of modern culture came into being. According to this doctrine, the coevolutionary brain–culture spiral that characterized hominids must have been driven primarily at the cognitive level. Thus, cognitive evolution triggers cultural evolution, which triggers further brain evolution, and so on. This is the conventional meaning of brain–culture coevolution.

However, the interaction between culture and cognition is more complex, and the influence sometimes runs in the other direction, from culture to cognition. Our brains and minds can be deeply affected by the overwhelming influence of symbolic cultures during development. I mean this, not in the superficial sense intended, for instance, by the Whorfian hypothesis about the influence of language on the way we think, but on a much deeper, architectural, level. Some cultural changes can actually remodel the operational structure of the cognitive system. The clearest example of this is the extended and widespread effect of literacy on cognition. In this case, we know that the brain's architecture has not been affected, at least not in its basic anatomy or wiring diagram. But its functional architecture has changed, under the influence of culture.

In this modified view, brain–culture interactions can cut both ways. Undoubtedly, certain brain modifications are a precondition of the emergence of complex culture and must precede its evolution. This order of precedence is confirmed by the archaeological record, which shows that cultural change often followed anatomical change, sometimes by many generations. This was true of advances in both toolmaking and the domestication of fire, which only emerged hundreds of thousands of years after the increased brain size of archaic *Homo* became a reality. But, at the same time, certain uses to which the human brain is put, such as literacy and distributed symbolic cognition, cannot occur without an appropriate level of cultural evolution and in this case, the brain is drawn along by cultural change. This is achieved by influencing development.

The resources of the infant brain can be radically redeployed under the guidance of cultural change, which can gain its own momentum. In turn, this phenomenon, rapid cultural change generation after generation, is made possible by the extreme plasticity of the human brain in epigenesis. This crucial characteristic has allowed the human brain to adapt to the ever-faster rates of change that have become typical of modern society. It may appear self-evident that our brains have proven sufficiently plastic to have allowed us to come this distance, but it is not clear how far this trend can continue. We undoubtedly have cognitive limitations as a species, both individually and collectively, and will come up squarely against them at some time or another.

Meanwhile, it is clear that, by means of this second kind of brain–culture interaction, our brain–cultural dynamic has become an integral part of the replicative machinery of the human species. Culture is the storehouse of crucial replicative information for certain aspects of our collective cognitive matrix, without which we cannot reproduce the cognitive systems by which we now function as a species. The memory repositories of culture allow our species to transmit across generations the codes, habits, institutional structures, and symbolic memory systems that are needed to operate a significant portion of the processes of modern cognition in human culture. This applies especially to the collective aspects of cognition, including the distributed storage and retrieval systems we deploy, but it also affects the functional architecture of the individual mind and brain.

But cognitive science still proceeds as if culture did not matter. The only major exception to this is developmental psychology. Developmental research is one of the few places in cognitive psychology where the impact of culture on cognition has been fully acknowledged and integrated into theory. Perhaps this happened because culture simply cannot be avoided or ignored when observing children in the real world. Whatever the reasons, this has been fortuitous for cognitive research and theory.

COGNITIVE SOLIPSISM

My own realization of culture's formidable epigenetic role came slowly and late, only after I had realized that neuropsychology, my home discipline, was saddled with the solipsistic assumptions that are common in standard-plan cognitive science. The central assumption of cognitive solipsism is that the mind may be, indeed must be, conceptualized as a system that is contained entirely inside a box. In the case of vertebrates like ourselves, that box happens to be the brain. The infant's mind is seen as a relatively self-sufficient entity, with a predetermined architecture consisting of various processors, capacities, and built-in preferences. Equipped with this, it faces the world as an autonomous entity, its hardware (and firmware) fixed in stone. Culture could not play a particularly important role in shaping the operational structure of such a cognitive system because, given normal development, its basic design and architecture are preset by its genes. Its unfolding is influenced by conventional epigenetic forces such as nutrition, sensory stimulation, and stress. Culture is just another of these forces, capable of depriving the system, or stimulating it, but not able to set any of its basic parameters. The infant's mind looks out on the surrounding culture and gradually deciphers it, learns from it, and influences it. But all the while, it is alone.

This isolated-mind doctrine contains some important truths, but as with all good things, it can be carried too far. The strong form of this doctrine holds that the mind exists and develops entirely in the head, and that its basic structure is a biological given, structured according to a set of innate neuropsychological universals. Within this framework, culture is necessarily assigned a secondary role. Culture fills in the blanks, giving a distinctive form to the mind's preset structures. For instance, it can provide specific grammars within the context of Universal Grammar, but cannot influence the basic operational structure of the language device. Culture reshapes the trivial details of mental life, such as the particular language one speaks, one's tribal identity, habits, customs, and beliefs, and the episodic specifics of personal experience. It might even influence the way we think, in the sense that it can train us in the strategies of rhetoric, for instance. But its influence stops there. It is restricted to providing what cognitive researchers would call *noise*. For them, the signal is the component structure of the mind. It is not for culture to determine.

Although this myth predominates in cognitive science and neuroscience, it has never been completely accepted in developmental psychology. This fact can be attributed largely to the influence of two individuals: Lev Vygotsky, who was one of the first to recognize the symbiosis of the developing mind with culture, and Jerry Bruner, who carried this important realization into the modern era. The legacy of their work is the wide acceptance of the idea that many of the operations and functions of the developing mind, including many of the actual operational algorithms of thought itself, develop only if the child has a close, continuous interaction with culture. Moreover, the nature of the cultural environment has a determining influence on the nature of the child's operational skills. Culture thus provides much more than the incidental details of mental life. It actually forms and structures the mind on a fundamental level. Fully realized, this idea challenges the myth of the isolated mind. This is not to say that it encourages group-think or a mysterious melding of individual minds into a collective mind. Rather, it suggests a change of emphasis in our theorizing. In accepting that culture plays a major role in the development of cognition, our focus must be widened permanently to include the cultural environment. The aloof, solipsistic Aristotelian mind, magnificent in its Olympian contemplation of the outside world, is dragged into the cultural streets, and forced to acknowledge that much of the representational machinery with which it contemplates the cultural world, and represents reality, had its humble beginnings in culture itself.

This idea has interesting implications when applied to human phylogenesis because it transforms the traditional elaborative role assigned to culture into a replicative one. If culture is essential in establishing the basic structure of the adult mind, it thereby becomes part of the mechanism of evolutionary replication and natural selection. Replicative mechanisms are central to evolutionary theory because natural selection acts on the entire process of replication, including its nongenetic components. The replicative mechanism of the human mind is, by definition, responsible for transmitting our cognitive architecture across generations. It determines the blueprint of the human mind. Modify it, and the blueprint of cognition is modified. In most species, culture, insofar as it exists at all, does not factor into the evolutionary picture in this way. But the modern mind depends upon a unique symbiosis of brain and culture, and in this context, traditional solipsism is unworkable. It is also unworkable in the sense that humans have constructed elaborate systems of distributed cognition, but this is a secondary aspect of the argument. The prehistory of the human mind, even at the earliest stages of hominid emergence, must acknowledge the evolution and role of symbolic culture as an integral part of cognitive evolution. This idea is fundamental to my own theory of human cognitive origins (Donald, 1991; 1993a, 1993b; 1995; 1997; 1998a, 1998b, 1998c).

THE INFLUENCE OF CULTURE ON COGNITIVE ARCHITECTURE: THE "LITERACY BRAIN"

What do I mean by the "replicative" role of culture in evolution? Many species need some form of early social interaction or facilitation to develop normally. But that does not imply anything more than a supporting role for social life in ontogenesis, similar to the role of, say, nutrition or sensory stimulation in development. However, unlike any of the latter, culture can have a qualitative impact on the component structure of cognition. Culture does not merely facilitate the development of a standard-plan cognitive profile. If culture can be shown to be primarily responsible for some truly novel aspects of human cognition, then, ipso facto, it is implicated in the reproduction of those novel features in future generations. It thereby becomes a carrier of essential replicative information, without which certain components of the system cannot be reproduced.

Are we just talking about memes here? Emphatically, no. This is not at all the same as the claim made by Dawkins (1989) when he proposed his concept of the meme. Memes are representational memory records—ideas and images—that move through cultures in waves. Ideas, such as democracy, nationalism, honor, and heroism, and images, such as the swastika, the ideal body shape, or the decorative trappings of class, are typical memes. They influence what we think and perceive and have a tremendous effect on behavior. For example, the meme "dying for one's country" has led to joyously suicidal behavior on the part of thousands of young men. But memes do not define the component structure of the mind. On the contrary, they are the natural products of conventional mental structure. Thus Dawkins remains a traditional cognitive solipsist.

I have made a much stronger claim for the impact of culture. Culture is a replicator, not only of memes, as Dawkins suggested, but of some of the key features of the operational system that generated the memes in the first place. Culture actually configures the complex of symbolic systems needed to support it by engineering the functional capture of the brain for this purpose in epigenesis. To be clear, I am using the word *culture* to refer to the entire interactive symbolic environment in which humans live and communicate. By the capture of neural structures, I mean simply that areas of the brain that would, in preliterate culture, have been dedicated to other use, have been appropriated by the demands of literacy. This has been mediated by basic neural-developmental processes such as synaptogenesis, displacement, and Hebbian learning (the strengthening of specific synapses by experience). Under some circumstances, these processes can establish, in the brain of the developing child, operational systems that make it possible to interact with, and use, the cognitive instruments of literate culture.

This principle has a great impact on human epigenesis, even though the basic wiring diagram of the nervous system has been largely predetermined in the genes. The central tenet of Edelman's notion of Neural Darwinism (1987) was that the functional capture of brain regions, especially of areas, such as the neocortex, which are far removed from the shaping influence of the peripheral nervous system, is governed by epigenetic events. This idea has been confirmed many times in the literature on developmental plasticity. For example, in the congenital absence of eyes and the active stimulation they mediate, those parts of the brain that normally form the visual system are not captured by vision, and they come "on the market," so to speak. Their functional fate is decided by a kind of local natural selection that takes place within the individual nervous system. Pathways that are normally encumbered for vision might be diverted in this case and employed by competition and displacement for other cognitive functions.

This process of capture and redeployment is much more flexible in the case of higher cognition, which is heavily dependent on recently evolved brain areas such as the tertiary areas of the frontal and parietal neocortex and the perisylvian regions. The brain is so plastic at this level that it is reasonable to expect that the functional capture of these areas might be subject to considerable individual variation. This confers a great benefit on humanity: extreme developmental plasticity and adaptability to many different environments. It also leaves human developing brains much more open to cultural influence because culture determines so much about the way we structure our system of skills, including some seminal skills that play a direct operational role in cognition.

Thus, by changing the kinds of cognitive environments to which infants are exposed, symbolic cultures can have a major epigenetic impact on the mind. In fact, over a period of many millennia, the pedagogical intervention of symbolic culture has undoubtedly evolved and institutionalized many novel skill structures in the human brain. The most obvious case in point is the complex of advanced literacy skills that are essential to running modern society. These skills demand a tremendous share of brain resources. Symbolic literacy simply cannot exist without installing, in thousands of developing children, an elaborate complex of lexicons, use rules, automated component subskills (such as decoding letters and symbols, finding words, and forming letters), and a number of memory management and attentional algorithms, each of which must be entrenched in its own neural architecture. This type of architectural redeployment of the brain, whereby an elaborate series of cognitive operations is formulated, trained, and structured by culture, is not unique, by any means, to the case of literacy. Literacy is just the most dramatic example. Most distinctively human skills depend on the existence of novel functional modules in the brain, with clinically dissociable components. This is true of most skill complexes that drive the modern world, including mathematical, musical, scientific, artistic, and managerial skills, all of which are functional impositions of culture that must be implemented in brains. As are mainstream literacy skills, they are part of a large hierarchy of automatic subroutines that are essential for a host of scaffolded intellectual operations whose existence is contingent on them.

Thus, brain and culture do not simply "coevolve" in modern humans, in the usual sense of that word. Conventional coevolutionary theories allow only for a tight, inflexible fit between brain and culture, in which the two have coevolved so closely that the form of each is greatly constrained by the other. This kind of theory is much favored by sociobiologists. In their view, humans are stuck with the fixed cognitive repertoire they evolved during the late middle and lower Paleolithic period (cf. Tooby & Cosmides, 1989). I do not deny the existence of such cultural and cognitive universals and species-wide adaptations, which characterize us as human, but it paints an incomplete picture to give them exclusive jurisdiction over cognitive architecture. There is an additional factor that affects brain–culture interactions, and it results from the juxtaposition of a super-plastic brain with our highly innovative symbolic cultures. Future generations can adjust to their drastically changed epigenetic environments without genetic change, through massive cultural intervention in their development. This greatly affects the deployment of our cerebral resources and changes the way our various cognitive games are played. The long-term outcome is a restructuring of cognitive skill that is so fundamental, when contemplated in purely cognitive terms, that we would normally expect such drastic changes only after changes to the human genome. Yet they were mediated entirely by culture.

Literacy, as we know it, is historically very new. It is about 5,000 years old, at most, and is still far from species universal. The spread of literacy has been so rapid that the human brain could not possibly have evolved an adaptation for it. Many individuals born into the New Stone Age have become highly literate in a single generation, and this surely negates the possibility of a special brain adaptation behind literacy skill. However, it is a mistake to underestimate the cognitive revolution brought about by literacy. In terms of its cognitive structure, full literacy involves an enormously intricate web of skills that have some novel properties. These skills must be assembled in hierarchies, largely automated in their operation, in the individual brain. This constitutes a very tangible functional brain system, and its dissociable subsystems can break down in clinical neurological syndromes, just as perception and language can. Yet the subtle architecture of the literacy brain is entirely a cultural imposition. All that complexity and exquisite structure is a product of cultural programming. In principle, if that kind of structure can be installed by culture, we cannot dismiss the possibility that language itself might be installed by similar developmental principles.

The breakdown of the literacy brain has been analyzed in neurological patients with acquired disorders of reading and writing, the so-called dyslexias and dysgraphias. This analysis has revealed a hierarchy of automatized component subroutines, including a very sophisticated control system for eye movements; a dedicated temporary buffer in short-term memory, sometimes called the graphemic buffer; and, depending on how many languages the reader has, input and output lexicons, each with its own automatic look-up addresses for thousands of words and each leading into a vast semantic system where the reader's knowledge is stored, sometimes semi-independently from the sound-based semantic system. It also includes several specialized output lexicons that control the operations involved in writing via different motor paths. There are many other features, such as the phoneme-to-grapheme mapping process that is needed to read certain languages.

These are all scaffolded systems with many layers of embedded production schemas and a hierarchy of memory "readout" systems that map the form of a planned phrase or sentence to actual production algorithms, for each letter of each word, in exactly the correct motor sequence. This enables the writer to produce a coherent text rapidly, without much deliberate thought on any level other than the semantic one. Early in acquisition, when readers are still without these automatic subsystems, they act like helpless neophytes, deliberating about every feature of every letter of every word, with a concomitant slowing of the thought process. But, after endless hours of rehearsal and pedagogical supervision, the process gradually becomes automatized, and thus fully "installed" through the functional capture of available brain resources.

In any normal childhood in a literate society, the child's brain must acquire many similar interconnected component subsystems. Music and mathematics demand a similar and parallel set of components, and most occupations, from chess playing to aeronautical engineering, involve decades of specialized training to establish an even more complex concatenation of complex systems in the brain. With practice, these become the well-worn paths of the expert, woven into an elaborate structure that mediates the rapid lexical, semantic, and syntactic reactions that any experienced reader needs. These connection patterns, which seem to be rather variable when compared across individuals, form the greater part of the real functional architecture of adult cognition in literate society.

These symbolically driven functional architectures have some very special properties. They are different from many other functional architectures of the brain, such as those for vision, hearing, somatic sensation, locomotion, long-term memory storage, arousal, and so on. These basic systems have their origins in genetic events with a very deep evolutionary history and associated neural structures that are dedicated to them. They are also neuropsychologically universal in any given species that has them. Although experience and stimulation may be needed to nudge them into development, culture plays no major role in actually setting them up. Accordingly, no one suggests that culture determines anything fundamental about vision or basic memory capacity. However, this is obviously not true of the functional architecture of literacy, and probably not of language. Enculturation is the actual source and replicative carrier of their architecture. And this is not to mention the large distributed cognitive systems of society that are also cultural in origin. These systems tie together individuals, machines, and external symbols into cognitive megastructures, whose novel properties have been described elsewhere (Donald, 1991; 1993b; 1998a). These are important and constitute another major contribution of culture, but are quite a different matter from the structuring effects of culture on individual brains.

APES, SYMBOLS, AND THE PROCESS OF ENCULTURATION

Our greatest intellectual accomplishments, and the ones that we tend to identify with the conscious representation of reality, are language and formal thought. They are both closely dependent upon culture and could not have evolved independently of it. I mean that literally. They could not have preceded culture, because their specific organization is entirely a product of culture. Although our brains have undoubtedly evolved a capacity for symbolic thought, this capacity is only vaguely defined in the nervous system itself. The brain is not, on its own, a symbolizing organ. The brain depends entirely on culture for the exploitation of its symbolic capacity, and some of its most impressive functions have a purely cultural origin. Symbolizing minds, as we know them, are not self-sufficient neural devices, as are eyes. They are hybrid products of a brain–culture symbiosis. Without cultural programming, they could never become symbolizing organs. They would become something else, very powerful perceptual-motor systems, like those of a superprimate, perhaps, but not truly symbolic.

To a cognitive neuroscientist like myself, it seemed very odd at the time I wrote my first book to propose that the most distinctive cognitive achievements of the human mind should be defined primarily in terms of an evolving symbiosis with culture. This places the human species in a completely unique position. Indeed, when it first occurred to me, the idea seemed too eccentric to bother pursuing. After all, I was trying to construct an account of cognition, not of culture. I was trying to establish a clear link between symbolic cognition and brain function. Any attempt to include culture as a major factor in cognitive evolution meant that we were looking at a very tangled causal chain that stretched all the way from neuron to culture and back again. But the idea endured, because it opened up an interesting possibility: that the rudiments of culture might actually have come first in our evolution, while symbolic thought, as we know it, came second, perhaps even a distant second, drawn into existence by a burgeoning cultural process whose roots were not primarily symbolic.

This contradicted the common assumption that cultural evolution is secondary to the evolution of symbols and languages. We tend to think that culture must be an invention of evolving minds, rather than vice versa. As with so many conventional ideas, this assumption seems solid enough. Surely we could not have evolved any kind of expressive culture without first having a capacity for symbolic communication. But this common assumption falls apart under careful scrutiny, because our best evidence suggests that symbol systems are always acquired through enculturation and are always simpler than the totality of the surrounding culture. Despite this, enculturation has been neglected as a possible formative process in its own right, a process that had a tremendous influence on cognition, while following, to some degree, its own evolutionary trajectory. Perhaps our neglect of enculturation is due to our great difficulty in objectifying our own intellectual dependency on culture, embedded as we are (especially scientists) in it. Given this bias, it is not surprising that the most striking evidences of the raw power of enculturation, data that we cannot ignore or deny, have come not from studying ourselves but from studying another species, the chimpanzee.

Chimpanzees that are raised in artificial ape/human cultures are often referred to as "enculturated" apes. They hold up a mirror to our own predicament. Like us, they are strangers in a strange land, raised in a culture that differs radically from their original, or natural, environment. The best-known studies of these extraordinary creatures have been carried out by Duane Rumbaugh and Susan Savage-Rumbaugh on a quasi-naturalistic reserve just outside of Atlanta, Georgia. They have raised bonobos (a distinct species of pygmy chimpanzee) as well as common chimpanzees in captivity, exposing these animals from infancy to the regular use of symbols. Some of these animals have acquired considerable symbolic skills without specific instruction, simply by cultural immersion. In the process of becoming symbol users, they have entered a sort of cognitive limbo, inasmuch as they have become exceptional in their natural habitat but remain strangers to human culture as well. They have achieved things that were believed, until the 1990s, to be beyond the reach of chimpanzees and bonobos. Their star bonobo, Kanzi, picked up a large working vocabulary and, without direct training, acquired a significant understanding of spoken English (Savage-Rumbaugh et al., 1993). This was an amazing achievement, and even though his linguistic skill appears to be quite limited when compared to a human adult, Kanzi can match 2½-year-old children in most tests of language comprehension. He can understand sentences such as "Can you put your shirt on? Can you put your shirt in the refrigerator? Do you want some more Perrier?" And so on. This shows that he understands the meaning of nouns, verbs, and prepositions, as well as word order. He has difficulty with more elaborate constructions, such as sentences with embedded clauses that separate the verb from its object. But even so, his understanding of English is sufficient to be quite useful to him in his daily life.

Based on these studies, some very strong claims have been made about a hypothetical ape language capacity; I do not agree with many of them. But, I cannot avoid making at least one major concession. Kanzi can do things that he was not supposed to be able to do, according to traditional doctrine. Moreover, this outcome is entirely the product of his special cultural environment. His biological inheritance has not been tampered with. He has exactly the same brain design as his wild-reared cousins. Yet, in some respects, he behaves like a different species. Many of his remarkable skills are completely absent in wild-reared bonobos. His capacity to use symbols and understand some spoken language could not have evolved directly in a species that lacked these skills in the wild. They were implanted in his brain by the cultural influence of another species, our own. This demonstrates convincingly that the enculturation process can successfully uncover and exploit cognitive potential that had remained untapped for millions of years.

The point is, a symbol-using culture can become an active, exploitative force in shaping the primate mind and can introduce apparently human cognitive features into the profile of nonhuman primates. Kanzi has learned to manufacture simple stone tools that are similar to the ones associated with the first hominids, present more than 2 million years ago. Moreover, he can use and manufacture them purposively and appropriately. For instance, if he breaks off a flake in order to cut a rope and it is not sharp enough, he will break off another one until he gets a cutting edge that actually works. Watching Kanzi make a stone tool, one has the feeling of witnessing a primordial scene that was first played out by our distant ancestors. Yet he is not human. He has none of the features—erect posture, changed vocal anatomy, increased brain volume, and so on—that define our direct line of ancestors.

Some of these enculturated apes have learned to use visual symbols to communicate with one another, although only under special circumstances. This was first shown by the Rumbaughs in the 1980s, when they demonstrated symbol-coordinated tool use in two chimpanzees named Sherman and Austin, who had earlier learned to use half a dozen tools, including keys, and to name them using symbol boards. Sherman and Austin were allowed visual contact with one another through a window, and were able to communicate using their symbol boards. They were also able to "mail" objects back and forth, from one room to the other, through a drawer that could be pulled through the wall. They shared a food locker, which was located in one room, while the key to the locker was kept in the other room. When one of them wanted to eat, he had to flash a request, using the visual symbols, to the other chimpanzee, who was the temporary caretaker of the locker. The caretaking chimpanzee would read the message, get the key, and send it through the porthole. Then, the requesting chimpanzee would open the locker and get the food, sharing with his colleague. They managed to coordinate their behavior in several different scenarios, involving several different tools, even though they were never explicitly trained to perform these specific exchanges. This was an impressive demonstration of symbolic communication between two members of a species that supposedly lacked any capacity for doing such things.

Kanzi's achievements have often been challenged and are regarded by many as a clever illusion, precisely because they do not occur naturally in the wild. Let us start by accepting this oft-heard comment at face value. In some respects, Kanzi is undoubtedly an illusion. In fact, he is from outer space, as far as most other bonobos are concerned. This is an important challenge, rather than a substantive criticism of the Rumbaughs' research, and it has very serious implications for our own species. Certainly, to our archaic forerunners, most of us would also appear to be from outer space. Our modern intellectual armamentarium has been constructed on the scaffolding of many previous cultures and has traveled a great distance. Thus, just as Kanzi, we are also illusory creatures, products of an incessant process of cultural revolution that has kept raising the intellectual bar higher and higher, pushing us toward cognitive heights that we were not really designed to reach (keep in mind that evolution is blind; it has no foresight).

There might be a hint about the nature of human cognitive evolution in the failure of enculturated apes to generate actual cultures. In some ways, apes have come close to human symbolic cognition as individuals, but they have failed completely on the cultural side of the equation. Despite the brilliant efforts of researchers such as the Rumbaughs and many others before them, apes continue to use symbols only for a pragmatic personal agenda. If symbolic skills alone had been enough to generate a truly symbolic culture, many apes would be much farther down the human road by now and would be moving toward collective representational systems. But they are not. Although individual apes have made significant advances, collectively they have never been inclined to construct their own symbolic cultures, not even on the small scale of, say, a small working or family group. Sherman and Austin, who could use symbols effectively to communicate with one another for pragmatic reasons, never extended their use of symbols to hold anything resembling a conversation. There is no evidence that they modified any of their traditional social behaviors, using symbols. In their case, competence in the use of symbols was not sufficient to generate a cultural revolution, not even a very small one. This negates any notion that symbolic skills have an immediate, transformative power to generate culture.

In short, there seems to be more to generating culture than a sprinkling of words and a smattering of grammar. This leaves us with a tricky chicken-and-egg question when examining our own origins. Which came first in human emergence, symbolic skill, or culture itself? Kanzi's symbolic skills are exclusively due to enculturation. So, obviously, are many of our own, the best example being all the skills associated with literacy. There were no true writing systems until about 5,000 years ago, and we have never had time to evolve a specialized capacity for reading and writing. All of what neuropsychologists know as the "literacy brain" is a product of culture (I mean that quite literally, as we shall see). The same principle applies to the neural origins of mathematics and musical skill, two very recent cultural innovations. These skills are products of cultural opportunism, not evolution. They illustrate the successful exploitation of raw cognitive potential that could not have been evident in the primordial cognitive profile of our species. Of course, there are individuals who have extraordinary talents in these areas, and this might mislead us to think that they must have special brain modules for musical talent, mathematics, and literacy. But they do not. Such modules never had the time to evolve, in the biological sense. These talents are simply products of genetic variation, happy convergences of factors that occur in a small minority of people. Rare convergences of genes can create the occasional Mozart. But these scarce opportunities have to be seized on by a culture that is positioned to exploit them. Without this exploitation, such talents would never become evident.

Unthinkable as it may seem, we are not even certain that spoken language, as we know it, was part of our primordial profile as a species. We have no firm empirical evidence by which we can dismiss the notion that language itself might be, especially in some of its most esoteric semantic and grammatical features, just another product of our deep symbiosis with culture.

THE OUTSIDE–INSIDE PRINCIPLE

However, the exploitative power of enculturation runs up against a wall at one point. We cannot invoke the power of symbolic culture to explain its own beginnings. The mystery of its origins deepens when we consider the brain design we have inherited. Unlike computers, which are physically open to a larger wired world, our nervous systems are private entities, physically isolated from one another. Our minds are thus locked up inside little boxes that cannot be wired directly to other minds. We can escape from those little boxes and from our intellectual isolation in only one way—through action. Our isolated nervous boxes can communicate only by projecting symbols into the world, by contracting muscles, and by waving limbs. The problem is that our brains can never produce truly symbolic acts unless they are imposed from the outside.

We can see this in the communicative helplessness of people who have grown up in isolation from culture. No matter how fiendishly clever they may later prove to be, they never invent symbols, not even for their own use, in isolation. The mental skills of isolated children are amazingly limited, and this situation can be reversed only by intense cultural immersion. We know this from studying the lives of deaf-blind children like Helen Keller, who lost both vision and hearing as an infant. Her later life revealed an extraordinary talent for language, but this talent was hidden during her period of isolation. She stagnated throughout the normal critical period for language and made no progress toward acquiring language until she was provided with a system of symbols by her famous teacher, Annie Sullivan (cf. Lash, 1980). Annie re-established that vital link with culture, first by giving Helen a system of simple hand signals, and then through a variety of other symbols, including several systems of raised print and Braille. After that momentous step was taken, Helen made good progress and eventually acquired not only English but other languages as well. In achieving this, she was totally dependent on constant contact with the surrounding world. Culture liberated her mind. It let her out of prison, allowed her to think, and gave her the equipment she needed to develop a more complex mental apparatus. All her depth and richness as an adult came through the liberating effect of culture.

The point is that isolated brains, even linguistically clever ones such as Helen Keller's, never invent languages, not even a "language of thought," for their own use, even though such a skill would obviously be highly adaptive. We know from the post hoc testimony of many other late-learning deaf signers (see, for instance, Schaller, 1991) that, prior to someone successfully establishing symbolic contact with them, they never even suspected the existence of language. They had no names for things and, thus, no labels to aid their memories, analyze their societies, organize their thoughts, or plan their lives. They had no notion of naming, even as a possibility. Names, symbols, and languages always come from the outside, from the individual's absorption into a symbolic culture of some kind, even if it is a very small culture of two people. Left to themselves, isolated human brains do not act as symbolizing or language-generating devices, any more than do the brains of other primates.

Thus, we arrive at the perennial catch-22 in theories of human cognitive origins: symbolic cultures cannot function without languages, and brains cannot generate languages without pre-existing symbolic cultures. Natural selection has somehow locked these two players into a strange symbiosis. But how could our brain's unique relationship with culture have started? There is only one possible solution. Short of invoking an evolutionary miracle, expressive culture must have taken the first step. Moreover, this step could not have depended upon any built-in tendency to symbolize reality. Some archaic cultural leap, deep in our prehistory, must somehow have set the stage for our later transition toward a symbolizing mind.

I have stated my own hypothesis elsewhere about the nature of that archaic first step (Donald, 1991), and I will not repeat it here. It involves a brain capacity that allows us to map our elementary event perceptions to action, thus creating, at a single stroke, the possibility of action-metaphor, gesture, pantomime, re-enactive play, self-reminding, imitative diffusion of skills, and proto-pedagogy, among other things. I call this complex "mimetic" skill and its cultural aspects *mimetic culture*. The rationale behind this notion derives from a principle first proposed by the Russian psychologist Lev Vygotsky in his pioneering studies of children, the so-called "Outside–Inside" principle. Vygotsky observed that children always copy the externals of language first and do not initially have inner speech, or silent forms of symbolic thought (see Vygotsky, 1986). The rule is that symbolic thought is first played out in action and only later internalized. Young children externalize every thought in action and carry out their verbal thinking out loud. Only much later are they able to think in silence or, in the case of deaf signers, without moving their hands. Symbolic thought thus originates in externalized acts and only gradually migrates inside the head to perform its magic in apparent solitude. The picture in adults can be deceiving; they might have acquired their skills in a solipsistic manner. But children give away the store. When they are first acquired, our own symbolic performances are completely public, even to ourselves. Only later do they become internalized. The direction of flow is clear: from the culture to the individual mind, that is, outside–inside.

In principle, the evolution of human symbolic skills might have emerged in an analogous manner, migrating from outside to inside. The analogy is a loose one because there was no symbolic behavior to imitate 2 million years ago, when the process probably began. But it must have started in this way because, if fully equipped modern human brains still cannot internalize symbolic skills without an externalizing phase, this principle would have been even more applicable 2 million years ago. Thus our symbolic origins must have been impressed on our brains from out there. Some of the externals of intentional action came first, before we had any form of inner language or any symbolizing system to mediate silent thought. Mimetic action is the best candidate for this. Thus, we find the deepest origins of our capacity for symbolic thought in action—in fact, in a primal, extraverted expressive process, mimesis, that was based entirely in externalized actions.

What mimesis achieved was nothing less than an escape from the isolation of the mammalian nervous system. In collective mimetic action, humanity created the cognitive fundamentals of culture, the communicative glue that still holds human society together on the most basic communicative level. These must have been in place, in externalized patterns of action, long before any form of internalized symbolic thought could have evolved. The action patterns of archaic humans must have originated in group action patterns, reflecting back on one another, creating ripple effects, novel variants, shared skills, conventions, customs, and proto-rituals, for a very long time before any truly symbolic processes emerged. And by extension, only much later, after further evolution, could these processes have been internalized.

CONSCIOUSNESS AND SELF-CONSTRUCTION

Before we can understand what this statement means, we need to know more about the nature of action and about culture. But above all, we need to pay attention to what we have discovered about consciousness. Consciousness has never gained a respectable place at the table in our long debate over human origins, but it is a key player, and it is time to give it the seat of honor. Our tangled phylogenetic history has given us a *hybrid* consciousness, that is, a multilayered, complex, and quite unique central process. In 1991, I had accepted that human consciousness was probably an outcome of our evolution and not so much a part of the process. At that point, I had not yet realized that consciousness might be the engine of our cognitive evolution. But I am now convinced that it is. Note that I am defining *consciousness* here in a pragmatic, inclusive sense, as conscious capacity. My reason can be stated very simply: this is the most useful definition that I can find.

Human conscious capacity is the generative core of symbolic culture and of all our distinctively human styles of cognition. When we evolved our very large brain, we acquired a much more powerful apparatus of consciousness. Thus, our capacity is useful and adaptive. It did not emerge as a mere evolutionary afterthought, as some have suggested. Nor was it an epiphenomenon, an inconsequential byproduct of other evolutionary events. Rather, it was the main event. Instead of evolving a specialized language brain, or an apparatus designed to build a symbolic thought capacity into the fabric of the brain, we evolved two more fundamental things: expanded conscious self-governance and a burgeoning cultural environment. As cultural knowledge structures became more complex, our co-evolving conscious capacity reflected that complexity, triggering a coevo-lutionary spiral that eventually culminated in high-speed modern lan-guage and all the spectacular cognitive pyrotechnics of the modern human mind. Ever since it began, our community of increasingly con-scious brains has coexisted with an exploding process of enculturation. All else followed from this elemental brain–culture chemistry.

One might reasonably ask, why? Why would conscious capacity be essential to cultural survival? The primary reason that conscious capacity is so important is that complex symbolic cultures are not easy to read. Symbol-using cultures hide their secrets from all but the most curious and attentive mind. Their surface appearance is highly deceiving. On the sur-face, humans appear to go about their business like any other social mam-mal, and, if this were true, human culture should be no more difficult to understand than any other. But on a deeper level, human culture is exceedingly tricky, devious, and resistant to discovery. Moreover, it is invis-ible. None of its major patterns are immediately present in perception. Without a powerful intellectual guide, it remains impenetrable, remote, and opaque. The cultural neophyte will find it full of blind alleys, decep-tions, indirect threats, tricks of memory, and shifting agendas. Above all, it showers the observer with blizzards of encrypted messages.

Human society is daunting enough even to those of us who are already skilled at surviving in it. But it must be terrifying to any creature with lim-ited mental equipment. Even to a human child, adult culture must be revealed only gradually, layer upon layer, with extensive mentoring. Learning a culture is not unlike deciphering the intentions of a group of alien beings that one is forced to live with but whose actions and inten-tions are seldom what they seem. Because of the survival value of the incessant plotting and scheming that is the normal business of human beings, every child needs an internal guidance system to enable its self-assembling little mind to navigate these daunting cultural labyrinths. Our children are normally well-equipped to handle this challenge. For most, childhood is a protracted Alice-in-Wonderland adventure, an exploration of fantastic cultural worlds replete with what might appear, to lesser minds, as unpredictable chaos.

To achieve a successful adaptation to this demanding cultural world, human beings are aided by powerful capacities that were specially evolved for living in culture. These are known in experimental psychology as exec-utive capacities. They constitute a central guidance system that allows human beings to manage and supervise their own cognitive activities while analyzing the second- and third-order patterns of culture. In this regard, we are much better equipped than apes. In fact, the major differ-ence between ape and human brains rests precisely on these capacities. If the reader can tolerate a bad pun which I found nevertheless irresistible,

I have labeled our unique complex or suite of executive adaptations as "the executive suite" (Donald, 1998b).

There are many components to the executive suite. They include memory, directional, and evaluative components. In the jargon of experimental psychology, all these components are identified with our conscious capacity. The *memory component* of human conscious capacity involves a greatly expanded working memory, a place in the mind where we can hold the images and ideas that may be relevant to whatever challenges we may be facing at any given moment. We need a great deal of working memory to learn something as complex as a language. The *directional component* gives us a certain cleverness in directing our attention selectively toward some of the least obvious features of the environment while ignoring others that are more perceptually attractive. This is needed to penetrate the intricate weave of social interactions and signals that characterize human society. The *evaluative component* involves cross-relating ideas in a highly efficient manner, across both time and space. This is needed very early in life, for instance, just to understand how a mother's actions today might follow from how she acted yesterday under quite different circumstances. This kind of cross-referencing is a tall order, and often impossible, for any nonhuman species. There are other components in the executive suite, but this will suffice to illustrate what it implies about autonomous cognitive self-regulation.

The kinds of functions that I have described, whether mnemonic, directional, or evaluative, are traditionally identified with consciousness, or more specifically, with what we call conscious capacity. They are essential for the mind to find its way through culture because human cultural environments are remarkably unpredictable at birth, and therefore a growing human mind must be maximally flexible and able to generalize rapidly from concrete instances and partial information. Our conscious capacity allows us to decipher the unpredictable forms of a surrounding culture. This is a critical skill, from the viewpoint of survival. If a child cannot make an initial connection with culture, the child cannot acquire the central skills that any symbolizing mind must have. My central thesis here revolves around that idea: conscious capacity is the key evolutionary feature of the human mind. It provides our connection with culture. At the same time, it is also the mediator for acquiring and assembling all our complex symbolic skills.

But its clinching achievement is an ability to generate a virtual infinity of skills. One culture invents sailing, another throat singing. One culture insists on a capacious oral memory to remember entire pharmacopoeias, whereas another demands great dexterity with external symbols to manage an electronic universe. We are asked to handle now broadswords, now biplanes, now remote microsurgical hands. Here we are asked to manage the politics of a tribal village with a memory that reaches back 10 generations, and there we live in a global culture with an infinity of instant information but no collective memory. All these specialized skills take years to acquire, under close conscious supervision and with deliberate instruction. Pedagogy and interaction are both essential to the process, because these skill complexes are always the product of more than one conscious mind. Specialized skills result from deep cognitive interactions between brains and constitute the cognitive core of any given human culture.

Indeed, such interactions constitute our main intellectual work. Our vital skills are watched, monitored, and worked over endlessly by the group. They are almost never species universal, automatic, or stereotyped, as are those of most species. Our expanded conscious capacity is essential for the self-assembly of all complex hierarchies of skill, including our most essential and most controversial skill, language. The latter has some universal features, as do many other skills, and these universals have to be explained. But in almost every important way, languages are culture specific. This reflects the most important fact governing our existence: unlike most species, we are self-invented to the core, peripatetic self-assemblers of minds.

This capacity for deliberate self-assembly is a direct product of our expanded executive brain. It allows us to supervise our acquisition of complex hierarchies of skill, including language. Without this, humanity would need to fall back on the evolutionary strategy of most other species, evolving a large number of innately programmed skills, built into our brains at birth, each with its own special modules. I do not deny that we have evolved some such programming, but it plays a much smaller role in the human case than in the case of other species. We get by with less fixed programming because we have added a new twist to the traditional Darwinian machinery of self-replication: a symbiotic relationship with culture and a conscious capacity to self-assemble cognitive architectures in our own brains. This relationship has liberated us from the cognitive isolationism of other species, and, to end on an optimistic note, may have given us the potential to eventually become masters of our own fate.

REFERENCES

Dawkins, R. (1989). *The selfish gene* (2nd ed.). Oxford, England: Oxford University Press.

Donald, M. W. (1991). *Origins of the modern mind: Three stages in the evolution of culture and cognition.* Cambridge, MA: Harvard University Press.

Donald, M. W. (1993a). Human cognitive evolution: What we were, what we are becoming. *Social Research, 60,* 143–170.

Donald, M. W. (1993b). Précis of *Origins of the Modern Mind* with multiple review and author's response. *Behavioral and Brain Sciences, 16,* 737–791.

Donald, M. W. (1995). The neurobiology of human consciousness: An evolutionary approach. *Neuropsychologia, 33,* 1087–1102.

Donald, M. W. (1996). The role of vocalization, memory retrieval, and external symbols in cognitive evolution. *Behavioral and Brain Sciences, 19,* 155–164.

Donald, M. W. (1997). The mind considered from a historical perspective: Human cognitive phylogenesis and the possibility of continuing cognitive evolution. In D. Johnson & C. Ermeling (Eds.), *The future of the cognitive revolution* (pp. 355–365). Oxford, England: Oxford University Press.

Donald, M. W. (1998a). Hominid enculturation and cognitive evolution. In C. Renfrew & C. Scarre (Eds.), *Cognition and material culture: The archaeology of symbolic storage* (pp. 7–17). Cambridge, England: Monographs of The McDonald Institute for Archaeological Research.

Donald, M. W. (1998b). Mimesis and the Executive Suite: Missing links in language evolution. In J. R. Hurford, M. Studdert-Kennedy, & C. Knight (Eds.), *Approaches to the evolution of language: Social and cognitive bases* (pp. 44–67). Cambridge, England: Cambridge University Press.

Donald, M. W. (1998c). Preconditions for the evolution of protolanguages. In M. C. Corballis & I. Lea (Eds.), *The descent of mind* (pp. 120–136). Oxford, England: Oxford University Press.

Edelman, G. (1987). *Neural Darwinism.* New York: Basic Books.

Lash, J. P. (1980). *Helen and teacher: The story of Helen Keller and Anne Sullivan Macy.* New York: Delacorte Press/Seymour Lawrence.

Savage Rumbaugh, E. S., Murphy, J., Sevcik, R. A., Brakke, K. E., Williams, S. L., & Rumbaugh, D. (1993). *Language comprehension in ape and child.* Chicago: Society for Research in Child Development (Research Monograph, Vol. 58).

Schaller, S. (1991). *A man without words.* Berkeley: University of California Press.

Tooby, J., & Cosmides, L. (1989). Evolutionary psychology and the generation of culture, part 1. *Ethology and Sociobiology, 10,* 29–49.

Vygotsky, L. (1986). *Thought and language* (A. Kozulin, Trans.). Cambridge, MA: MIT Press. (Original work published 1934).

Part II

PERSONAL, SOCIAL, AND AFFECTIVE DEVELOPMENT

Chapter 3

Emotions and Social Norms

Martha C. Nussbaum
The University of Chicago

GRIEF AND SOCIAL NORMS

Tomas, a 5-year-old Ifaluk boy, contracted meningitis and was comatose within 24 hours. Relatives and friends began to gather at his parents' home. Female relatives washed the feverish body until the efforts seemed futile; then male relatives took turns holding the semirigid form, weeping as they cradled it. "At the moment of death, a great wailing went up. The dead boy's biological mother, seated on the floor mats near him, rose to her knees as if she had been stabbed and pounded her fist violently against her chest. The adoptive mother . . . began to scream and throw herself about on the ground." The whole house was filled with crying, "from low moaning to loud, wrenching and mucus-filled screaming to wailingly sung poem-laments, and continued without pause through the night. Both men and women spent tears in what seemed . . . equal measure." (The Ifaluk believe that those who do not "cry big" at a death will become sick afterwards.) Anthropologist Cathy Lutz (1988) found the proceedings "shocking": like many young Americans, her only contact with death had been "the subdued ritual of one funeral" (pp. 125–127).

One afternoon in Bali, Norwegian anthropologist Unni Wikan's housekeeper, a young Balinese girl, came to her to ask for several days off. She was smiling and laughing. Asked for her reason, she told Wikan that she wanted to attend the funeral of her fiancé, in a distant part of the island. Wikan immediately suspected deception: she could not believe that this cheerful bouncy girl had recently suffered a major bereavement. Several days later, the girl returned, even more cheerful and energetic than before. Certain that the girl had gone on some pleasant holiday at her expense, Wikan considered dismissing the girl for lying. Talking to others, however, she discovered that the girl was telling the truth: her fiancé, whom she had loved very much, had indeed died of a sudden illness. Over time, Wikan came to understand that the Balinese believe sad feelings dangerous to a person's health. If you brood and let yourself grieve, you weaken your life force and become prey to malign forces. It is therefore best to respond to loss by distracting oneself, focusing on happy events and acting cheerfully (Unni Wikan, personal communication, September 1997; see also Wikan, 1990).

Human beings experience emotions in ways that are shaped not only by shared human circumstances and capacities but also by individual history and social norms. My own grief at my mother's death was at one level a universal human response to the death of a loved parent, a response shaped by deep needs and attachments that are in some form ubiquitous in human societies.[1] It was also shaped, however, by more local norms about the proper way to mourn the loss of a parent. These norms, as I experienced them through my own inclinations, were unclear and, to some extent, inconsistent with elements of the Ifaluk and the Balinese uneasily thrust together. One is supposed to allow oneself to "cry big" at times, but then American mores of self-help also demand that one get on with one's work, physical exercise, and commitments to others, not making a big fuss. Thus I considered canceling the lecture I had been writing, out of respect for my mother and my grief. I wanted to give some sign that, only one week after the funeral, I could not go on as if everything were all right. Canceling seemed one substitute for dressing in black, an expressive gesture no longer available. But I was told by friends that canceling a big lecture would be a bad thing. One does not defect from a commitment that way, they said, and one should be able to rise to the occasion. Besides, they said, it would be good for my psychic health to focus on something that I could control, in which I was not helpless. These contradictory instructions came, as well, from my own history, as I asked myself what my mother would have wanted of me (prolonged sadness, or so I felt), and what my father would have said (that a person of dignity carries on in the face of misfortune, head "bloodied but unbowed.") At times I focused on thoughts of loss and had periods of intense weeping; but I also prided myself on making the lecture as good as it could be, tirelessly

---

[1]This example is fully described in chapter 1 of Nussbaum, *Upheavals of Thought* (in press), the manuscript from which this chapter derives.

revising it, distracting myself from thoughts of grief. I felt guilty when I was grieving because I was not working on the lecture; and I felt guilty when I was working on the lecture because I was not grieving. The night before the lecture my hosts wanted to take me to a festive dinner, but there I drew the line. Eating a celebratory meal seemed to me disrespectful. Some of my hosts understood these feelings, but others thought me peculiar. I ate quietly in someone's home, insisting on baked chicken with no sauce.

In the larger project of which this chapter is a part, I develop a cognitive theory of emotions as "upheavals of thought," evaluative forms of perception and judgment that involve the recognition that a person or object matters deeply in relation to one's own goals and projects.[2] The view I defend insists on the universality of certain human emotions. Based, as they are, on vulnerabilities and attachments that human beings can hardly fail to have given the nature of their bodies and their world, emotions such as fear, love, anger, and grief are likely to be ubiquitous in some form. I argue, moreover, that they are elements of our common animality with considerable adaptive significance, so their biological basis is likely to be common to all.

But this does not mean that emotions are not differently shaped by different societies. The capacity for language is common to all, and any infant can learn any language—but languages nonetheless differ greatly, both in structure and in semantics and, to some extent, in expressive range. I now ask to what degree emotional repertories also differ and to what extent these variations are caused by societal rather than individual differences. It is evident that the behavior associated with emotion differs greatly in my three cases of bereavement. But it is likely that the differences run deeper, affecting the experience of the emotion itself. All three bereaved people have suffered an important loss, going to the heart of their goals and plans. But the response to the loss takes a very different form and not only outwardly. The Ifaluk mother believes that she will be ill if she does not dwell on her grief and indulge in sad thoughts. Wikan's housekeeper believes that she will be ill if she does indulge in sad thoughts, and therefore she tries not only to behave cheerfully but also to distract herself with happy thoughts. I oscillated between the belief that it

---

[2]This "eudaimonistic" feature of the emotions (their connection to one's picture of flourishing or *eudaimonia*), must be carefully distinguished from egoism, or an instrumental attitude to objects. Emotions in my view may ascribe intrinsic worth or value to persons and objects, although they do so from the point of view of the person's own attempts to construct a rich and meaningful life. Thus, I loved my mother for her own sake and thought her a person of enormous worth in her own right; but the fact that she was the object of my intense emotions is connected to the fact that she was *my mother*, not someone else's mother, and thus a most central part of my own life.

was a sign of respect and love to the dead to focus on loss and sadness and the belief that one should distract oneself and go about one's business, showing that one was not helpless. These differences marked not only my behavior but also my inner experience.

A cognitive/evaluative conception of emotion is neither necessary nor sufficient for the recognition of significant social variation, or, as it is frequently called, "social construction." If one held a mechanistic or hydraulic conception of emotion, it would be difficult but not impossible to hold that societies mold emotions in different ways. Plato, in the *Laws*, holds that emotions are unreasoning movements in the organism, and yet he offers advice to pregnant women about how to soothe and mold the emotions of their fetuses by regular rhythmic movement and other noncognitive techniques. Nor is a cognitive/evaluative view sufficient for the recognition of "social construction": for one might hold that the relevant cognitions are universal and shaped by our common situation as vulnerable beings in a world we do not control. Or one might hold that there is significant variation among emotional repertoires but that the primary source of variation lies in the developmental history of individual children with their parents.

On the other hand, taking up a cognitive/evaluative view makes it easy to see how society could affect the emotional repertory of its members. If we hold that beliefs about what is important and valuable play a central role in emotions, we can readily see how those beliefs can be powerfully shaped by social norms as well as by an individual history; and we can also see how changing social norms can change emotional life. This was, of course, central to the ethical program of the original Stoics, who used their cognitive/evaluative conception of emotions to show how societies might rid themselves of some pernicious forms of anger, envy, and fear. Although they themselves tended to focus on large general areas of emotional life that to some extent all societies share, their view naturally lends itself to the recognition of differences between one set of social norms and another. The Stoics did not care much about these differences because they held the extreme view that all emotions are bad, and thus all known societies are profoundly diseased. If one should reject that extreme view and yet still hold that there are some emotions that are socially pernicious, social variation would become of major significance. For one will then want to look and see what different societies do about emotions, and whether there are better or worse ways of constructing an emotional taxonomy. We face these normative issues much later; but we can only face them well if we have some sense of the degree and nature of emotions' social variability.

Theorists of emotion frequently fall into one or the other of two extreme camps on this issue. Some theorists completely ignore the role of society and treat emotional life as universal in all salient respects. This is a common position in evolutionary psychology and also in psychoanalysis, where the role of cultural factors in shaping the developmental process is only just beginning to be discussed. Psychoanalytic thinkers are usually practitioners with a culturally narrow sphere of reference. They frequently have difficulty distinguishing the universal from the local in what they observe, and do not often even raise the question. We notice local Viennese cultural patterns in Freud's patients, features of British emotional life in Bowlby's and Winnicott's patients, American styles of parenting (focused on both empathy and independence) in Mahler's and Stern's parental subjects, and so forth; but few analysts build the recognition of cultural difference into their account.

At the other extreme, anthropologists sometimes speak as if the emotional repertory of a society were socially contructed through and through and as if there were few limits imposed on this construction by either biology or common circumstances of life. At the very least, there is often a certain lack of curiosity about what this commonality might be. The tendency to present cultures as emotion systems with little overlap is exacerbated when the researcher describes a culture in general terms, ignoring the variety of its individual inhabitants. Recently more complex conceptions of culture with an emphasis on plurality, conflict, and porous boundaries have been emerging in anthropology; these have paved the way for more balanced and nuanced accounts of a society's specific emotional range.

A good account of social variation in emotion, then, should neither exaggerate difference nor overlook it—a platitude easy to endorse in theory but far more difficult to realize in practice. A helpful starting point is to reflect about human/other animal differences that play a role in the social construction of emotion. We can then proceed to identify some salient sources of social variation; this, in turn, puts us in a position to describe the most common types and levels of variation.

HUMAN/ANIMAL DIFFERENCES:
TIME, LANGUAGE, AND NORMS

In nonhuman animals, the capacity for *temporal thinking*—for memory, for expectation, for conceiving of a life as a temporal process with a beginning, a development, and an end—is obviously limited. These limits are different in different species, but even in dogs and primates, temporal thinking plays a far smaller role than it does in the life of a normal human adult, for whom time is a background grid on which the self orients itself and without which it cannot experience itself as a continuous self.[3] To the

---

[3]This is, of course, a theme much developed by Proust, especially in the opening section of his novel.

extent to which an animal lacks awareness of the passage of time, it must also lack a sense of habit and routine, something that is also of great consequence for the sense of self and the emotional life.

To the extent that time is lacking, the capacity of other animals for generalizing is limited. All animals recognize at least some objects as instances of types seen before. Thus, their very ability to survive requires the recognition of "food," of dangerous predators (general schemata for which are probably innate), and of members of their own species. But types of generalizing that require a sophisticated awareness of historical patterns or of social structures will elude them.

Putting these two elements together, one finds that there are thoughts of potential import to emotional life that nonhuman animals are unlikely to be able to form: for example, the idea of membership in a distinctive group with a distinctive history, perhaps a history of glorious deeds, perhaps a history of oppression; the idea of being a member of a species that has done great evil and can also do what is right; the idea of planning or striving for the realization of national or global justice; and the idea that certain calamities are the common lot of one's species.

Animals also vary in the degree to which they have causal concepts; and again, most species have them to a lesser degree than human beings. Emotions such as shame and anger depend on causal thinking ("He did that to me," "I disappointed him in this way"). Many animals lack the basis for such emotions. Even when an animal does have some causal concepts (as a dog, for example, can clearly connect a person with abuse or with the bringing of food), there are some causal stories that they probably will not tell themselves—such as stories concerned with their own childhood history—which are fundamental to many human emotions.

All normal humans can imagine what it is like to be in the shoes of another, and from early childhood, they receive constant practice in this ability. Such perspectival thinking is fundamental to human emotional and moral life. Dogs have a limited degree of this ability, in the sense that they respond to cues of sadness sent by their owners and offer them consolation. Apes have more sophisticated forms of the ability and are able to engage in imitative play, to recognize their images as such in a mirror, and in other ways to manifest a sophisticated awareness of positionality and self–other relatedness (see de Waal, 1989, 1996; de Waal & Lanting, 1997). The degree to which a creature possesses these abilities is fundamental to its capacity for compassion and love.

Some emotions will prove altogether unavailable to many animals, to the extent that the sort of thinking underlying them proves unavailable: hope, for example, with its robust sense of future possibility; guilt, which identifies a past wrongdoer with the agent's own present self; romantic love, to the extent that it involves a temporal sense of aim and aspiration and a fine sense of particularity; compassion, to the extent that it calls upon a sense of general possibility and fellow feeling; and even some forms of anger and grief, to the extent to which they require causal and temporal judgments. Apes and dogs can have some of these, or to some degree; but many animals lack them entirely.

Only humans, it seems, form theories of the world. Religion, metaphysics, philosophy, and science are human phenomena. But this, too, makes a great difference to the emotional life, giving the human being not only new emotional objects (Nature, God), but also a framework of understanding within which causal and temporal thinking will operate. The nature of this framework shapes the emotions. Thus anger is shaped by views about who is responsible for what and how the causality of evil works. Fear is shaped by thoughts about what harmful agencies exist in the world, how harmful they are, and how to ward them off.

All these cognitive differences between humans and animals create differences in the concept of self, and of the relation between self and other. The way we see ourselves depends not only on our innate cognitive capacities, but also on our specific conceptions of temporality, of causality, and of general notions such as species, nation, family, god, spirits, and the universe. It depends upon our idea of our distinctness from others, and on the degree to which we consider ourselves members of groups along with others. Animals have comparably rudimentary self-conceptions; in many cases, none at all.

The emotions' eudaimonistic character rests upon a sense of the self, its goals and projects. It will therefore vary with the conception of self in each species. For all animals, some parts of the world stand out as salient, as connected with urgent needs of the self. But the human animal is much more likely to have a relatively organized and comprehensive conception of such goals, to think of them as forming a network, and to include among them persons and things at a distance, either spatially or temporally.[4] Furthermore, humans have an unparalleled flexibility in the goals they pursue.

From this follow a number of implications for the logic of the emotions. First, that in the human case there is logic in them, to an extent unknown in the rest of the animal world. Humans may form inconsistent goals and have emotions accordingly; but the awareness of an inconsistency is likely to be a reason for deliberation, self-criticism, or revision in a way that it will not be in the other species.

More generally, human emotions, unlike animal emotions, are subject to deliberation and revision in connection with general deliberation about

---

[4]Good accounts of goal hierarchies are in Ortony, Clore, & Collins (1988) and Lazarus (1991).

one's goals and projects. If, like Seneca, one believes that a person of dignity should depend on nothing and no one outside himself, and yet one is at the same time so passionately attached to one's status and reputation that one is furious at being seated in a less than high place at a dinner party (see Seneca, *De Ira*, III.36 ff), this is an inconsistency: for one both believes and does not believe that a certain external item is of enormous importance. Sort this out and get your life in order, Seneca tells himself. This does not mean that it will be easy to get rid of anger, grief, or fear where these do not accord with one's reflective sense of value: for the judgments these emotions embody may lie very deep in the personality and be settled parts of one's sense of self. But they are in principle available for deliberation and "therapy," as part of my general deliberation about *eudaimonia*. This deliberative activity is initiated in interactions with others and is carried out in substantial measure in the context of such interactions.

Human deliberative sociability also affects the range of emotions of which humans are capable because it permits the object of an emotion to be a group: the city, country, or nation itself and, possibly even the whole of humanity—abstractions of which no other animal is capable. Some social and interactive emotions involve complicated forms of reciprocity that are peculiarly human. Thus, animals may have attachment, but few will have love in the sense in which Aristotle defines it, that is, as requiring mutual awareness, mutual good intentions, and reciprocity.

And because humans are more fully social, they are also more fully capable of being alone—therefore of the exhilaration of solitary contemplation, of awe before the silence of nature, of peaceful solitary joy at the air and light that surrounds them, but also of loneliness, of the gloomy horror that can seize one in the middle of a forest, in whose shadows one finds images of one's own death. It seems likely that the capacity to be alone (even in the presence of others) is fundamental to human emotional development and an important determinant of adult human emotional relationships.

In short, in an ethical and social/political creature, emotions themselves are ethical and social/political, parts of an answer to the questions, "What is worth caring about?" and "How should I live?"

Language, I have said, is not everything in emotion: emotions can be based on other forms of symbolic representation. But the fact of language does change emotion. The fact that we label our emotions alters the emotions we can have. We do not simply apply terms to antecedently organized items. In the process of labeling, we also organize, bounding some things off from others, sharpening distinctions that may have been experienced in an inchoate way. From then on, we experience our emotions in ways guided by these descriptions.

A person who does not know the emotional "grammar" of his or her society cannot be assumed to have the same emotional life as one who does know this "grammar." To be able to articulate one's emotions is *eo ipso* to have a different emotional life. This does not mean that one cannot fear without being able to name one's fear, and so forth; I have said that there are many reasons why an emotion, especially a background emotion, might remain unconscious in a person who could readily recognize and label the emotion in the right circumstances. But a person who never develops fluency with the emotion words at all, and with the criteria of their application, is likely to be different "inside" from the person who does.

All these differences—but especially those connected with labeling and deliberation about the good—give us reason to look at the role played by society in constructing emotions. Animals have emotions about other animals with whom they share a society; but human societies transmit practices of emotion labeling and normative evaluation that actually enter into the content of the emotions their members will have. The thesis of *social construction*, in its most plausible form, is the thesis that these practices make a difference to a society's emotional repertory.[5]

SOURCES OF SOCIAL VARIATION

Human life has some invariant features that are dictated by the nature of our bodies and of the world within which we live. We are physically weak among the species, and cognitively mature at an early age while we are still physically helpless. There are many things that are really dangerous to us and which we therefore have good reason to fear, assuming that we are attached to our own survival, as we innately are. Thus it would be a remarkable society that contained no fear, and a highly unsuccessful one. But certain specific fears are also ubiquitous and dictated by our animal heritage: the fear of the snake, for example, appears to be innate and based on perceptual schemata that have adaptive significance. Fears of thunder and lightning, of sudden loud noises, of large animals—all these are, once again, ubiquitous and highly functional. (It is now thought that children all pass through a long sequence of fears, and that most fears are eventually mastered after being activated. Thus a child who fears large dogs would be a child who had never unlearned a fear with an innate

---

[5]For this thesis, see, in psychology, Averill (1980, 1982); see also Lazarus (1991); in anthropology, especially Briggs (1970), a remarkable account of the Utku, an Eskimo people who try to avoid anger and aggression; see also Lutz (1988), Rosaldo (1980; 1984), and Harré (1986).

basis, not a child who had learned an atypical fear.) Similarly, all known societies contain some varieties of anger, hope, and grief. Strong attachments to parents or caretakers are also ubiquitous, as are the early bases of imaginative empathy and social compassion.

What features of societal difference might plausibly be invoked in arguing for inter-societal differences in the emotional life? First, there are physical conditions. Some societies face danger from the elements on a much more regular basis than do others. Lutz plausibly argued that Ifaluk culture—an island culture based on a fishing economy—is especially preoccupied with the dangers of nature and that its emotional repertory has developed in response to this preoccupation. Some societies face hostile enemies more regularly than do others. Thus a young Roman male under the Empire would be taught that his task in life was to beat down all the barbarian enemies of Rome, and this would inform emotional development and response. Some societies, and groups within societies, have opportunities for leisure that others do not. This, again, will shape the range of emotions that will be developed and expressed: certain sorts of highly self-conscious romantic love seem to require a relatively unharried middle-class, or even aristocratic, life. Some people live crowded together; others spend a good deal of time in solitude. Thus, Finnish people intensely cultivate and prize emotions connected to the solitary contemplation of the forest, one's own smallness and insignificance in the face of monumental nature; the conditions for these specific experiences are unknown in Calcutta. Some need to cooperate closely in order to survive at all, whereas others may go their own way, pursuing self-directed projects. The Utku Eskimos studied by Jean Briggs needed fine-tuned cooperation at all times in order to hunt in the inhospitable climate to get enough food to live; therefore, they could not afford hostility, which would do little harm in the old U.S. West with its wide-open spaces giving people room to avoid each other.

Second, societies differ in their metaphysical, religious, and cosmological beliefs. The fear of death, which in some form is ubiquitous, will be powerfully shaped by what one thinks death is and whether there is an afterlife. The Hindu theory that we should renounce selfish urges and desires shapes the emotional lives and even practices of childrearing (see Kurtz, 1992) of people who believe it. The belief that an enemy's curse can cause death shapes emotional life so profoundly that, as Seligman has shown, it may produce a sense of extreme helplessness resulting in sudden death (see Seligman, 1975).

Grief is deeply affected by these metaphysical differences. Although people who have a confident belief in the afterlife still grieve for the deaths of loved ones, they usually grieve differently, and their grief is linked to hope. Not so the Ifaluk, for whom any death tears a hole in the fabric of the community, jeopardizing its safety. The Balinese theory of the vital force and its enemies shapes Balinese grief, teaching people to view it as a dangerous threat to health. So too, in somewhat related ways, does the U.S. theory (of Protestant European origin) that one can conquer luck through work: grieving is thus sometimes felt as a sign that one is not making sufficient effort. (An idiosyncratic offshoot of this view is found in the metaphysics of Christian Science, whose members believe that bodily disease is caused by personal deficiencies in religious willing. This view leads to a radical denial of grief.)

Third, practices also shape emotional life, usually in ways that are closely connected to physical conditions and metaphysical beliefs. For example, practices of childrearing differ in significant ways, probably with significant effect on emotional development. Chinese infants are typically encouraged to be immobile. Their limbs are tightly wrapped; styles of interaction discourage initiative and promote peace. American children, by contrast, are given a lot of stimulation and encouraged to move; their limbs are free. Again, a typical Indian infant is constantly carried by its mother on her hip during the first months of life and is given the breast on demand; at the same time, the mother spends little time talking to her child or interacting with it, frequently because she has other children and tasks to attend to and also because her dwelling is likely to be highly porous, with people from extended family and village moving in and out (Kakar, 1983; Kurtz, 1992). American infants, by contrast, usually have long periods of physical separation from the mother's body and frequently cry before feeding; at the same time, the mother interacts a lot with the infant, smiling and talking—partly because she spends long stretches of her time alone with the infant, in a single-family dwelling where privacy is the norm, and is less likely to have many other children to attend to. All these differences influence development, although the nature of these differences is hard to pin down.

Weaning practices, once again, vary greatly. American mothers usually wean gradually, after the child is well accustomed to solid food. Utku children are weaned abruptly in favor of the newborn baby: they suddenly find themselves turned away from the breast and see another child in their place. Briggs not implausibly connects this difference to the intense sibling jealousies that characteristically erupt.

In later childhood we also find large cultural differences. In ways that shocked Briggs, Utku children are permitted to display aggression against siblings because of the Utku theory that children do not have reason or the ability to control their passions. American parents tend to expect more control, believing that children are capable of control. American children generally see their mothers daily throughout their childhood. The Indian male child, by contrast, is often moved suddenly, at around age 6, from the constant company of his mother to a male world where he rarely sees the mother. Similarly, British children of the upper classes are frequently sent quite suddenly from the sheltering atmosphere of the nursery to boarding school at age eight, a world that is still often single sex and highly hierarchical. Again, such differences affect emotional development, although, again, it is difficult to isolate these factors and to say precisely what their influence is.

In all cultures, practices of childrearing mark at least some differences between boys and girls, although the degree of these differences varies with culture and individual. The practice of training males for separation from the mother and females for continuity with the mother's domestic function profoundly shapes gender development in many societies (see Chodorow, 1978).

It is extremely important not to generalize prematurely about such cultural practices. Any cultural group, studied in sufficient detail, exhibits many different practices, even in these familiar areas of child development. (Male–female differences, for example, are too rarely studied with the care they deserve.) Halberstadt's studies of American children from different ethnic and economic backgrounds show a wide range of family styles in the areas of communication and expressiveness—as we would naturally expect, since we are used to the fact that people we know are different from one another, that WASP families are different from Jewish families, and so forth. Some families talk a lot and some do not; some tell each other what is on their minds, others bottle up grievances (Halberstadt, 1991; see also Parke et al., 1992). We should not make the mistake of thinking that members of a distant culture, especially one as vast and diverse as India, are more homogeneous than we know members of our own culture to be. Many generalizations that are made about "the Indian child," however suggestive, rest on a very small sample and do not adequately reflect cultural, religious, and regional differences—or differences of sex, because all the studies have focused exclusively on boys.[6] Briggs' study of the Utku and Lutz's of the Ifaluk are different because they attempted to examine all individuals, albeit within a very small population; the studies carry conviction in part because they do point to significant differences among families and individuals.

Fourth, language differences probably shape emotional life in some ways, but the role of language has often been overestimated. It is very difficult to estimate it correctly. For example, one should not make the common error of supposing that if there is no single term in a language for an experience, that experience must be lacking. This is just as wrong as the idea that, if a word is the same, the experience is likely to be the same.

---

[6]See Kurtz (1992), who pointed out that the studies that have given rise to the sweeping hypotheses of Kakar and others rest on a handful of scattered observations.

Aristotle already pointed out that certain patterns of virtuous conduct that he could clearly describe and exemplify from his culture had no one-word name in his language. This "namelessness" probably has some significance. For example, the fact that there was no name for a moderate disposition of character with regard to anger and retaliation forced Aristotle to co-opt the concededly imperfect term "mildness" and probably reflects the fact that his culture placed an unusually high value on retributive conduct speaking about it far more than about mild conduct. Nonetheless, his audience was expected to recognize what "mildness" was, and that "mildness" was not quite the right term for it (because the "mild" person will take revenge when his family is damaged).

So too with emotion terms. The fact that Greek and Roman cultures have many fine-grained words for different varieties of anger shows us that they were unusually preoccupied with that emotion. But once we read their accounts, we understand how they were individuating the kinds and recognize examples of these kinds in our own world. Thus it would take further argument to show that the presence of a large number of distinct words really makes a difference in the emotional life itself. Cicero (*Tusculan Disputations*, IV) pointed out that Latin has only a single word for love, *amor*, whereas Greek has several; but he expected his readers to be familiar with different types of love identified by Greek discussions: they are just subtypes of *amor*, to be marked off by further qualifying words.

Language is most revealing as a source of difference when we find a culture classifying together things that we would usually classify apart. Thus, Lutz showed that the Ifaluk word for love, *fago*, is also the word for compassionate care for the weak, sadness at the lot of the unfortunate, and so forth. *Fago* thus covers part of the territory of "compassion," and yet it is the central term for personal love. Lutz plausibly argued that Americans focus on romantic love as the paradigm case of "love," whereas the Ifaluk focus on maternal nurturance and, more generally, meeting the basic needs of another as the paradigm experience of *fago*. This probably reveals (or helps to constitute) at least some difference in the emotional life. Americans probably do think of romantic love as more central in their conception of what life is about than do the Ifaluk, and their emotional experience varies accordingly. Language, of course, does not shape these differences by itself. In this case, we can understand the difference as growing largely out of differences in physical condition. A society preoccupied with survival may have less time for romantic love than a prosperous society and is more likely to focus on compassionate care as a core emotion. But it is likely that the culture's vocabulary also shapes, to some extent, its members' sense of what is salient in experience.

Finally, and perhaps most important of all, *social norms* pertinent to the emotional life vary. If emotions are evaluative appraisals, then cultural views about what is valuable can be expected to affect them very directly. Thus a culture that values honor highly and attaches a strong negative value to slights to honor will have many occasions for anger that an equality-focused culture such as that of the Utku will not have. The Stoics were correct to think that the more one values external goods that are not stably within one's control, the more occasions one has for all sorts of emotions, such as fear, grief, anger, envy, jealousy, and hope. (As Seneca said, "You will cease to fear, if you cease to hope.") Societies have different normative teachings with regard to the importance of honor, money, bodily beauty and health, friendship, children, and political power. They therefore have many differences in anger, envy, fear, love, and grief.

TYPES AND LEVELS OF VARIATION

First and most obvious, criteria for the appropriate behavioral manifestation of an emotion such as fear or anger are socially taught and may vary considerably from society to society. The Ifaluk learn to "cry big" at a loss, the Balinese to smile and act cheerful, and the English to manifest composed restraint. Cathy Lutz found Ifaluk wailing shocking, but an American resident might also be shocked by British decorum. To the Utku, Western people are childish in their volatile expression of anger and sorrow; they are called an uncontrolled and bad-tempered race. To a Finn, the happy greeting of an American runner, smiling on the path, seems an intrusion bordering on hostility: one does not smile in the forest, nor does one invade the contemplative space of another.

In some cases, we should probably imagine that emotional experience remains very similar, and it is only the outward manifestation that is different. As we can tell from literature, letters, and personal friendship, British and American grief are probably not very dissimilar, although the rules for public manifestation are somewhat different. In other cases, the behavioral rules probably alter the experience itself. Finns certainly do experience profound joy, but the merry casual joy of the outgoing exuberant American, who waves at a fellow runner, is a type of joy not clearly available to people who have learned to be extremely shy and introverted and who associate the forest with profound thoughts about helplessness and the shortness of life. Few Finnish emotions are casual or easily tapped.[7] This makes an experiential difference.

Second, we find social variation in the *judgments about the worth of an entire emotion category*. Briggs' Utku Eskimos teach that anger is always inappropri-

---

[7]For 8 years I spent 1 month every summer in Finland, and I still return there almost every year. My remarks are based on personal observation.

ate, because it is always inappropriate, at least for an adult, to care deeply about slights and damages. Although they do backslide and certainly experience anger,[8] Utkus always feel it a sign of immaturity, which infantilizes the possessor. Adults should put away such childish things. In this, if not across the board,[9] they are true Stoics. Although it is difficult for the anthropologist to get at the distinction between displaying and having an emotion, Briggs' argument is convincing on this point, since she was careful to engage in prolonged conversation with her family about norms of human goodness. Especially revealing was their discomfort at the incident in the Bible in which Jesus drives the money changers out of the temple. As good Christians they had to endorse this, but they really had trouble fitting it into their normative picture of Jesus' character (not just his public demeanor). Their explanation: he did scold the money changers, but not out of anger—he did it in order to improve them, since they were being "very bad, *very bad*, and refusing to listen to him" (Briggs, 1970, pp. 331–332; emphasis in original). In general Jesus is praised for his lack of anger. (Briggs noted that the Utku, ashamed of being angry, gave their dogs unusually severe punishments—not admitting to anger and treating it as a form of training. Nonetheless, she plausibly saw in the striking harshness a backdoor outlet for emotions of anger and frustration that could not be acknowledged to one's fellow humans.)

Contrast the attitude to anger in the Rome described by Seneca, where it was expected that a truly manly man would be extremely attached to his honor and therefore eager to get angry at any slight or damage. Anger is classified in both Greek and Roman Stoic taxonomies as a pleasant emotion directed at the future, because of the pleasure of contemplating a revenge. This is a specific cultural idea. Even though modern Americans are closer to the Roman than to the Utku in violent behavior, our norms about the appropriateness of anger are much more ambivalent. In years of polling my classes as to where they would categorize anger along the Stoic good-present, good-future, bad-present, bad-future axes, I have found not one student (apart from experts in Stoicism) who classified anger in the good-future category as the Greek and Roman philosophers all do. Our Christian heritage has at least some impact on our view about anger, if not always on our actions.

Such differences in normative judgment affect experience itself. For an Utku, being angry will be hooked to shame and the feeling of diminished

---

[8]Briggs' findings are misreported in Pinker, who attacks her for allegedly claiming that the Utku "have no word for anger and do not feel the emotion" (Pinker, 1997, 364–366). Briggs describes at length a complex set of terms for various types of angry emotion and behavior, finding at least five terms in the language that refer to angry emotion (Briggs, 1970, 328–337).

[9]They are permitted to have strong attachments that are associated with longing, loneliness, even grief.

adulthood; for a Roman, it will be hooked to a feeling of manly pride and
to a quasi-erotic excitement, as he prepares to smash the adversary. Americans are raised with conflicting signals, and different Americans are
raised differently, with gender differences being especially prominent
among the sources of variation. I learned to find anger terrifying and
came to believe that it meant that I would do something irrevocably
destructive; this means that I rarely experience it directly, but discover its
presence through headaches, patterns of behavior, and so forth. My lecture audiences, especially the males in them, often report that they experience anger as a painful sort of boiling or exploding; this is still quite far
from the Greco-Roman view that anger is a terrific and delightful thing,
dripping "sweeter than honey" before the heart.[10]

So too with other emotions. We may expect the experience of erotic
love in a society that has internalized the Augustinian view of original sin
to be very different from the experience of love in a society that has no
such teaching. People often do learn to feel ashamed of and troubled by
their own arousal, and this affects the experience of both sex and erotic
love. Similarly, again, the Balinese judgment on grief—that it is dangerous to the health—affects experience as well as behavior. My father's view
that one should not be bowed down by life made his grief rather close to
Balinese grief, and very different from the grief of someone who believes
it right to enter fully into the experience of helplessness and hopelessness.

Societies may also differ more subtly in their normative judgments
about an emotion type, simply by giving an emotion greater or lesser
prominence. It is evident that the modern United States gives roman-
tic/erotic love an unusual degree of prominence, as the result of a long
Western European heritage. And love is a different experience when it is
believed to be a central source of meaning in life. The Ifaluk certainly
experience romantic love, but that is not what they think life is primarily
about: it is about basic material stability and survival.

In a remarkable comparative study of childrearing practices, Kurtz (1992)
suggested that Western romanticism affects the early behavior of (middle-
class) mothers and children through norms of closeness and fusion. He
observes that an American mother will typically gaze often into her baby's
eyes, smile, respond—creating, over time, a richly responsive interpersonal
world (see also Stern, 1977, 1985). A mother in India, by contrast, is more
likely to carry her baby on her hip, letting it feel the solidity of her bodily
presence but rarely looking into its eyes as she goes about her chores. Even
when the child is at the breast, eye contact is much less elaborate than in the
American case. She gives the child a sense of material stability and security,

---

[10]Aristotle, *Rhetoric* II.2, quoting Homer. Aristotle does not deny that anger is painful: he
holds that it has both aspects.

but seems less interested in cultivating an intensely personal kind of loving interaction with it. (To some extent, as we have seen, these differences are the product of family size and physical circumstance.) Kurtz concludes that American practices lead to exaggerated expectations of perfect intimacy and harmony that cause difficulties in later romantic life; Indian practices seem to him more sensible and realistic (Kurtz, 1992). But whatever one's normative judgment, one can see how our idea that romantic love is necessary and central may color many aspects of the emotional life and, indeed, shape its very foundations.

All five sources of emotional variation play a role in these differences of normative judgment. Physical conditions shaped the Utku desire to distance themselves from anger, the American leisured life that focuses so much on love, the Ifaluk life that has more room for compassion than for romance. Metaphysical beliefs (or their absence) shape the Balinese distaste for grief and the American connection between love and salvation. Practices and routines also contribute, as when a mother looks into her infant's eyes because that is what she has seen others do or a Roman man threatens an adversary because that is the way things are done in his social set. Language probably plays some role: thus the absence of a special term for romantic love and the fact that the term *fago* is taught in connection with core experiences of nurturance or need fulfillment may help explain why the Ifaluk do not share the U.S. belief that romantic love is the center of the universe. And finally, of course, social norms—about what all people in a culture should be like, and about what men and women should be like, about what different social classes should be like—pervasively shape judgments about emotion categories, either for society as a whole or for particular social actors.

Next, societies impart different views about the appropriate objects for an emotion, again, views that shape experience as well as behavior. The doctrine of "reasonable provocation" in the Anglo-American criminal law embodies social norms about the occasions on which a "reasonable man" will get violently angry. These include the adultery of a spouse (but not of a fiancée) and a blow to the face (but not a boxing of the ears) (see Kahan & Nussbaum, 1995). Although judges knew well that people got violently angry at many other provocations, the assumption behind the doctrine was that social norms should guide norms of sentencing: the well brought up person responds with violence to only some provocations. Today the doctrine remains, but the objects have changed. A man's wife is no longer taken to be his property; therefore, adultery is no longer imagined as "the highest invasion of a man's property," and violent anger at adultery is less likely to win a reduction in level of homicide. New objects of proper anger have, however, been added to the menu: in particular, the anger of a battered woman against her abuser.

These are differences within a single society; there are also intersocietal differences. Romans approved a far larger menu of objects for extreme, even murderous, anger than do modern Americans. Seneca's *On Anger* is full of stories of trivial provocations that arouse murderous responses— the idea being that these are what the society teaches as acceptable, although the reader is supposed to see them, ultimately, as unacceptable. Anger is also often taught differently to different social actors. Many studies show that angry and aggressive behavior by American boys is subtly encouraged and little discouraged, whereas similar behavior by girls is sharply discouraged. We can easily find similar differences in the objects of fear, pity, and other central emotions.

The appropriate objects of grief might be thought to be rather uniform in all cultures that think grieving appropriate at all; but even here there are differences. Lutz (1988) suggested to her Ifaluk hosts that the death of a very elderly woman was not so bad because it would "put her out of her misery"—thus expressing an American judgment that has much currency, although it is far from universal. The Ifaluk were shocked and even incredulous: "the death of a person of any age tears a hole in a wide-ranging network" (p. 110).

Finally, emotion taxonomies themselves vary across societies. I have said that all known societies have some variety of the major emotion types: love, fear, grief, anger, jealousy, envy, compassion, and some others. But even at the level of the big generic categories, we do not find a perfect one-to-one correspondence across cultures, since cultures organize in different ways the elements that individuate emotions from one another. Thus Ifaluk *fago* contains elements both of personal love and of compassion, the core idea being a nurturing attitude focused on the object's neediness or vulnerability. Cultures that connect love with the high value or specialness of the object more than with its neediness cannot connect the two emotions in the same way: to that extent, the list I just gave of the "big generic categories" is a sectarian list. Similarly, one may doubt whether the anger that the Romans classified as good/future is exactly the same generic emotion as the anger that my students uniformly classify as present/bad.

If this is so at the generic level, it is much more likely to be so at the level of particular species. The precise species of guilt and shame about the sexual body that many Christian cultures experience and cultivate has no precise one-to-one equivalent in ancient Athens, since Athenian culture lacked the Christian metaphysical belief in original sin. Species of erotic and romantic love are especially various, even within the Western tradition. Ancient Greek *erôs* is not mutual: it is an intense erotic longing for an object, which includes the thought of possession and control of the object. It is explicitly contrasted with *philia*, a type of love that need not be sexual (although it may be), and that centrally involves reciprocity and mutual benefit; also with *agapê*, a selfless and usually nonsexual benevolent love. Although a language without a plurality of love words could articulate these distinctions (and Latin authors try, using only the term *amor*), the contrasts in concept both represent and shape, it seems, real contrasts in experience: a Greek does not expect erotic love, as such, to pursue mutuality. (Contrast the modern U.S. conception of erotic love with its heavy emphasis on mutuality and reciprocity.) Again, medieval courtly love has some distinctive features that were not present in ancient Greece and that are not present in the modern America: the idealization of the female object, seen as chaste and unapproachable, the paradigm of selfless devotion to and risk in the service of this perfect being. Modern American conceptions of love contain features of ancient *erôs* and of courtly love, but they are also powerfully shaped by romantic paradigms of love as a ceaseless striving culminating in death or extinction. Most other societies would be seen to contain similar layers of historical complexity and interweaving, if we understood them well enough.

CULTURE AND UNDERSTANDING

Culture provides a crucial part of the explanation for an individual's emotions. But social constructionists frequently suggest several more ambitious theses: that cultural forces leave no room for individual variety and freedom; that they make the details of a personal history etiologically unimportant; that they create mutually inaccessible worlds. By now we have reason to question all these claims.

The claim of mutual incomprehensibility is, of course, belied by the very act of sensitive culture description and by the long history of imaginative receptivity that precedes any good anthropological emotion study. Jean Briggs found much about the Utku initially opaque. Nor did time altogether dispel mystery: she remained baffled by the moodiness and inconsistency of her host, Inuttiaq. But, as she also realized, people are mysterious and inconsistent, some more so than others. When she got to the point of treating Inuttiaq as a person, rather than as a cultural text, she could allow him to be as mysterious as any of her Western friends and not consider this a failure of method.

Both biology and common circumstances, I have argued, make it extremely unlikely that the emotional repertories of two societies will be entirely opaque to one another. It is no surprise that cross-cultural communication often focuses on generic experiences that derive from this common situation. Thus the works of Sophocles and Euripides cross cultural boundaries with tremendous power, since they focus on myths of loss and family conflict that are easily recognizable by others. Homer's *Iliad* has been used successfully in treating Vietnam war veterans who suffer from post-combat trauma—because its stories of rage and fear are recognizable across cultural differences. So too the *Mahabharata*, which attracted huge audiences when presented in New York by an international cast in a production by Peter Brooks intended to underline the work's human universality. Briggs (1970) found that Italian opera provided a valuable common ground between Western and Utku emotion concepts. Since the Utku in general, and Inuttiaq in particular, were great lovers of Verdi and Puccini, moments in the works could be used to discuss specific emotions. Inuttiaq's favorite was *Il Trovatore*, which he called "the music that makes one want to cry" (p. 154). The world of Verdi's mythical Italianate Spain is enormously different from the world of the Utku hunters. But at another level grief for the loss of a mother and thoughts of revenge against those who have damaged her are not in the least foreign to any society.

Some forms of life are, as such, unavailable to us. Medieval courtly love is not a live option in the present day, since we cannot share the metaphysical beliefs and practices necessary to sustain it. We can understand it reasonably well through literary and historical imagining, but we can imagine ourselves in that world only at a very general and partial level, focusing on ideas of sacrifice, idealism, devotion, and the "gentle heart" that are still available to us. In the same way, some contemporary emotion concepts may prove unavailable to us, in the sense that we cannot well imagine what it would be for us to have these concepts. I think, however, that there are very few cases of this kind, if we understand the logic behind another culture's emotions at a deep enough level. Although I do not intend to enter deeply into anthropological debates about the universality of rationality, I am convinced, with Donald Davidson (1986), that the very act of interpretation requires assuming that things make sense, and thus communication presupposes something like a common rationality. In just this way, the Balinese idea of the vital force looks at first blush strange and superstitious—until we recall that we believe something very like that about the effect of stress on the immune system. There usually will be reasons of habit and deep personal history that prevent us from actually taking on a different set of emotion concepts, but they do not seem unimaginably foreign and uninhabitable.

As for individual variety and freedom, some social constructionist accounts err in this area, sometimes under the influence of Michel Foucault—who, whatever his genius, was not terribly interested in individual diversity. We should not go as far as psychoanalyst Donald Winnicott (1965), who wrote that cultural differences can be studied simply "as an overlap of innumerable personal patterns" (p. 15). Culture itself has an explanatory role to play: the fact that something is a widely endorsed cultural norm gives people a reason for following it that is not reducible to an overlap of individual endorsements. Nonetheless, Winnicott is right to stress that culture only exists in the histories of individuals, that individuals vary greatly, and that the existence of diverse personal patterns creates spaces for diversity in the culture itself. People usually see this where their own culture is concerned. They intuitively understand it to be highly variegated—not a power machine that stamps out a series of identical humans as so many cookies from a cookie cutter, but a scene of vigorous debate and considerable diversity, where these very features create spaces within which the individual has at least some leeway to move around. They are also intuitively aware that individual parents are the first and in some sense the primary medium of culture transmission and that culture is transmitted only when it enters the life of the individual child. Individual parents and individual children vary greatly, and parents have at least some latitude to choose what elements of culture will enter the lives of their children.

When we consider other societies, especially distant societies, we do not always remember these facts. We tend to speak of "the Utku view of anger," or, more absurdly (given the size and diversity of the society) "the Indian view of the child." And we do not always grant to others prerogatives we usually take for granted in ourselves—of criticism, change, and the conscious shaping of moral development.

This brings us back to the eudaimonistic character of the emotions. The cognitive/evaluative view implies that emotional content is itself part of a creature's pursuit of flourishing. Given the fact that human beings deliberate ethically about how to live, it implies that emotions are part and parcel of ethical deliberation. If we see emotions as impulses, we will think that we can educate or change them only by suppression. Thus Kant thought that virtue must always be a matter of strength, as the will learns to suppress inclinations, rather like a cook holding down the lid on a boiling pot. But in daily life, we endorse a different picture: we believe that emotions have an intentional content and that people can do a good deal to shape the content of their own, and especially their children's, emerging emotions. Thus the recognition of social construction should lead to a recognition of space and freedom rather than the reverse.

This freedom is not boundless. An American who spends time with the Utku and judges that Utku ideas about anger are valuable cannot simply go home and turn America into Gjoa Haven.[11] Her stance toward America and toward herself will be very much like that of Seneca toward Rome— that of a social critic who can try to shape the course of the moral development of the next generation, even while struggling with her own deeply

---

[11]My example is hypothetical. Briggs does not make the normative judgments I explore here.

implanted cultural impulses. But she certainly need not judge that she has a fate that dooms her to (what she now thinks is) excessive anger. As her conception of *eudaimonia* changes on reflection, so too her emotions may gradually alter—although their deep roots in childhood make alteration a gradual and partial matter. Perhaps more important, she can consciously shape her interactions with children, transmitting the norms that she reflectively endorses.

Indeed, a great advantage of a cognitive/evaluative view of emotion is that it shows us where societies and individuals have space to make improvements. If we recognize the element of evaluation in emotions, we also see that they can themselves be evaluated—and in some ways altered if they fail to survive criticism. Social constructions of emotion are transmitted through parental cues, actions, and instructions, long before the larger society shapes the child. We teach children what and whom to fear, what occasions for anger are reasonable, what behavior is shameful. If we believed that racial hatred and aggression were innate, we could at best teach children to suppress these impulses. But according to the cognitive/evaluative theory, there will be no racial hatred if there are not certain perceptions of salience—that people with different skin color are threatening, dangerous, or evil. By shaping the way children see objects, we contend against these social conventions.

The recognition of "social construction" does entail a recognition that our emotions are made out of elements that we have not made ourselves. This, of course, any view of emotion would have to grant, one way or another. But the social constructionist view I have defended says that these elements are of a particular sort: they are intelligent pieces of human normative activity, of the sort that can in principle, within certain limits, be changed by more intelligent human activity. That does not mean that we can expect group hatred and other pernicious emotions to disappear from our world: but it gives us strategies by which we can considerably reduce their power.

REFERENCES

Averill, J. R. (1980). A constructivist view of emotions. In R. Plutchik & H. Kellerman (Eds.), *Emotion: Theory, research, and experience: Vol 1* (pp. 305–339). New York: Academic Press.
Averill, J. R. (1982). *Anger and aggression: An essay on emotion.* New York: Springer.
Briggs, J. L. (1970). *Never in anger: Portrait of an Eskimo family.* Cambridge, MA: Harvard University Press.
Chodorow, N. (1978). *The Reproduction of mothering: Psychoanalysis and the sociology of gender.* Berkeley and Los Angeles: University of California Press.
Davidson, D. (1986). *Inquiries into truth and interpretation.* Oxford, England: Oxford University Press.

Halberstadt, A. G. (1991). Toward an ecology of expressiveness: Family socialization in particular and a model in general. In R. S. Feldman & B. Rimé (Eds.), *Fundamentals of nonverbal behavior* (pp. 106–160). Cambridge, England: Cambridge University Press.

Harré, R. (Ed.). (1986). *The social construction of emotions.* Oxford, England: Basil Blackwell.

Kahan, D. M., & Nussbaum, M. C. (1995). Two conceptions of emotion in criminal law. *Columbia Law Review, 96,* 269–374.

Kakar, S. (1983). *The inner world: A psycho-analytic study of childhood and society in India* (2nd ed.). Oxford, England: Oxford University Press.

Kurtz, S. (1992). *All the mothers are one: Hindu India and the cultural reshaping of psychoanalysis.* New York: Columbia University Press.

Lazarus, R. S. (1991). *Emotion and adaptation.* New York: Oxford University Press.

Lutz, C. (1988). *Unnatural emotions: Everyday sentiments on a Micronesian Atoll and their challenge to Western Theory.* Chicago: University of Chicago Press.

Nolan-Hoeksema, S. (1990). *Sex differences in depression.* Stanford, CA: Stanford University Press.

Nussbaum, M. (in press). *Upheavals of thought: A theory of the emotions.* Cambridge and New York: Cambridge University Press.

Ortony, A., Clore, G. L., & Collins, A. (1988). *The cognitive structure of emotions.* Cambridge, England: Cambridge University Press.

Parke, R. D., Cassidy, J., Burks, V. M., Carson, J. L., & Boyum, L. (1992). Familial contribution to peer competence among young children: The role of interactive and affective processes. In R. Parke & G. W. Ladd (Eds.), *The family-peer relationships: Modes of linkage* (pp.). Hillsdale, NJ: Lawrence Erlbaum Associates.

Pinker, S. (1997). *How the mind works.* New York: Norton.

Rosaldo, M. Z. (1980). *Knowledge and passion: Ilongot notions of self and social life.* Cambridge, England: Cambridge University Press.

Rosaldo, M. Z. (1984). Toward an anthropology of self and feeling. In R. A. Schweder & R. A. Le Vine (Eds.), *Culture theory: Essays on mind, self, and emotion* (pp. 137–157). Cambridge, England: Cambridge University Press.

Schweder, R. A., & Le Vine, R. A. (Eds.). (1984). *Culture theory: Essays on mind, self, and emotion.* Cambridge, England: Cambridge University Press.

Seligman, M. E. P. (1975). *Helplessness: On depression, development, and death.* New York: Freeman.

Stern, D. N. (1977). *The first relationship: Infant and mother.* Cambridge, MA: Harvard University Press.

Stern, D. N. (1985). *The interpersonal world of the infant.* New York: Basic Books.

de Waal, F. B. M. (1989). *Peacemaking among primates.* Cambridge, MA: Harvard University Press.

de Waal, F. B. M. (1996). *Good natured: The origins of right and wrong in humans and other animals.* Cambridge, MA: Harvard University Press.

de Waal, F. B. M., & Lanting, F. (1997). *Bonobo: The forgotten ape.* Berkeley and Los Angeles: University of California Press.

Wikan, U. (1990). *Managing turbulent hearts: A Balinese formula for living.* Chicago: University of Chicago Press.

Winnicott, D. W. (1965). *The maturational processes and the facilitating environment: Studies in the theory of emotional development.* Madison, CT: International Universities Press.

Chapter 4

Continuities of Selfhood in the Face of Radical Developmental and Cultural Change

Michael J. Chandler
The University of British Columbia

Christopher E. Lalonde
The University of Victoria

Bryan W. Sokol
The University of British Columbia

Our *text* for this chapter is the underexamined notion of self-continuity (i.e., the art of counting one's self only once), and our *purpose* is to bring out both common and distinctive ways in which young persons, representative of markedly different cultures, usually succeed, but occasionally fail, in somehow regarding themselves as one and the same numerically identical individual despite their awareness of often dramatic personal and cultural change. The *point* of our rehearsing these matters is to use them as a way of drawing attention to what we judge to be better and worse ways of dealing with the recurrent culture versus transculture polemic that crosscuts the whole of this volume.

The particular villain of this piece is that exclusionary brand of neosituationalism that has, of late, motivated a renaissance of interest in cross-cultural work within the developmental disciplines by succeeding in shaming much of the field into settling for a warmed over version of the classical duality between "Nature and Nurture" that only "Nurture" could win. We mean to speak against this stark antinomy by championing a kind of "levels analysis" that aims to give equal pride of place to both the universals and particulars of development. We intend to do this, at least in part, through example, by directing your attention to the notion of self-continuity, and by demonstrating that it, at least, is a concept that is necessarily transcultural in its formal design features, and, at the same time, also fully determined by the vagaries of culture.

In taking up the notion of self-continuity, we intend to further focus attention on the grisly fact of suicide among young people from both Canada's cultural mainstream and from the badly savaged culture of Canada's aboriginal or "First Nations" peoples. Our point is to demonstrate that the risk of suicide that is run by such young people is importantly determined by the personally and culturally different ways in which they undertake to satisfy the common obligation to work out some diachronic sense of identity that allows them to survive as continuous or numerically identical individuals, despite the inevitability of personal change. In taking up this agenda, we mean to proceed through a series of three steps.

AGENDA

First, we want to broadly sketch the rough outlines of the culture versus transculture polemic that currently divides our field and to run up a cautionary flag meant to warn you off of the dangers of settling for some fickle choice between these two oppositional alternatives.

Second, we want to go on to quickly particularize what might otherwise risk becoming a flight of abstraction by focusing attention on the target issue of self-continuity, a concept that we mean to mark as one more of those Janus-faced matters, that, in one of its countenances, directly reflects the cultural context in which it is situated, and, in the other, reveals itself to be one of those existential matters that, as birth and death or solidarity and loneliness, necessarily recurs in every culture.

Finally, we want to report on an ongoing program of research meant to track the developmental course of the self-continuity "warranting practices" of young persons drawn from Canada's cultural mainstream as well as their aboriginal counterparts, all with an eye toward better understanding the life or death consequences of successes or failures in the maintenance of a sense of personal and cultural persistence.

THE PITTING OF UNIVERSALITY AND PLURALITY

Let us begin, then, by first critically examining what we plan to hold up as the common but misguided practice of pitting universality against plurality. As is generally recognized, the developmental sciences are suffering through yet another in what has shown itself to be an ongoing series of pendulum swings that repetitiously sets human nature against contingent circumstance in some either/or form of bivariate opposition (Chandler, 1997). According to the latest version of this increasingly radicalized nature/nurture polemic, more or less everything of moment is understood to be either the automatic consequence of some small handful of innate (and therefore "universal") modularized structures, or is otherwise seen to come down to only culture. Not surprisingly, the neonativists who live on the "wet-lab" side of this either/or paradigmatic divide are quick to remind us of our million or more years of common hominid history, and the stark improbability of all of this yielding nothing that deserves to count as real "human nature." For their own part, the "neosituationalists" or "cultural relativists" lined up on the opposite side of this ideological divide adopt much the same scolding tone, but used this time to heap shame upon the heads of all those who dare to intimate that there might still exist something (anything) that is actually common to all cultures. As seen from the postmodern vantage of such *fin-de-millennium* parlor nihilists (Chandler, 1997), the traditional search by developmentalists for "existential themes" likely to recur in every culture, or to define some universal trajectory in human growth, is not only viewed as a fool's errand, but, worse still, is thought to betray a kind of residual ethnocentrism, some lingering colonialist mind-set, that works to limit human freedom and to trivialize all cultures save one's own. All such retrograde universalistic assumptions, it is argued, not only perpetuate long since discredited modernist illusions about so-called human nature, but leave all those who promote them self-accused of an unreflective prejudice that is so shabby and so shot through with ideological contaminants that they need to be understood as collaborators in some repressive Orwellian plot of the political right. Although perhaps understandably provoked by the all too familiar tendency on the part of some to proclaim the discovery of yet another new developmental universal hidden away like a prize in whatever adventitious sample of young persons comes most easily to hand, such understandable resentment alone is insufficient, in our view, to justify the bleak vision of subjugated selves currently being promoted by the advocates of the new situationalism.

Several things seem wrong with any such high-contrast, oppositional picture of universals and particulars, not the least of which is the fact that it is inimical to, and effectively empties out, most of what has traditionally proven really interesting about the study of human development. More to the present point, however, is the fact that there appear to be any number of good reasons as to why no such mirror-image, either/or account will ultimately work. Beyond the observation that the new cultural determinism looks surprisingly like biological determinism stood upon its head, one might well list out, by way of objection, the facts:

1. Any such attempt to discount apparent transcultural universality by evoking some "universal law of difference" amounts to a performative contradiction (i.e., the suggestion that it is in our nature to be

infinitely open to the influence of the environment is no less a commentary on human nature than is its opposite number).

2. Such expressions of thoroughgoing social determinism presuppose that culture directly impresses itself upon presumably passive individuals without the necessity of interpretation.

3. Such claims merely threaten to relocate the epicenter of essence away from the individual person, and into the culture.

4. No evident "stop rule" exists to prevent big cultures from being progressively downsized to the point that we are once again reduced to studying just you versus me (Habermas, 1989).

5. The idea that persons are simply clay in society's hands is no less ideological, and no less likely to be enlisted as a tool of political oppression, than its opposite.

ESCAPING THE NATURE/NURTURE POLEMIC

If that is enough said about why simply trading old monologic lamps for new hardly qualifies as much in the way of real progress, then the serious task at hand would seem to become that of finding some better way of conceptualizing how it might be that at least some components of development actually reflect both a fully determinant human nature and, at the same time, have culture written all over their faces.

Any argument to the effect that the defining course of development—in this case identity development—is somehow set by certain universal design characteristics constitutive of the whole of human kind and, at the same time, is thoroughly determined by the vagaries of culture can only hope to succeed through some divide and conquer strategy that locates putative universals in one place and contingent consequences somewhere else. Because the available maneuvering room is as tight as it is, such sorting strategies have tended to spread out either "horizontally" or (in a way that we find more uplifting) "vertically."

The most ready-to-hand of these orthogonal alternatives has been to proceed horizontally, by simply dragging out our well-oiled analysis of variance techniques and apportioning to both culture and its opposite their own seemingly fair share of responsibility for this or that aspect of personhood. We could, in so doing, get lucky by finding that the neosituationalists and the neonativists are both entitled to something like 50% of the available variance. Although no one would walk away empty-handed from such a Solomon-like dividing of the spoils, such a hatchet job would continue to leave us with two competing camps caught up in yet another of those forced-choice, "whatever makes you rich, makes me poor," scenarios. Invoking the language of contemporary object relations theory, Overton (1997, 1998) has stigmatized all such horizontal instantiations of the traditional nature/nurture polemic as "split positions," equivalent in form to the old domestic Donnybrook in which I insist that I drink because you yell, and you argue that you yell because I drink. Because such confrontational politics ensure that every putative gain in understanding in one quarter automatically qualifies as a countervailing loss in the other, there is, we would urge, a renewed obligation on us all to somehow rise above any such zero-sum game.

The more stand-up alternative to all such horizontal nature/nurture dualities is to attempt some more vertical form of levels analysis according to which distinctions are drawn, not between one's various collateral attributes, but rather between (a) those formal, abstract, "computational" (Marr, 1982; Norman, 1982), or "design features" (Dennett, 1987) that specify what function this or that psychological mechanism is meant to serve, (b) those more "functional" or "procedural" or "algorithmic" means—as they have been variously called—through which such designs are actualized (Overton, 1991), and, finally, (c) those particular physical mechanisms, or bits of psychological "hardware," by means of which such procedures are concretely implemented. Clocks, for example, if they are to satisfy the purposes for which they are intended, must all share the common design feature of somehow lending a measured beat to the passage of time, quite apart from the procedural and hardware questions of whether they are "digital" or "analog," or whether they accomplish their functions with batteries, tightly wound springs, or the slow measured burning of ropes. In ways, then, that are analogous to Aristotle's classic claim that a full explanation of any phenomenon requires an account of formal and final, as well as efficient and material causes (Overton, 1991), many contemporary cognitive scientists and theorists of mind (e.g., Dennett, 1987; Marr, 1982; Norman, 1982; Searle, 1984) have, of late, also come to insist that all well-rounded explanations must necessarily include not only hardware and procedural explanations, but also pattern, design, or competence explanations that seek to make clear what it is that particular psychological mechanisms are supposed to be able to do.

The special merit of applying such a levels analysis to the problem of arbitrating what is context or culturally specific and what is potentially common or universal is that one and the same psychological mechanism—the self, for example—can be meaningfully understood to be both culturally specific at one level of explanation and universal at another. At the hardware level, for example, Lillard (1998) has informed us that in some, for us exotic, cultures it is imagined that the seat of the self is to be found in the nose or some other dangling appendage. Similarly, our own data, to which we shortly turn, makes the case that, at the procedural level,

Euro-American cultures tend to promote a structural or essentialist strategy for computing self-continuity, whereas certain aboriginal communities support a more narratively based, functional approach to the problem of personal persistence. None of these strongly situated, culturally based variations need be understood, however, as detracting from the possibility that, at a different and more patterned level of analysis, self-continuity continues to be a necessary transcultural design requirement for any workable conception of self- or personhood.

SELF-CONTINUITY ON THE COMPETENCE, PROCEDURAL, AND HARDWARE LEVELS

Armed with something akin to Dennett's (1987), Overton's (1991), or Marr's (1982) hardware, procedures, and competence framework, we now mean to turn full attention to the topic of selfhood in general, and the problem of self-continuity in particular, all in an effort to better understand how representatives of distinct cultural groups might proceed in similar and different ways to warrant the necessary assumption of their own numerical identity. In going about this task we mean to organize our remarks as follows. First, we plan to argue, both on formal grounds and on appeal to a certain amount of newly minted empirical evidence, that, by focusing on the pattern, design, or competence level of explanation, it is possible to describe what amounts to a transcultural program aimed at specifying a common problem space within which any person of any stripe must define the meaning of selfhood. Next, we describe a set of preliminary findings that offer good reasons to believe that mainstream Canadian youth, on the one hand, and First Nations adolescents, on the other, adopt quite different procedural approaches or employ different algorithmic strategies in attempting to solve the generic self-continuity problem. Finally, we report out on some collected epidemiological data (Chandler & Lalonde, 1998) that help to drive home the point that different culturally sanctioned procedural solution strategies to the problem of self-continuity are differently vulnerable to particular kinds of challenges to identity that historical circumstances can set in one's paths.

THE FORMAL PROBLEM SPACE OF THE SELF

Taking this list from the top, we begin by reflecting on the general problem space over which any conceivable notion of selfhood is presumably obliged to operate and by considering the possibility that there may well exist certain constitutive conditions, or system imperatives, that any workable account of identity needs to satisfy before it could potentially calculate anything that would be recognizable as a fully fledged person. Before going very far down this road, that is, before openly suggesting anything as politically incorrect as the possibility that there may be some transcultural design characteristics to the self, it is probably best to start by happily conceding the point that, in different times and in different places, persons have and do continue to hold quite radically different ideas about the hardware and procedures that go into making up a self. If this proposition was ever in serious doubt—which seems unlikely—research and observational data accumulating at least since the 1940s has left no real room for continuing uncertainty. It just *is* the case that humankind has already proven itself capable of holding to views about itself that not only are strongly different from our own Euro-American, post-Enlightenment thoughts on the matter, but also are often so different as to strike the cross-culturally challenged as totally preposterous. Selves located in noses, you say with a snort, how absolutely quaint or charming or ludicrous. Put off you may be, but what you are not is *surprised*. The idea that available conceptions of selfhood vary cross-culturally has long since become old news (e.g., Shweder & Bourne, 1984). What we are not so sanguine about is the precise *sense* in which the meaning of selfhood requires being understood as subject to the vagaries of culture, and it is in this place of uncertainty that any hope of winning the argument that something about selfhood is common to the whole of humankind must somehow try to gain its explanatory foothold.

Although there are other contenders for the transcultural part in the production of selfhood (self-unity and personal agency, for example), an obvious first-draft choice among these various candidate design features is clearly the notion of self-continuity. The considerable agreement that exists on this point arises out of the seemingly inescapable fact that every society would seem to require, as a condition of its continuing existence as a moral order, some degree of social responsibility on the part of its constituency (Hallowell, 1955) and, consequently, the availability of some mechanism for both counting its members responsible for their own past actions and for ensuring some degree of commitment to a common future (Harré, 1979). For this reason it is widely thought to follow that *any* shared conception of selfhood capable of supporting *any* cultural form of life whatsoever would, at a minimum, need to allow persons to be identified and redescribed at different moments in time (Strawson, 1959). That is, every society must, as a necessary condition of its own maintenance, somehow make whatever conceptual provisions are necessary to permit its members to understand themselves to persist in a way that is sufficiently self-same to allow all of their various temporally distinct ways of being to be counted as paraphrases or alternative expressions of one and the same continuous individual. On this authority any putative self (and, in fact, any candidate culture) that lacked this constitutive quality of presumed persistence—what Taylor (1991) has called the bare reflexive awareness of one's self as a continuing subject—would fail to be recognizable as an instance of what we ordinarily take selves to be (Cassirer, 1923).

For all of these reasons it has been widely argued that: (a) the requirement that persons be seen to persist in time is an immanent providence at work in all human affairs (Shotter, 1984); (b) the fundamental logic of identity necessarily understands the subject as self-identical (Haber, 1994); (c) a sense of personal continuity is not an elective "feature" of the self but a "constitutive condition" of its coming into being (Habermas, 1991), and so needs to count as one of those things that every one needs in some measure in order to qualify as a person (Cassirer, 1923); (d) personal persistence stands as a necessary condition over which even the term *self* could reasonably be allowed to operate (Shotter, 1984), automatically rendering any claims to selfhood that did not include such a temporal dimension fundamentally nonsensical (Luckman, 1979); (e) any notion of selfhood that was not held to be abiding in this diachronic sense would consequently have no functional value in the operation of any human social order (Hallowell, 1976); and finally (f) any society that failed to make provisions sufficient to permit the reidentification of persons across time would simply fail to function. On these and related grounds, a long list of otherwise apparently committed cultural relativists (e.g., Geertz, 1973, 1975; Hallowell, 1976; Shweder & Bourne, 1984) have come to agree that self-continuity is "universal in the human experience" (Levine & White, 1986, p. 38) and thus "ubiquitous to all of humankind" (Harré, 1979, p. 397; Chandler & Lalonde, 1998).

Now, of course, none of this is automatically true just because so many contributors to this literature have assumed it to be so. Perhaps we have all, once again, simply become infected with some new strain of lingering colonialist sentiment that causes us to misread simple contingencies and practice effects as evidence for some deep-running transcultural computational form. Clearly, something stronger than abstract formalisms or mere hearsay is needed if you are to go away persuaded that something about the design of selves is really exceptionless and so universal after all.

Without being necessarily convinced that this is the sort of disagreement that can be effectively attacked by throwing data at it, we do have one line of empirical evidence that does speak to this question. It comes from a program of research that has as its goal the possibility of bringing out the changing ways in which young persons of various stripes undertake to warrant whatever convictions they may have about the basis for their own self-continuity. To do this we have spent time with upwards of 200 "normal" and psychiatrically hospitalized adolescents, first reading with them various "Classic Comic Books" (e.g., Victor Hugo's *Les Miserables* and Charles Dickens' *A Christmas Carol*), that depict examples of persistent identity in the face of personal change before then going on to press them for their own reasons for believing that, despite dramatic transformations, they themselves still deserve to be counted as the selfsame continuous and numerically identical person. Without going into detail about the age-graded changes that we have observed in the various strategies that more or less mature young persons differently employ in warranting their own and others persistence through time (see, for example, Ball & Chandler, 1989; Boyes & Chandler, 1992; Chandler & Ball, 1990), we do want to draw attention to the unique ways in which an available subgroup of suicidal adolescents have dealt with this assessment task.

But what bearing, you might well ask, does the topic of youth suicide have upon the foundational matter of self-continuity and on the variable ways that individuals of different developmental stations or different cultures undertake to warrant their own sense of personal persistence? The answer, we suggest, lies in the fact that somehow being able to throw a bridge across the distinctive expressions of selfhood that differently manifest themselves at separate moments within the ontological course needs to be understood as the link that welds together one's past, present, and future into an enduring sense of personal identity worth caring about. That is, self-continuity is that glue that not only holds us responsible for our own past actions but also provides the key to understanding why we are entitled to our own just desserts and why we ordinarily have a legitimate stake in our own as yet unrealized future. Why, you might wonder, is the prospect of our own death at some future moment a matter of special interest? Why do we not picture the death of that person we will later become in the same dispassionate way that we read about some drive-by shooting in some distant city or in the same detached way that military pilots must think about their high altitude bombing missions? The answer, we suggest, is that, we ordinarily understand ourselves as projecting both forward and backward out of the specious present, such that, later down the road of serial reincarnation of ourselves, we, like some shopworn ship of Theseus, will still be us—precious us. In short, the reason that we do not happily shuffle off this mortal coil when the going gets tough is because we count the dead person in question to be our own closest continuer, an extension of ourselves into some as yet unrealized future.

Two available sets of facts add to the good prospects of this attempt to reread youth suicide as an expression of disruptions to the standard self-continuity warranting practices of more successfully developing persons, one of which is known by practically everyone. The other is contained within a series of our own publications (i.e., Ball & Chandler, 1989; Boyes & Chandler, 1992; Chandler, 1994a, 1994b; Chandler & Ball, 1990; Chandler

& Lalonde, 1995, 1998). The common knowledge is that young persons (adolescents and young adults) actually do undertake to kill themselves at a prodigious rate some 10 to 20 times that of still younger and older persons—a fact that, in and of itself, cries out for a developmental explanation (Ball & Chandler, 1989). The second is that, in the course of their own sharply accelerating process of identity development, adolescents do regularly and repeatedly shift the grounds on which they attempt to argue or "warrant" the presumptive basis for their own self-continuity. In addition, and more to the present point, in the process of tacking back and forth between these less and more mature ways of warranting their own self-continuity, that is, in trying to clear the hurdles separating a series of increasingly complex and formally adequate ways of thinking about their own personal persistence through time, young persons do repeatedly find themselves with both developmental feet off the ground and, during these precarious transitional moments, occasionally trip and fall. In so doing, they temporarily end up (victims of their own progressive development) without any workable means of understanding their own continuity in time, their own reason to be invested in the person they are otherwise slated to become. At such awkward and potentially lethal transitional moments, suicide is a solution strategy with no appreciable downside and an outcome that often seems preferable to the more boring or heart-wrenching of teenage moments.

On the strength of this hat trick of evidence (i.e., on the strength of the facts that: [a] in the absence of any workable means of warranting one's own self-continuity, the concept of selfhood becomes nonsensical and all reasons for investing in one's own future become problematic; [b] adolescents are regularly in the business of transiting between one and another way of warranting their own self-continuity and sometimes temporarily lose their way in the process; and [c] adolescents attempt to take their lives at a rate that is many times higher than that of other age groups), we undertook to look at the ability of suicidal adolescents to warrant their own self-continuity in time.

Stripped of all of those details better suited to a journal format, this, in short, is what we found (see Ball & Chandler, 1989). First, to a person, ordinary adolescents (labeled Control in Fig. 4.1) always had at their disposal some more (Level II) or less (Level I) mature way of warranting their belief that they are continuous in time. Second, in almost every case, psychiatrically hospitalized but nonsuicidal adolescents (Low Risk), although regularly less "mature" in their approach to the problem of self-continuity than their nonhospitalized age mates, were, nevertheless, still able to find good reasons as to why the persons they had been, were now, and would later become were the self-same numerically identical person. Finally, and in remarkably sharp contrast to those prepared to go on liv-

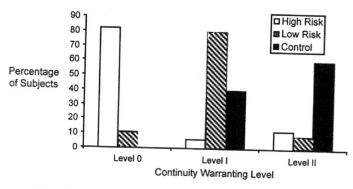

FIG. 4.1.   Continuity warranting level by suicide risk status.

ing, some 84% of the seriously suicidal adolescents tested (High Risk) came up empty. That is, they were totally unable to find any grounds whatsoever for warranting the necessary belief that they were continuous in time or connected to their own prospective futures (Level 0). None of this is, of course, ironclad evidence in support of the broad proposition that self-continuity is a universal design feature of self- or personhood, but it is arguably a step in that direction.

CULTURE AS THE SETPOINT FOR THE CHOICE BETWEEN ALTERNATIVE ALGORITHMS FOR CALCULATING SELF-CONTINUITY

If, as we have shown, there are empirical as well as formal reasons to support the claim that self-continuity is a necessary constitutive condition of any coherent conception of selfhood and, consequently, of any collective moral order, then we have advanced our assertion that numerical identity is a nonelective design feature of all workable accounts of human individuality and thus belongs in the bag of transcultural things that turn out to be true for all people in all times. What all of this leaves unsettled is the location of the proper place in which to preserve the otherwise uncontested fact that, at some other level of analysis, the meaning of selfhood is also one of those things that is known to *vary* dramatically from one culture to the next.

The answer, we suggest, is that it is at what Dennett (1987) and Overton (1991) refer to as the functional or procedural level of description that culture works to "select" the broad outlines of the particular operational strategy (i.e., digital, analog, or what?) that its members actually employ in directly computing their own self-continuity. That is, given the assertion that anyone, however situated, must, on pain of otherwise ceasing to be any sort of understandable person whatsoever, somehow learn to count themselves as continuous in time, it still follows that members of different cultures are nevertheless free to generate their own functional procedures and their own notational system and algorithmic heuristics for calculating how it might be that individuals who are first one way and then another can, nevertheless, end up being counted as one and the same numerically identical person.

If something like this is so, then what remains to be determined is precisely what choices one culture as opposed to another has made in arming its members with alternative procedural means for somehow finessing the problem of computing sameness in the face of exceptionless change. At present, we have at our disposal small bits of information that could help to answer this question as it differentially pertains to young persons drawn from Canada's cultural mainstream, on the one hand, and their aboriginal, or First Nations counterparts, on the other.

In particular, what our ongoing research has suggested is that, when obliged to lay out their own conceptual strategies for winning the argument that they and others are continuous in time, standard issue Canadian youth almost invariably begin and, more often than not, end by rooting their convictions that they are diachronically continuous on the presumptive fact that there must be some *essential* aspect or feature of their identity, situated at some more or less subterranean level of internality, that manages to stand apart from the ravages of time and works to vouchsafe the problematic matter of their own personal persistence. What tends to change in the course of ontogenetic development, this research suggests, is the level of abstraction at which such structural claims for the existence of some unchanging personal essence are pitched. Young 9- or 10-year-olds, for example, simply turn a blind eye toward everything about themselves that is different and instead focus their attention exclusively on one or more of their surface attributes (their finger prints, their DNA, etc.) that they imagine somehow stand outside of time. Older adolescents, by contrast, tend to create an identity structure with some depth and invoke a kind of phenotype/genotype distinction that allows them to write off evident change as merely superficial, while still preserving what they take to be an unchanging subterranean core of their identity. Only the oldest, and among them only the best and the brightest, ended up calling into question this common essentialistic strategy, conceding that perhaps, after all, everything about themselves is subject to change. Forced to abandon their former structural or essentialist strategies, these young people (all whom were in their late teens and at strongly formal operational levels of reasoning by standard measures) sharply shifted the ground on which they made their case for personal persistence, opting instead for some more functional or narratively based self-continuity warranting practices. By these new lights, they and others were assumed to be self-same across time, not because some more or less deep-seated part of them had escaped change, but rather because the person they once were and the person they had subsequently become were functionally related by some narrative connection assumed to exist between admittedly different installments of their identity. That is, they judged themselves to be diachronically continuous either because their past was assumed to be the determinant cause of their present (i.e., "I am the person I am today because of that terrible/special thing that happened to me in the past") or because, applying a more presentist form of historiography, they reasoned that they could narratively reinterpret their past in light of their evolving present. That is, they effectively joined Dennett (1978, 1987) and Flanagan (1996) in assuming that the self amounts to a "narrative center of gravity" in one's own life.

What is perhaps most remarkable about this later group of more developmentally advanced young persons—that is, those who came to adopt a more narratively based conception of their own persistent identity—is just how hard they were swimming against the main cultural stream. Without really trying to provide the full grounds for saying so, it is, we think, uncontroversially true that, certainly since the Enlightenment, and probably as far back as Plato or the origins of Christianity, our Western culture has been an essentialist culture, committed to what Polkinghorne (1988) described as a "metaphysics of substance." As a result, we are all quick to assume that "foundational" matters of great importance are always buried deep beneath obfuscating layers of phenotypic opacity, all of which must be swept aside or tunneled through before ever getting to the real heart of any matter. Small wonder, given all of this, that the young subjects of our research, rooted as they are in our own essentialist Euro-American culture, should begin their search for the "roots" of their own identity by "going deep" in search of some unchanging structure and that those uncommon forays into some more narratively based constructions of self-continuity that do occur always seem to come late and always in the wake of insurmountable difficulties in warranting personal persistence on a more structural, essentialistic basis.

Although the amount of data that we have in hand is too small to warrant statistical treatment, the kind of evidence that is coming in about the self-continuity practices of young aboriginal or First Nations Canadians suggests a very different picture than that afforded by their non-Native counterparts. These young persons all belong to a culture that, on report, is committed not to some foundationalist approach to truth or an essentialist approach to meaning, but to what Polkinghorne (1988) referred to as a "metaphysics of potentiality and actuality" and, consequently, are given to a more narratively based way of framing problems. That is, the First Nations of Canada, with their oral history and storytelling tradition, represent a culture whose standard notational schemes and algorithmic strategies should predispose them to attempts to solve the common computational problems of self-continuity through strategies that "go long" rather than "go deep," by linking earlier and later occurring personal ways of being through some narrative framework that connects past and present in a more "leading to" or "interpretive" fashion.

It is precisely this reliance on a narratively, rather than an essentialist based, self-continuity warranting strategy that our data so far suggest. That is, when tested with what are meant to be more culturally appropriate story materials, young First Nations persons almost never attempt to warrant their own or others self-continuity by searching out some potentially hidden essentialist core. Rather, from the outset, they undertake to frame some story that will narratively link their earlier and later ways of being. It is not, of course, that these young persons all succeed in authoring anything that would ordinarily qualify as a mature form of autobiography. That is, they do not begin by relating self-narratives that take the complex form of *bildungsroman*, or other transformational stories of character development (Lightfoot, 1997; Rorty, 1976). Rather the early efforts of the youngest of these native respondents are more often like early picaresque novels, or Medieval romances, in which the episodes of their own and other people's lives are simply strung together like beads on a string, *sans* real plot or coherent change of characters. As such, the procedural ways that First Nations youth do go about the business of warranting their own or others' self-continuity are, according to our data, qualitatively different from the ways of proceeding that are common to their culturally mainstream counterparts. They adopt from the outset a leading to form of narrative-like self-accounting that is, in its mature expression, only an endgame achievement in the development of non-Native youth. In short, First Nations youth pursue a computational algorithm that plays analog to our own digital. It is in no way our point to try to argue that one of these strategies is naturally more adequate than the other. Rather, our claim is only that, at the functional or procedural level of description, different cultural groups can and do understandably vary in how they undertake to vouchsafe their own self-continuity.

HARD TIMES AND THE DIFFERENTIAL COSTS
OF NARRATIVE AND ESSENTIALISTIC SOLUTIONS
TO THE SELF-CONTINUITY PROBLEM

Finally, we want to alert you to the possibility that, although there may not exist some blind scale of justice on which to weigh the relative merits of this or that culturally specific procedural strategy for solving what, in this case, is the universal obligation to compute some workable self-continuity warranting strategy, there is also no guarantee that such contrastive heuristics will prove uniformly adequate in dealing with the specific kinds of adversities that historical circumstance happens to throw into one's path. That is, under the press of this or that practical circumstance, digital sometimes just is better (or worse) than analog. Something like this is also pointedly the case in view of the different historical circumstances in which Aboriginal and mainstream Canadian youth are obliged to negotiate their own convictions about self-continuity.

By most accounts, we are all, to one degree or another, living through a time of dramatic cultural change. However true this might be for rank-and-file Canadian youth, a case can still be made that their culture's predilection for a more essentialistic approach to the common problem of self-continuity, although not without certain alienating costs of its own, works in their favor by partially insulating them from at least the surface structure of rapid cultural change. That is, if the culturally sanctioned direction of your search for some means of warranting your own personal sense of sameness across time happens to carry you away from the situationally troubled surface and toward some quieter, more subterranean pool of abstraction where the core of your self is alleged to be found, then count yourself temporarily lucky for being born into a place where "going deep" may just happen to be contingently better than "going long."

If, by contrast, you happen to live in a culture, as do contemporary First Nations youth, the fundamental meaning of which is understood to reside in the continuity of its own narrative history; if your culturally sanctioned ways of thinking about your own self-continuity are similarly prescribed to be narratively based; and, finally, if, after 10,000 years of adaptive success, your culture, nevertheless, has been declared "stone aged" and moribund—that is, if your cultural practices have been criminalized and beaten out of you through generations of residential schools and genocidal approaches to your language and cultural life—then woe be on you and your chances of declaring your personal existence as having any worthwhile or enduring meaning. This, of course, is precisely what has happened to the culture of every aboriginal group across North America and beyond.

Given this shameful history and the connections we have already drawn between culture, self-continuity, and suicide, one would naturally expect that the rate of suicide among Canada's First Nations youth would be dramatically higher than that of their non-Native counterparts. In fact, the trouble is worse than one's worst expectations. The overall rate of suicide among Canada's First Nations persons is three to five times higher than the national average (see Fig. 4.2), and, in fact, is the highest of any culturally identifiable group in the world (Kirmayer, 1994). Worse still, the rate of suicide among First Nations youth is another five to ten times higher than this already alarming statistic (Cooper, Corrado, Karlberg, & Pelletier, 1992). Given these current trends and before everything is over,

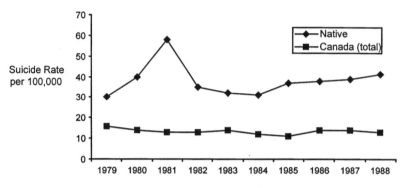

FIG. 4.2.   Suicide in Canada (1979–1988).

1 in every 20 of this generation's First Nations youth will end up dying at their own hand (Chandler & Lalonde, 1998).

Looking into this bleak picture, we have completed an epidemiological study (Chandler & Lalonde, 1998) that tried to get beyond the usual "pan-Indian" level by asking about the potentially differential rates of suicide that characterize specific tribal groups. The results of this inquiry are perhaps surprising. Among the 30 some Tribal Councils that organize British Columbia's 196 aboriginal bands, the rates of suicide turn out to be extremely variable. Over the 5-year window of the study (i.e., 1987—1992), more than half of the province's native bands suffered no youth suicide at all and, consequently, have overall suicide rates well below the national average. Others have suicide rates that are 500 to 800 times that of the nation as a whole (see Fig. 4.3).

On the strength of the proposition that suicide is a manifestation of failed attempts at sustaining a sense of personal self-continuity as well as the expectation that, at least among First Nations peoples, the culturally sanctioned procedure for computing personal persistence is narratively based, and so automatically linked to the narrative continuity (or discontinuity) provided by their own cultural heritage, we have attempted to relate the known variability in the suicide rates of various First Nations communities to some index of the degree to which these groups have been left without any sustainable culture whatsoever.

In view of the fact that the "ethnic cleansing" to which each of these aboriginal groups has been subject is, in most respects, more tragically similar than different and because their traditional cultures have been almost uniformly swept away, we looked for any kind of markers that might index community-based efforts to rebuild or rehabilitate a culture that was otherwise on the cusp of being lost. Given available resources, we have identified six such possible indexes of cultural reconstruction, including the facts that

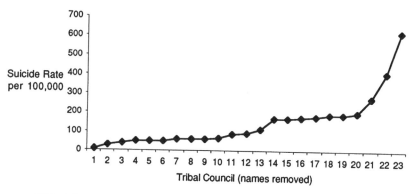

FIG. 4.3. Native suicide rate by tribal affiliation (British Columbia, 1987–1992).

some but not others of these cultural groups are in the midst of litigating for self-government or aboriginal title over traditional lands, and that some have met with more success than others in introducing native values into and exercising local control over their own public health and educational and judicial systems. Figure 4.4 draws out the strong statistical relation of these six markers of cultural rehabilitation to known rates of suicide, whereas Figure 4.5 depicts the cumulative effect of these markers. What these comparisons serve to make clear, we think, is that, in working to inculcate a sense of connectedness to one's own cultural past, communities can succeed in constructing safety nets that help to catch young people who slip while trying to navigate those standard developmental transitions that recurrently threaten to cost every young person a sense of enduring self-continuity.

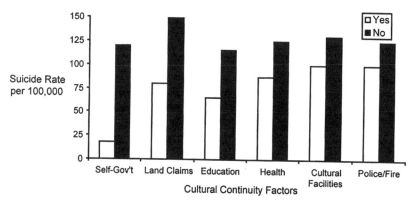

FIG. 4.4. Relations between suicide rates and measures of cultural reconstruction.

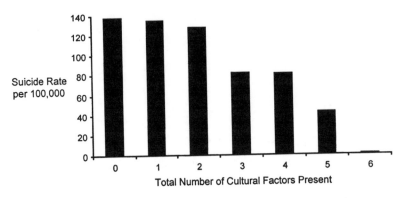

FIG. 4.5.   Cumulative effect of measures of cultural reconstruction.

CONCLUSION

What we take from all of this is that the subject of selfhood and its development is neither the exclusive province of those in search of some broad transcultural competence theory of identity development nor some wholly owned subsidiary of those neosituational theorists committed to showing how the concept of the self is the contingent consequence of socially constructed and, thus, culturally variable systems of belief. Rather, the task of working out what it could possibly mean to have or be a self needs to be viewed as existing within a problem space that occupies at least three different levels of description. At the most abstract of these levels—Dennett's or Overton's competence level, or Marr's level of computational description—there are strong empirical as well as formal reasons for supposing that, however culturally situated, any workable conception of the self, on pain of otherwise failing to satisfy those minimal design requirements necessary for the maintenance of any social or moral order, must be designed in such a way as to address the universal problem of sameness within difference, and so allow individuals to understand themselves as somehow continuous in the face of inevitable personal change. Nothing about such claims in favor of the existence of transcultural commonalities needs to be seen, however, as in any way impugning the reputation of different claims and different lines of evidence all pointing to the undeniable fact that different communities make available to their members culturally contingent ways of constructing the self. Without careful attention to the different levels of problem description on which such claims operate, we risk once again trafficking in that same spent culture versus transcultural polemic that has cost us our professional reputations so many times before.

REFERENCES

Ball, L., & Chandler, M. J. (1989). Identity formation in suicidal and nonsuicidal youth: The role of self-continuity. *Development and Psychopathology, 1*(3), 257–275.

Boyes, M. C., & Chandler, M. J. (1992). Cognitive development, epistemic doubt and identity formation in adolescence. *Journal of Youth and Adolescence, 21*(3), 277–304.

Cassirer, E. (1923). *Substance and function.* Chicago: The Open Court Publishing Company.

Chandler, M. J. (1997). Stumping for progress in a post-modern world. In A. Renninger & E. Amsel (Eds.), *New directions in the study of change and development* (pp. 1–26). Mahwah, NJ: Lawrence Erlbaum Associates.

Chandler, M. J. (1994a). Adolescent suicide and the loss of personal continuity. In D. Cicchetti & S. L. Toth (Eds.), *Rochester symposium on developmental psychopathology: Disorders and dysfunctions of the self* (pp. 371–390). Rochester, NY: University of Rochester Press.

Chandler, M. J. (1994b). Self-continuity in suicidal and nonsuicidal adolescents. In G. Noam & S. Borst (Eds.), *Children, youth and suicide: Developmental perspectives* (pp. 55–70). San Francisco: Jossey-Bass.

Chandler, M. J., & Ball, L. (1990). Continuity and commitment: A developmental analysis of the identity formation process in suicidal and non-suicidal youth. In H. Bosma & S. Jackson (Eds.), *Coping and self-concept in adolescence* (pp. 149–166). New York: Springer-Verlag.

Chandler, M. J., & Lalonde, C. E. (1995). The problem of self-continuity in the context of rapid personal and cultural change. In A. Oosterwegel & R. A. Wicklund (Eds.), *The self in European and North American culture: Development and processes* (pp. 45–63). Dordrecht, The Netherlands: Kulwer Academic Publishers.

Chandler, M. J., & Lalonde, C. E. (1998). Cultural continuity as a hedge against suicide in Canada's First Nations. *Transcultural Psychiatry, 35*(2), 193–211.

Cooper, M., Corrado, R., Karlberg, A. M., & Pelletier Adams, L. (1992). Aboriginal suicide in British Columbia: An overview. *Canada's Mental Health, 19*, 19–23.

Dennett, D. (1978). *Brainstorms.* Hassocks: Harvester Press.

Dennett, D. (1987). *The intentional stance.* Cambridge, MA. MIT Press.

Flanagan, O. (1996). *Self expressions: Mind, morals, and the meaning of life.* New York: Oxford University Press.

Geertz, C. (1973). *The interpretation of cultures: Selected essays.* New York: Basic Books.

Geertz, C. (1975). On the nature of anthropological understanding. *American Scientist, 63*, 47–53.

Haber, H. (1994). *Beyond postmodern politics.* New York: Routledge.

Habermas, J. (1989). *The new conservatism: Cultural criticism and the historians' debate* (S. W. Nicholsen, Trans. & Ed.). Cambridge, MA: MIT Press. (Original works published 1985 & 1987)

Habermas, J. (1991). The paradigm shift in Mead. In M. Aboulafia (Ed.) *Philosophy, social theory, and the thought of George Herbert Mead* (pp. 138–168). Albany: State University of New York Press.

Hallowell, A. I. (1955). *Culture and experience.* Philadelphia: University of Pennsylvania Press.

Hallowell, A. I. (1976). *Contributions to anthropology: Selected papers of A. Irving Hallowell.* Chicago: University of Chicago Press.

Harré, R. (1979). *Social being: A theory for social psychology.* Oxford, England: Blackwell.

Kirmayer, L. (1994). Suicide among Canadian aboriginal people. *Transcultural Psychiatric Research Review, 31*, 3–57.

Levine, R. A., & White, M. I. (1986). *Human conditions: The cultural basis of educational development.* New York: Routledge & Kegan Paul.

Lightfoot, C. G. (1997). *The culture of adolescent risk-taking.* New York: Guilford.

Lillard, A. (1998). Ethnopsychologies: Cultural variations in theories of mind. *Psychological Bulletin, 123*, 3–32.

Luckman, T. (1979). Personal identity as an evolutionary and historical problem. In M. von Cranach (Ed.), *Human ethology: Claims and limits of a new discipline* (pp. 56–74). New York: Cambridge University Press.

Marr, D. (1982). *Vision: A computational investigation into the human representation and processing of visual information.* New York: Freeman.

Norman, D. A. (1982). *Learning and memory.* San Francisco: Freeman.

Overton, W. F. (1991). Competence, procedures, and hardware: Conceptual and empirical considerations. In M. Chandler & M. Chapman (Eds.), *Criteria for competence: Controversies in the conceptualization and assessment of children's abilities* (pp. 19–42). Hillsdale, NJ: Lawrence Erlbaum Associates.

Overton, W. F. (1997). Beyond dichotomy: An embodied active agent for cultural psychology. *Culture and Psychology, 3*, 315–334.

Overton, W. F. (1998). Developmental psychology: Philosophy, concepts, and methodology. In W. Damon (Series Ed.) & R. M. Lerner (Vol. Ed.), *The handbook of child psychology: Vol. 1. Theoretical models of human development* (5th ed., pp. 107–188). New York: J. Wiley.

Polkinghorne, C. (1988). *Narrative knowing and the human sciences.* Albany: State University of New York Press.

Rorty, A. O. (1976). *The identity of reason.* Berkeley: University of California Press.

Searle, J. (1984). *Minds, brains and science.* Cambridge, MA: Harvard University Press.

Shotter, J. (1984). *Social accountability and selfhood.* Oxford, England: Basil Blackwell.

Shweder, R. A., & Bourne, L. (1984). Does the concept of the person vary cross-culturally? In R. A. Shweder & R. A. Levine (Eds.), *Culture theory: Essays on mind, self, and emotion* (pp. 158–199). Cambridge, England: Cambridge University Press.

Strawson, P. F. (1959). *Individuals.* London: Methuen.

Taylor, C. (1991). *The malaise of modernity.* Concord, Ontario, Canada: House of Anansi Press.

Chapter 5

The Culture Concept and the Individualism–Collectivism Debate: Dominant and Alternative Attributions for Class in the United States

Claudia Strauss
University of North Carolina at Chapel Hill

Some cultural psychologists have proposed that there is not a universal path of human development but rather development of two types, unevenly distributed around the world: an individualist (or idiocentric or independent) path characteristic of the industrialized West and a collectivist (or sociocentric or interdependent) path characteristic of nearly all other societies (Greenfield, 1994; Harkness, Raeff, & Super, 2000; Kagitcibasi, 1996; Kim, Triandis, Kagitcibasi, Choi, & Yoon, 1994; Markus & Kitayama, 1991; Shweder & Bourne, 1984; Triandis, 1995). Although this distinction draws on anthropological observations and theories, most anthropologists at the end of the 20th century react to this division as a relic of an earlier way of thinking.[1] This chapter explains why general cultural characterizations of this sort—indeed the very concept of culture—have been questioned by anthropologists; proposes a better way of thinking about culture; and illustrates the complexities of culture with research about the ways U.S. Americans explain economic standing. I argue (similarly to Turiel, 1996; see also Killen & Wainryb, 2000; Wainryb, 1997) that there are conflicting cultural models to explain economic standing in the United States. Some of these are individualist, others collectivist, and still others are mixed or hard to classify. I depart from the work of Turiel and others, however, in showing that individualist cultural models of class standing were psychologically

---

[1]One of my anthropological colleagues, on learning of my interest in this topic, reacted that this way of thinking was "prehistoric." Another warned me about "essentializing."

dominant in the United States near the end of the 20th century and probably still are in many respects. The new way of thinking about culture proposed here helps to explain why defenders and critics of the individualism/collectivism distinction both have part of the truth.

THE INDIVIDUALISM/COLLECTIVISM DEBATE

Discussions of psychological differences between individualist and collectivist societies are burgeoning. The individualist/collectivist distinction has been seen as useful for understanding cross-national differences in public policies (Triandis, 1995) and organizational behavior (Hofstede, 1980, 1991) as applicable to the education of immigrants to the United States (Greenfield & Cocking, 1994), and as a corrective to Western psychological theories (Markus & Kitayama, 1991). Triandis (1995) distilled much of this literature, presenting four attributes that are supposed to distinguish individualist (I) from collectivist (C) societies: (a) interdependent self definitions (C) versus independent self definitions (I); (b) priority given to group goals (C) rather than to personal goals (I); (c) focus on norms and duties (C) versus personal needs and rights (I); and (d) emphasis on maintaining interpersonal relationships (C) versus maintenance of such relationships only if they are personally advantageous (I; pp. 43–44).[2] Advocates for this distinction recognize intracultural variation, but argue that these cultural syndromes lead to overall tendencies toward differences between the thoughts, feelings, and motivations of people growing up in Europe, the United States, Australia, and New Zealand (I societies) and those of people in every other part of the world (C societies). (Hunter-gatherer societies, which tend to be I in many respects, are said to be an exception to this geographic distribution; Triandis, 1995, p. 26.)

Other I/C research allows for different types of individualism and collectivism. Chen, Meindl, and Hunt (1997) proposed that crosscutting the individualist/collectivist division is a "horizontal" (valorization of sameness or equality)/"vertical" (valorization of difference) dimension. To take an example given by Triandis, competitive upper-middle-class U.S. Americans are vertical individualists whereas Swedes tend to be horizontal individualists—highly independent but not liking people to "stick out" (Triandis, 1995, p. 45). Kashima et al. (1995) found that relatedness (agreement with statements such as "I feel like doing something for people in trouble because I can almost feel their pain") was different for males and females in their Australian, mainland United States, and

---

[2]It is important to distinguish these collectivist attributes from generosity or selflessness. It is common for elderly people in the United States to refuse to live with their children because they do not want to be a burden on them. This is unselfish, while individualist.

Japanese samples,[3] but not cross-culturally as a main effect. On the other hand, factors they labeled *collectivism* (e.g., "I am prepared to do things for my group at any time, even though I have to sacrifice my own interest"), *agency* (e.g., "I don't change my opinions in conformity with those of the majority"), and *assertiveness* (e.g., "I assert my opposition when I disagree strongly with the members of my group") did differ cross-culturally. Alipuria (1997) pointed out the striking difference between childrearing patterns of two collectivist societies: India and Japan. Hindu Indians have been characterized as practicing diffuse mothering (encouraging the child to form affective bonds with adult female relatives in the extended family but discouraging close mother–child bonds; Kurtz, 1992; Seymour, 1983; but see Nuckolls, 1996), whereas Japanese mothers are said to encourage a sense of fusion between mother and child (Alipuria, 1997, p. 34, citing Markus & Kitayama, 1991; see also Allison, 1996; Lebra, 1994).[4] Thus, some I/C advocates highlight differences within the broad individualist/collectivist categories, while maintaining the importance of the overall I/C division.

Other psychologists and psychological anthropologists have challenged arguments for general differences between individualist and collectivist cultures. Spiro (1993), for example, pointed out that ideologies about the self seem to differ more cross-culturally than do phenomenologies of self or lay ideas about self. His discussion draws on the observations of numerous anthropologists, including Ewing (1991), Hollan (1992), McHugh (1989), Parish (1994), and Wikan (1987); see also Lindholm (1997). Killen and Wainryb (2000), Nucci (1997), Turiel (1996, 1997), and Wainryb (1997) stressed the conflicting moralities that can coexist within a society as well as cross-cultural universals in moral reasoning.

ANTHROPOLOGICAL WARINESS

Most of the proponents of the I/C thesis are psychologists, not anthropologists.[5] This may seem surprising, given anthropologists' central concern with cultural differences. A quick intellectual history of cultural anthropology is

---

[3]It is interesting that there were no gender differences in relatedness in their Korean sample.

[4]See also Kusserow (1999) and Tobin, Wu, and Davidson (1989) for interesting discussions of other distinctions within or between I and C societies. Kusserow discerned class-differentiated patterns of child rearing in the United States that led to three types of individualism, which she labeled "hard defensive," "hard offensive," and "soft offensive." Tobin et al. presented contrasting collectivist approaches to early childhood education: a Chinese model that stresses conformity and a Japanese model that stresses group feeling but allows for considerable differences in individual behavior.

[5]Shweder (Shweder & Bourne, 1984; Shweder, Mahapatra, & Miller, 1990) is the most prominent anthropological proponent of the thesis. See also Kurtz (1992) and Marsella, DeVos,

necessary to explain why most anthropologists are receptive to the I/C argument that Western psychological theories need to be reexamined in the light of cross-cultural differences but are suspicious of the I/C construct itself.

The discipline's tendency toward cultural particularism (i.e., emphasis on cultural uniqueness) would account for a good part of this split reaction to the I/C thesis. Cultural particularism predisposes anthropologists to suspect that Western psychological theories are ethnocentric and limited, but it also makes anthropologists queasy with any division of world cultures that puts all of Asia, Africa, and Latin America in one category.

The I/C thesis might have been more acceptable in an earlier period in anthropology. Earlier, anthropologists' cultural particularism vied with a concern for larger explanations. The result was acceptance of grand divisions between "folk societies" and "civilization" (Redfield, 1953), that is, between societies characterized by "mechanical solidarity" (likeness, conformity) and relationships based on "status," and normative "holism" on the one hand and those characterized by "organic solidarity" (complementary but differing roles) and relationships based on "contract," and normative "individualism" on the other (Durkheim, 1893/1933; Maine, 1861; Dumont, 1970, respectively). The textual turn in anthropology, with its accompanying valorization of interpretation over explanation (Geertz, 1973), has put large explanatory schemes of any sort out of favor. Furthermore, there is an uncomfortable similarity between the newer relativist I/C dichotomy and the older evolutionist ones in which Individualism was not just different from Collectivism but more advanced. Clifford Geertz probably speaks for the majority of contemporary anthropologists in rejecting "stark 'great divide' contrasts between 'modern' and 'premodern' societies, the one individualistic, rational, and free of tradition, the other collectivistic, intuitive, and mired in it" (Geertz, 1994, p. 3, quoted in Killen & Wainryb, 2000, p. 5; but see Shore, 1996, especially chaps. 5 to 8, for a qualified endorsement of general "primitive"/ "modern" differences in thought).

An even more radical challenge has arisen not just to "West versus the rest" dichotomies but even to general characterizations of a single culture. Persistently throughout the 20th century and increasingly toward the end of the century, concerns were raised about the very concept of culture. The charges that have been leveled against the culture concept include the following: It implies stasis (Wolf, 1982; Clifford, 1988); it implies homogeneity within the group whose culture is described (Roberts, 1961; Wallace, 1970); it implies thematic consistency, disregarding both contextual variability and

---

and Hsu (1985) for closely related discussions. Probably more anthropologists support a version of the I/C thesis that applies just to differences between their culture area and the West. For example, Lebra (1994) contrasted Japanese and U.S. parent–child relationships in a way that is compatible with the I/C thesis but without defending its applicability to other societies.

heterodox ideas (Bakhtin, 1981); it implies motivational force, ignoring doctrines to which people pay lip service only (Spiro, 1987); it implies definite boundaries between entities (the culture of the x, the culture of the y), overlooking exchanges of ideas, objects, and practices (Wolf, 1982; Appadurai, 1990); it elides the way representations are disseminated by dominant groups and resisted by nondominant groups (Gramsci, 1971; Foucault, 1972); it misses the way cultural descriptions sometimes reflect the anxieties of analysts about their own societies more than behaviors in the society being described (Said, 1978) or capture only the official rules proffered by informants, ignoring actual practice (Boas, 1911/1938; Bourdieu, 1972/1977; Malinowski, 1922/1961); and it creates a fictional single entity out of a diverse set of objects, practices, and mental representations (D'Andrade, 1995).

It follows that attempts to characterize cultures as individualist or collectivist will, from some quarters in anthropology, raise questions that derive from these concerns: Is this a timeless feature of the culture or one that is changing? Is it true of certain subgroups only in the society? Does it overlook contextual variation in behavior? Is it the tendentious representation of cultural apologists, one that ignores what people really do? And so on. Debates about the culture concept have even been invested with a larger moral resonance, as indicated by the title of a panel at the 1996 annual meeting of the American Anthropological Association: "The Concept of 'Culture': Moral Pluralism or Racism in Another Guise?" Nowadays Japanologists debate characterizations of Japanese groupism or holism (e.g., Kuwayama, 1992; see Kelly, 1991, and Rosenberger, 1992, for overviews); Sinologists demonstrate the difficulties of reducing Chinese history and culture to a simple sociocentric summary (see Elvin, 1985; Oxfeld, 1992); and South Asianists point to Indians' life histories (Mines, 1988) and examples of political resistance by women and lower castes (Omvedt, 1980) to show that Indians are not necessarily all the contented holists they have been portrayed as being (e.g., by Dumont, 1966/1970; but see Kurtz, 1992, for a strong defense of Dumont's characterization).

Intriguingly, it seems that characterizations of U.S. Americans as individualist are not as controversial in anthropology and U.S. studies as are characterizations of non-Westerners as groupist, collectivist, or holist. True, there have been criticisms of one-sided characterizations of U.S. individualism (e.g., Hollan, 1992; Holland & Kipnis, 1994; Quinn, 1996; Strauss, 1997), vivid portrayals of subgroup collectivism (e.g., Stack, 1974, 1996) as well as feminist discussions of male–female differences (Gilligan, 1982, but see Miller, 1997).[6] Still, as Moffatt's review of ethnographic writ-

---

[6]Killen and Wainryb (2000) cite a great deal of literature (e.g., Mills, 1956; Reisman, Glazer, & Denney, 1953; and Whyte, 1956) that discussed aspects of conformism in U.S. society. These findings, however, are consistent with an ideological emphasis on individualism

ing about U.S. culture noted, accounts of the "saliency of a distinctively American individualism" (Moffatt, 1992, p. 215) represent the mainstream approach of this research.

There are three plausible explanations for this continued emphasis on U.S. individualism. First, anthropologists are often driven by the desire to challenge the naive ethnocentrism typical of Westerners who value their own practices and beliefs over those of other societies. Descriptions of non-Western collectivism are thus suspect if they imply mindless or spineless compliance (although less so if they suggest close interpersonal ties and "it takes a village" nurturing lacking in competitive, capitalist societies). Descriptions of Western, especially U.S., individualism, on the other hand, are often cultural critiques and thus are consistent with this overriding critical agenda. Ethnographers of the United States often follow the lead of Alexis de Tocqueville, the 19th century French observer of social norms in the United States, who admired egalitarian social relations in this country but worried about the "habit of always considering themselves as standing alone" that "threatens in the end to confine [every American] entirely within the solitude of his own heart" (Tocqueville, 1835/1840/1956, p. 194). Although I suspect this is part of the reason why anthropologists are less hesitant to offer overall characterizations of U.S. culture than of other cultures, investigating this supposition is beyond the scope of this chapter.

A second possible reason for the persistence of Tocquevillian accounts of the United States is that individualism is a socially dominant value in this country. As a dominant value, it is frequently represented in sources that are highly visible to both native and foreign observers of the United States, making it easier to observe than nondominant alternatives.

A third possible reason is that Tocqueville was right: There is a sense in which the dominant ideology of individualism does lead to an American "habit of always considering themselves as standing alone." I argue that the latter two reasons are both partly correct.

REDEFINING CULTURE

What notion of culture is compatible with both the claims that individualist ideologies are contested in the United States and that individualism is dominant in this society? Naomi Quinn and I have argued for the follow-

---

and were in fact noticed in the 19th century by Tocqueville, who commented, "I know of no country in which there is so little independence of mind and real freedom of discussion as in America" (1835/1840/1956, p. 116). Tocqueville explained U.S. conformism as the result of the way democracies expect inner conformity to majority opinion in the place of the behavioral acquiescence that is sufficient in authoritarian societies (p. 116). See Mead (1965, p. 87ff) for related commentary about U.S. patterns of childrearing.

ing redefinition of the culture concept, which would allow for both of those observations:

> Culture consists of the human production of objects, events, and practices, as well as the cognitions, emotions, and motivations people share as a result of these common experiences.[7] (adapted from Strauss & Quinn, 1997, p. 7)

In other words, instead of starting with a society (the !Kung, Japan, the United States) and assuming public practices and mental structures are shared in it, we start with either a set of public practices or a set of mental structures and ask who shares it.[8] Even people living at the same time in the same area will be exposed to a variety of ideologies and experiences (arising from particularities of their family, ethnicity, gender, class, education, religion, ideological and mass media exposure, as well as lifestyle choices), each of which has distinctive psychological effects. There is no need for these experiences to be consistent with each other or limited to a spatiotemporally contiguous population. For example, followers of a certain musician could share the experience of listening to that music despite being in different continents. Still, this is not to say that the situation is chaotic, with no general patterns emerging for cross-cultural differences or intrasocietal similarities. People who live in the same natural, political, economic, and social environment often share some internally motivating and durable ways of thinking and acting (Strauss & Quinn, 1997, chaps. 4 & 5).

Drawing out the last point, we need to distinguish between ideas and practices that are socially *dominant* and those that are *alternative* (cf. Bourdieu, 1972/1977, pp. 168–169; Gramsci, 1971; Williams, 1977). Socially dominant ideas and practices have high cultural standing, that is, they are espoused by the relevant powers-that-be in authoritative accounts and are supportive of major social institutions. In the field of medicine, for example, biomedicine is dominant in the United States and other approaches to healing are alternative. Alternative ideas and practices can be formerly dominant but now embattled (e.g., theories of male superiority); newly emergent (e.g., mind–body medicine); countercultural, that is, shared by a wide subgroup (e.g., free love in the 1960s); or marginal, that is, shared by a small subgroup with little influ-

---

[7]Thus, the sorts of schemas Piaget considered (for space, matter, etc.) would not be considered cultural, since they could be learned through interaction with the natural world rather than the humanly created one. We could rule these out by excluding panhuman cognitions, emotions, and motivations, but that would eliminate some practices and schemas that are cultural (e.g., knowledge of how to make fires or cook, Brown, 1991).

[8]Cf. the "epidemiology of representations" suggested by Sperber (1985) and the "population psychology" proposed by LeVine (1982).

ence or status (e.g., Heaven's Gate cult; cf. Williams 1977 on "dominant," "residual," and "emergent" ideologies).

Dominance, it is important to note, is not the same as predominance. *Predominance* is a simple quantitative concept: the predominant concepts and practices in a society are the ones held or displayed by the greatest number of people.[9] The core of the notion of social dominance, by contrast, is not high frequency but high status. Widespread ideas and practices are not always dominant in this sense: for example, a majority of U.S. Americans believe in the existence of unidentified flying objects, despite repeated official denials of their existence (Norback, 1980). Yet (just focusing on ideas—the realm of practices is more complicated), although predominant ideas need not be socially dominant, we might expect that socially dominant ideas would be predominant. Given their key role in legitimating social institutions, socially dominant ideas are typically widely disseminated and taught in ways intended to make their messages durable (Strauss & Quinn, 1997, pp. 93–98), making it highly likely that they will be included among the (possibly contradictory) beliefs held by most people in the society. Moreover, we could postulate that socially dominant ideas should have a special place in the belief systems of most people (Strauss, 1992). For example, they might come to consciousness sooner than alternative ideas, particularly if the context clearly relates to the issues addressed by the dominant ideology. Finally, we might expect socially dominant ideas to be held with about equal frequency by members of nondominant and dominant groups, and alternative ideas to be held with differing frequencies by members of nondominant and dominant groups. (Nondominant and dominant along the dimensions relevant to the ideology, that is. Women physicians are nondominant with respect to gender ideologies but—compared to the population without medical degrees—dominant with respect to medical ideologies.) This should be so because alternative ideas are distributed via media and methods that reach specialized audiences, whereas socially dominant ideas are so widely and frequently represented that everyone is likely to be exposed to them. If socially dominant ideas meet these criteria (predominance over alternatives in individuals' responses; greater salience [e.g., earlier mentions] than alternatives in individuals' responses; and expression at more similar rates than alternative ideas by members of dominant and nondominant groups), we could say the ideas are psychologically as well as socially dominant. Some of the research reported next considers whether individualist explanations for class standing in the United States are psychologically dominant in these ways.

---

[9]The point I am making here is similar in some ways to Wainryb's (1997; Killen & Wainryb, 2000) critique of purely proportional solutions to the difficulties of classifying societies as either individualist or collectivist.

U.S. AMERICANS' CLASS ATTRIBUTIONS

It is uncontroversial that individualist explanations of class standing (in particular, the view that anyone can become wealthy and achieve the American dream if they want to, so a person's own actions and traits explain their socioeconomic status) are socially dominant in the United States. This economic individualism is espoused by the relevant powers-that-be (e.g., Presidents, successful businesspeople, and celebrities) in authoritative accounts (presidential addresses, textbooks for young people, and advice books for adults) and is supportive of major social institutions (the neoliberal state, including low marginal tax rates on upper income brackets and comparatively miserly social welfare programs; Hochschild, 1995; Huber & Form, 1973; Lipset, 1996; Triandis, 1995). Individualist explanations for class standing are also widely represented in magazine stories and movie plots, pep talks at sales meetings, and the stories people hear and tell about relatives, friends, and acquaintances who got ahead by hard work or who failed because they were lazy.

At the same time, individualist explanations are not the only ones present in the United States. There is a long-standing U.S. populist tradition of distrusting the rich and powerful, which can lead people toward explanations that focus on social forces instead of or in addition to ones focusing on individual traits (Kazin, 1994; Goodwyn, 1978). Sayings such as "The rich get richer, and the poor get poorer," labor union appeals, conspiracy theories, anti-establishment talk radio and movie plots, and private conversations (especially among people who have not realized the American dream) make available to many people structural explanations for the distribution of wealth as does exposure to alternative social theories for some of the college educated. (Structural accounts are ones that focus on the importance of social structures, social connections, and social forces.[10]) Structural theories are more collectivist than individualist in focusing on external, contextual explanations and seeing people as members of groups instead of as atomistic individuals.

What are the psychological consequences of these public representations? Do individuals internalize alternative as well as dominant individualist understandings of the causes of economic standing, resulting in a dual or mixed set of cognitive schemas? There is a fair amount of previous research in social psychology, sociology, and political science on these questions. Sev-

---

[10]Religious and other teachings regarding the importance of caring for the poor may reflect a different, communitarian, alternative to individualism. (Communitarian ideologies are ones that stress the mutual obligations and responsibilities of members of a community.) On the other hand, religious teachings can also reinforce individualist understandings if they assume that wealth is a sign of individual virtue (Weber, 1904–1905/1958; Kluegel & Smith, 1986).

eral researchers have found evidence for a pattern of "dual consciousness" in the United States that mixes individualist and structural explanations for class standing (Bobo, 1991; Hochschild, 1981; Hunt, 1996; Kluegel & Smith, 1986; Mann, 1970; Strauss, 1990). Most previous research has found evidence for the predominance of individualist explanations (e.g., Feagin, 1972; Kluegel & Smith, 1986), although one survey, by Hunt (1996) in Southern California in 1993, found that, averaging across items, 52% of the respondents rated structural explanations for poverty very important, whereas only 42% gave the same rating to individualist items (1996, p. 300). Hunt attributes these findings to recession and other crises in California around the time of the survey. The question of class variation in individualist/structural attributions has also been investigated, with inconsistent results. Kluegel and Smith found that *structural* explanations for both poverty and wealth were more likely at lower levels of income, but *individualist* explanations for poverty were not correlated with income (1986, p. 91). Hunt (1996), on the other hand, found increasing income and education correlated with decreasing levels of both individualist and structural responses. With only a few exceptions (e.g., Feldman & Zaller, 1992; Hochschild, 1981; Lamb, 1974; Lane, 1962), this research has been based on closed-question survey research, thus has not allowed for the discovery of mental models beyond the "individualist," "structural," (and sometimes, "fatalist," Feagin, 1972; Zucker & Weiner, 1993) explanations that researchers already know.

A different set of relevant studies bears on what is known as the *fundamental attribution error*, that is, the tendency of subjects to prefer dispositional attributions, which explain behaviors as the result of agents' stable internal traits, over situational attributions, which explain behaviors as the result of contextual factors (Ross, 1977). This is relevant because individualist economic explanations would be a type of dispositional attribution, whereas structural explanations would be a type of situational attribution. There is a fair amount of research showing that Westerners (or, at least, U.S. Americans) are more prone to the fundamental attribution error than are non-Westerners (Miller, 1984, 1987; Morris & Peng, 1994; L. Newman, 1993). In an interesting study of natural discourse, Morris and Peng (1994) found that articles in *The New York Times* and the Chinese-language *World Journal* on two mass murder incidents differed, with the Chinese-language newspaper articles favoring situational attributions for both shootings, and the U.S. English-language newspaper articles favoring dispositional attributions when the perpetrator was a Chinese immigrant (outgroup member) but mitigating situational attributions when the perpetrator was a U.S. American (ingroup member; an example of the "ultimate attribution error," Pettigrew, 1979).[11]

---

[11]See Fletcher and Ward (1988) for a review, including some results that do not fit this pattern. Ross and Nisbett (1991) discuss class differences in attributions.

As does the class-standing literature cited earlier, the attribution literature considers only a small set of alternatives: dispositional versus situational attributions, largely ignoring mixtures of these; subtypes of each; and explanations that do not fit easily into either category. The research discussed next presents all the causal models underlying my interviewees' explanations for class standing as well as some causal models that arise in other contexts. A finding of alternatives to individualist models or dispositional attributions would not refute the I/C thesis, some advocates of which have acknowledged lack of uniformity and contextual shifts in the display of I/C traits. On the other hand, the diversity of understandings that exists within societies and within individuals has not been explored in depth by such theorists. Furthermore, advocates of the I/C thesis have equated predominance with dominance. My research considers predominance as only one measure of dominance and looks as well at salience of individualist explanations and more agreement about them by members of dominant and subordinate groups than there is about nonindividualist explanations.

METHOD

In 1985, I conducted semistructured interviews with 5 working-class and 5 middle-class adults in Rhode Island (two women, eight men; all Euro-Americans).[12] I met with each interviewee for six sessions of 1½ hours each, to explore his or her ideas about economic individualism. This topic was explored in the context of questions about my interviewees' experiences with a chemical company that employed some of the interviewees and was situated in the neighborhood where others of them lived, as well as discussions of other issues related to their work lives, their life histories, and other current events. All questions were open-ended, and, typically, I let interviewees talk as long as they wanted on not only the initial topic but also others that came to mind while they were speaking. However, the last interview I conducted with each person consisted of a series of questions that I asked of everyone. In 1990 I conducted a follow-up interview with each of them in which I repeated some of my standardized questions. I also completed three interviews each with two more interviewees, both working-class women. All the interviews were tape recorded and transcribed.

Before focusing on attributions for class standing in particular, I considered a more general question: What is the full range of causal models implicit in my interviewees' explanations of any social behavior or status? As

---

[12]Nine of these were born in the United States; one immigrated from Eastern Europe in her teens.

an initial attempt to answer that question, I analyzed the complete tran-
scripts of the interviews with "Carol Russo." Russo, a working-class mother
in her 40s when I first interviewed her in 1984 in the pilot phase of this
research, frequently illustrated her comments with examples from the lives
of friends, relatives, acquaintances, and people she had read about in the
newspaper or heard about on the radio or television, producing a larger-
than-average number of attributions. Furthermore, because I conducted
three interviews with her in 1990 (in addition to six interviews in 1984), I
have an extensive corpus of her discourse on which to draw.

After deriving a set of explanatory models from Russo's discourse on a
wide variety of topics—many of which were initiated by her—I considered
the overall frequencies of those causal models and any others present in
all interviewees' responses to the set of standardized questions regarding
class standing that I asked in 1985 and repeated in 1990: "What things
keep people from getting ahead in the world?" "Who or what is to blame
for this, if people can't get ahead?" "What things help people to get
ahead?" and "Is the system fair? Does everyone pretty much have an equal
chance to get ahead?"[13] Answers to these standardized questions were not
probed or interrupted, except for occasional clarifying questions.[14]

MULTIPLE CAUSAL MODELS

I found seven types of causal models underlying my interviewees' attributions.[15] Two could be considered individualist, two collectivist, and the
remaining three are mixed or difficult to classify along those lines. One
difficulty I encountered in trying to classify explanations as individualist
or collectivist was the assumption, made by many attribution researchers,
that individualist attributions are dispositional ones (stable as well as
internal). Yet, the most common individualist model focuses on factors
(effort and choices) that, although internal, are not stable. Therefore,
instead of limiting individualist explanations to dispositional ones, I

---

[13]An alternative wording used for some interviewees was, "Does everyone pretty much
have the same chance to get ahead?"

[14]There were only two instances of interruption to ask for an explanation or example
among the 38 responses I obtained in 1985 and two again among the 48 responses in 1990.

[15]Initially I worked with Weiner's (1986) three dimensions of attribution (locus, stability,
and controllability) and hired three Duke undergraduates to code all responses along each
of those dimensions, both for "the response that seemed to come to the speaker's mind first"
and then for the response as a whole. (Intercoder agreement was 80% for 1985 initial
responses; 83% for 1985 responses as a whole; 81% for 1990 initial responses; and 83% for
1990 responses as a whole.) The subsequent shift to seven causal models required a recod-
ing, and given the merely suggestive nature of the data with a small sample, I did all the coding, taking care to code contrary to the hypotheses in any ambiguous cases.

included in this category any explanations that focused on internal attributes of the actor, whereas collectivist explanations covered any models that focused on external features of the situation. Whenever possible, each model is illustrated first with an example from Russo, then with an example from other interviewees' responses to the getting ahead questions.

(Internal Attribution) Individual Effort and Choices

This is the classic U.S. belief that, as one interviewee puts it, "you can achieve anything your mind can conceive." My interviewees sometimes acknowledged that ability makes a difference. However, at least for economic mobility, the relevant abilities were usually thought to be skills that could be acquired with higher education. Pursuit of higher education and scholarships to pay for it, if need be, was seen as the individual's choice. Some interviewees challenged the premise that everyone should get ahead economically, but they usually still assumed that an individual's mindset is decisive in the achievement of whatever goals a person has (cf. Linde, 1993, pp. 201–203):

> CS: Who or what is to blame for this, that is, if people don't get ahead in the world?

> Russo: I think largely themselves, you know. There's all kinds of ways—I've come across so many people in my life—I always thought, well, you know, the rich people go to school and that's not true. A very good friend of mine who I graduated high school with, oh was smart, a very, very smart person. Her father did not educate her, he educated his son but he didn't educate her. So she was knocking around different jobs which she did well in—you know, secretarial stuff, but she was *bored*. And she put herself through college. And I really have to hand it to her, she did very well. And it was by her own merit and her positive thinking.

> CS: Who or what is to blame for this, that is, if people don't get ahead in the world?

> Jim Lovett (working class, late 50s): I don't know that you could *blame* anyone. You, you are the one to blame. It's you. Because . . . you can achieve anything your mind can conceive. If you can think, if you have an idea. In your head. And if you think about it hard enough. And you want it bad enough. Then you can achieve it. There's nothing on this, in this country or on earth that if you were willing enough to work at it, that you cannot achieve it. So we all have the potential of being a millionaire, if that is your goal.

> CS: Who or what is to blame for this, that is, if people don't get ahead in the world?

> Linda Petty (working class, late 20s): Themself. Yea. Themself. I think there's enough opportunity out there. Enough, you know, a lot of things

going on just by watching the TV, you should be able to get something out of it to say, okay, it's my life and I'm going to do it or I'm not going to do it. I think you can choose. I know at one point when I was really down and out [*after the birth of her second severely disabled child, during a period when her husband was out of work*] and I just didn't seem like I was getting anywhere, my counselor said to me, "You make this choice. You either choose to be like this or you choose to be happy. You make the choice." And I never had had it brought to me like that before, but it was true, and it was, I was the only one that could do it, no one was going to, you know, say, "You're going to be happy." I had to say, "I'm going to be happy; I don't care what it takes." But I think no, it's yourself. I really believe that.

(Internal Attribution) Individual's Fixed Nature

Explanations of this sort encompass both biological determinist models and ones that assume fixed internal traits without explaining their origin.

> Russo: There must be a chromosome missing in these people who can just go out and kill people.

> Russo [*on an abusive man*]: He's not going to change. That's my opinion because I don't believe in rehabilitation.

> CS: Is the system fair? Does everyone pretty much have the same chance to get ahead?

> Frank Hollingworth (middle class, late 40s): [deletion] they may not, as far as heredity is concerned, your genes and so forth . . .

> CS: Who or what is to blame for this, that is, if people don't get ahead in the world?

> Tony D'Abrosca (working class, late 50s): [deletion] Some are handicapped. I am, in a way. I have asthma and I have a speech impediment. I couldn't go too far with that.

(External Attribution) Social Forces

At the same time many interviewees also offered structural explanations, noting the way life chances are affected by fairly stable social factors such as inegalitarian institutions, personal connections, or the prejudicial attitudes of people in power. Interviewees used Social Forces explanations regardless of their political orientation. Thus, Susan Maxfield's discussion of racism and Daniel Collins's criticism of what he perceives to be unfair affirmative action policies are both examples of Social Forces explanations.

> Russo [*on looking for a job after her children were grown*]: [T]here's all this wonderful stuff, oh, stay home with your children, bring up your children, and after, they don't want you. And like one of my friends said to me, I said, "I

can't believe it. I know I'm qualified for that job and I didn't get hired." She said, "Carol, you don't have nice buns." (laughs) You know, that's . . . exactly, that's the bottom line.

Michael Fields (middle class, early 40s): I don't think the American Dream of working hard and getting to where you want to go is applicable to all people because there are barriers. I mean, I witnessed that in my job. There are certain jobs that you can have 2000 qualified people who apply for it, because somebody knows somebody, they get the job, whether they are qualified or not.

CS: Who or what is to blame for this, if people can't get ahead?

Susan Maxfield (middle class, early 30s): I don't know. I think it all goes back to slaves and slavery, and bringing people over from Africa, I mean that was just a horrible situation and I just think that ever since then, I really felt badly for the black people. It seems like that they just can't get ahead, that there is so much racism now.

CS: Is the system fair? [etc.]

Daniel Collins (working class, early 40s): Nope. It all depends on the mood of government . . . or big business. You know, if government says, Well, we have 80% Whites and 20% Black or 10% Black and 10% Hispanic and we have to increase our workforce and we have to stay within the boundaries—like the large corporations, they only have to hire a certain percent, to get their federal contracts and whatnot. I don't think that's fair. I don't think that's fair at all. If you're willing to go out there and work, be you white, black, green, yellow, man, woman, child, as long as you're willing to go out there and work and earn a, you know, give a good day's work for a good salary, there shouldn't be any restrictions at all. And there is.

(External Attribution) Chance

Another sort of external model emphasizes the role of chance events, randomly changeable rather than stable external forces. There are no clear examples of this in Russo's discourse, but several in other interviewees' responses:

CS: Who or what is to blame for this [if people don't get ahead]?

Hilda Grafstein (middle class, late 60s): [deletion] You got to be in the right place at the right time, and lucky.

CS: What things help people to get ahead?

Michael Fields (middle class, late 30s[16]): [deletion] So what does it take? It takes a lottery. Or a rich inheritance. I mean it too, right? You don't need any personal ambition, you don't need any drive or determination, you

---

[16]Ages stated for a given interviewee vary if one of the statements quoted was made in 1985 and another in 1990.

don't need anyone else on the outside, you don't need, you don't need to do a thing. You just have to go to the closest lottery agent and buy a ticket.

(Mixed or Hard-to-Classify Attribution) Involuntary Psychological States

According to this model, some social behaviors have causes that are internal but feel external. In other times and places, the sense of one's actions being under the control of an internalized but alien force would be described as possession. Spirit possession discourse is rare at this time in the United States; it has been replaced by references to mental illnesses, both chronic (including addictions) and temporary (e.g., temporary insanity). There were no examples of this model in responses to the standardized getting ahead questions, but a few in Russo's discourse on other topics:

> Russo: [*speaking about a Boston professor who killed a prostitute*] Someone said, "Well, he should have pleaded guilty for reasons of insanity." He was obsessed by her.

> Russo: [*speaking about young women she saw soliciting in New York City*] What happened to them [deletion] that they would be so desperate and [the bus driver] said most of them are drug addicts. [*Spoken in the context of exonerating the women because they were in the grip of their addictions.*]

(Mixed or Hard-to-Classify Attribution) Upbringing Determines Dispositions

This model muddies the internal/external distinction by explaining behavior in terms of stable internal traits that were in turn the product of external circumstances:

> Russo: [S]ome poverty-stricken woman, all she know's how to do is have kids. One after another. [deletion] and she's never been educated to the fact that she should get off her butt and go to work. So she brings up like five or six kids the same attitude and *they* do the same thing again.

> CS: Who or what is to blame for this, if people can't get ahead?

> Al Choquette (middle class, early 40s): [deletion] I think that, you know, it's a breeding type of thing. It's what your parents expect of you and then what you expect of your kids and what they expect of their kids and right on down the line.

For some interviewees, the fact that one's dispositions are shaped by early upbringing makes it difficult to assign blame.

Russo: [*on her daughters*] I drive them to school. It's really my fault; I'm making cripples out of them.

CS: Who or what is to blame for this, if people can't get ahead?

Susan Maxfield (middle class, early 30s): [deletion] That's a tough question. It really is, because . . . I don't know. If you're born in that, in that environment and you go to school until the fourth grade and then your parents say, "Well, you don't have to go anymore," I mean, that's not my fault. It's your parents' fault. But the, whose fault is it that they don't care about it? It's *their* parents' fault. I guess. It opens up a Pandora's Box.

CS: What things keep people from getting ahead in the world?

Frank Hollingworth (middle class, late 40s): [deletion] [I]t just to me stems back to education. And I don't mean formal necessarily, I mean right in the home, when a child is reared and brought up and so forth. The education that that child gets in that environment may be such that they find that later in life they're not as far ahead as they'd like to be, and they say, Gee, the reason I'm not is I should've taken college courses, I should have paid attention in school, you know, maybe we didn't have the counseling and so forth, but doesn't that stem from the lack of education from the people who raised them perhaps?

(Mixed or Hard-to-Classify Attribution) Dispositions
Interact With Social Circumstances

The previous explanation (Upbringing Determines Dispositions) posits a sequence unfolding over time: external factors shape the dispositions a person develops and then displays later. Some interviewees noted that internal and external factors also interact at any given moment because social pressures do not operate inexorably, but rather set up a system of incentives to which individuals will respond differently, depending on their values and abilities. Sometimes these interactions are implied more than they are stated. For example, in the first of the following quotes Russo begins by discussing purely contextual factors affecting politicians' behavior. The final line, "What is in it for him?," however, contains the implicit moral judgement that a less selfish person would not have become "polluted."

> Russo: [*on politicians*] I said, "I wonder if there should be a school, just to groom people to become—What [deletion] a abbey? You know, like keep them so pure and wonderful? And so clear. But they just become so polluted. You know. If someone has a job, a political job, he's just going to be wooed and dined and, whatever the words are, so he can be nice to somebody else. What is in it for him?
>
> CS: I guess some people would say that if it's mostly poor people who are [*selling drugs*] for money [deletion] give those people better jobs, or something. . . .

Russo: I don't believe that. The money's too easy. Who'd want to go to work? [deletion] You know, really it's the person. I just feel that I couldn't bear to do something [*i.e., sell drugs*] as much as I would like money just like the next guy—how would you destroy a person?

Linda Petty (working class, late 20s): [*on people who receive welfare but do not use it to become self-supporting*] And those people are real, they get me upset because they're perfectly capable of going out and doing something with their life and once you get on welfare, you can get grants for school and everything, and they refuse. And I just think that that sort of system is wrong, and the system should say, "No, you're capable of going to school and we're willing to pay for you to go to school. We'll put your child," you know, "you could go to daycare," and I know a family that—and she refused. And at that point, I think they should turn around and say, "Well, you don't get the money," you know. I mean, make them do something.

INTERNAL EXPLANATIONS AS PSYCHOLOGICALLY DOMINANT?

Clearly multiple models, some internal, some external, some mixed, are present in my sample as a whole and even voiced at different times by the same person. Still, are internal explanations for class standing psychologically dominant in the three ways predicted: (a) greater overall frequency; (b) greater salience within responses; and (c) voiced at equal rates by members of dominant and nondominant groups? For my sample the answers are clearly yes for 1985 and partly so in 1990. Following these results I consider whether these findings can be generalized.

Overall Frequency

Table 5.1 presents the proportional representation of each type of explanation relative to all explanations given by interviewees in responses to the four getting ahead questions (n = 21, 15, 23, and 20 for Q1 to Q4 in 1985; n = 24, 22, 28, and 21 for Q1 to 4 in 1990). Internal attributions were clearly predominant in 1985: 43% of all the explanations attributed economic success or failure to internal factors, whereas 28% cited external factors, 13% were mixed, and the rest were uncodable.[17] Unexpectedly, however, in 1990 external attributions slightly outnumbered internal attributions (41% external, 38% internal, 14% mixed, and the rest uncodable).

---

[17]The most frequent type of uncodable response was an unelaborated reference to the importance of education that left unexplained if this is an internal attribution (individuals are responsible for acquiring greater education); external attribution (today's society demands advanced educational credentials); or a mixture of these.

TABLE 5.1
Proportion of References to Various "Getting Ahead" Explanations

	1985					1990				
	Q1	*Q2*	*Q3*	*Q4*	*T*	*Q1*	*Q2*	*Q3*	*Q4*	*T*
INTERNAL										
Individual Effort and Choices	.43	.40	.30	.35	.36	.25	.41	.32	.33	.33
Fixed Nature	.09	.07	.04	.10	.07	.04	.09	.03	.05	.05
EXTERNAL										
Social Forces	.24	.20	.22	.30	.24	.37	.41	.28	.38	.36
Chance	0	0	.13	0	.04	.04	.05	.07	.05	.05
MIXED										
Involuntary Psychological States	0	0	0	0	0	0	0	0	0	0
Upbringing Determines Dispositions	.09	.20	.09	.05	.10	.08	0	.14	.09	.08
Dispositions Interact With Social Forces	0	.07	.04	0	.03	.08	.05	.07	.05	.06

In both 1985 and 1990 the two most frequently given explanations were Individual Effort and Choices and Social Forces. As Table 5.1 indicates, these two models accounted for 60% of all explanations in 1985 and 69% in 1990, and on the average across all questions no other explanation appeared in more than 10% of the responses; hence all further analyses reported compare those two explanations only.

Salience Within Responses

Many interviewees gave an individualist response first to one of the standardized getting ahead questions, then qualified their initial response, or added to it, by referring to social forces or chance. I noticed that pattern in some of Russo's responses:

CS: Who or what is to blame for this, that is, if people don't get ahead in the world?

Russo: I think largely themselves, you know. [*8 more lines in this vein; see first quote under Individual Effort and Choices*] The only problem I think about as women, is that a lot of times women give up their livelihood or their life to become a mother and a wife and it's so wrong.[*continues with the example of a woman she knew who had wanted to be a lawyer but did not, because her husband objected*]

CS: What things keep people from getting ahead in the world?

Russo: I think sometimes their own mind. [*10 more lines in that vein*] Of course, for people to be successful, there is always, it's easy [*i.e., it helps*] to have family money.

Russo even commented on these differences in salience when, in an earlier interview, I asked, "What do you think determines how well a person does in life in this country?" She replied,

I'd love to believe . . . education. I'd really love to, like I keep pushing my daughters, education, education. **But a little further down in my mind** I say to myself, sometimes it's who you know.[Emphasis added]

I found the same pattern with some of the other interviewees:

CS: What things keep people from getting ahead in the world?

Michael Fields (middle class, early 40s): Mostly themselves. I shouldn't say mostly themselves. I think, well, okay, mostly themselves and then I think discrimination in all forms, ethnic, color, race. I guess socioeconomic status.

Hilda Grafstein (middle class, early 60s): Not getting ahead? Who's to blame? I don't know, probably the person themselves. It could be that, on the one hand, or it could be again opportunities that are not always there for the person to get ahead.

To test the generality of this pattern, the order of multiple explanations within responses was recorded. Table 5.2 shows the percentages of Individual Effort and Choices and Social Forces explanations given first, relative to all explanations given first (n = 12, 8, 10, and 11 for 1985; n = 12, 13, 12, and 12 for 1990).[18] In 1985 Individual Effort and Choices was a first response more than twice as often as Social Forces. (See Table 5.2.) In 1990, despite the fact that Social Forces explanations slightly outnumbered Individual Effort and Choices explanations overall, Individual

---

[18]N was less than the number of interviewees for Q2 in 1985 because two responses were missing. N was greater than the number of interviewees in several instances because if two explanations were included in the initial sentence (e.g., "I don't know, it could be personal, it could be opportunities") both were coded as 1's. In such cases, it seemed clear that the two explanations were equally salient, so the fact that the internal explanation was mentioned first was unrevealing.

TABLE 5.2
Proportion of Individual Effort and Choices and Social Forces Explanations Given First

	1985					1990				
	Q1	Q2	Q3	Q4	T	Q1	Q2	Q3	Q4	T
Individual Effort and Choices	.58	.50	.50	.36	.48	.33	.61	.50	.42	.46
Social Forces	.17	.13	.30	.27	.22	.50	.33	.25	.42	.38

Effort and Choices explanations were still voiced initially more often than Social Forces explanations on average across questions (46% vs. 38%), although the tendency was not as striking as in 1985.

Voiced at Equal Rates by Members of Dominant and Nondominant Groups

For ideas about class standing, middle-class interviewees were considered to be the dominant group and working-class interviewees the nondominant group.[19]

To examine the hypothesis that dominant and nondominant groups would differ more in expression of alternative (Social Forces) than dominant (Individual Effort and Choices) ideas the following procedure was used: for each question the percentage of middle-class interviewees who offered an Individual Effort and Choices response was compared with the percentage of working-class interviewees who offered Individual Effort and Choices responses; then the percentage of middle-class interviewees' Social Forces responses was compared with the percentage of working-class interviewees' responses of that type.[20] As Fig. 5.1 indicates, the results were as predicted. In both 1985 and 1990 for every question the difference between these percentages for Individual Effort and Choices was equal to or smaller than the difference between these percentages for Social Forces explanations.

---

[19]Gender and race might also make a difference, but I did not have sufficient numbers of female interviewees to analyze gender independently or in interaction with class, and all interviewees in this study were Euro-American.

[20]For this analysis, percentages within each class were calculated relative to numbers of interviewees, rather than numbers of explanations given, because working-class interviewees tended to give more explanations per person than middle-class interviewees.

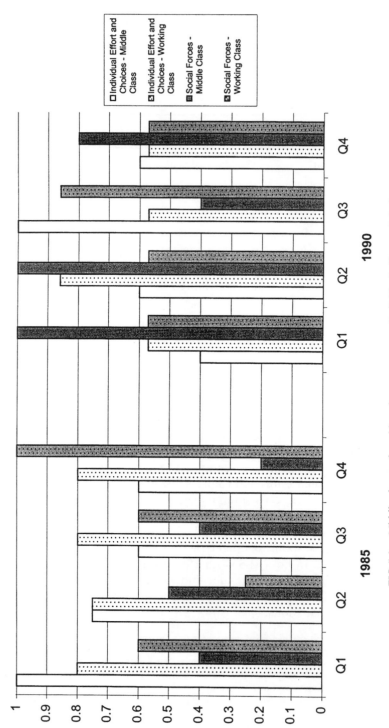

FIG 5.1. Middle class and working class percentages: Individual effort and choices versus social forces.

106

DISCUSSION

What would account for the differences between my 1985 and 1990 results? The 1990 sample included two additional working-class women; omitting them from the sample does not restore the predominance of the Individual Effort and Choices model, however.[21]

One possibility is that some interviewees changed perspective as they grew older (see Noricks et al., 1987, on the collectivist tendencies of older U.S. Americans). Another possibility is that the 1985 interviews made structural explanations more salient, and repeating the same questions in 1990 reactivated those schemas. A third possibility is that the weaker dominance of individualism found in 1990 reflects larger historical forces. There is evidence from other research for this third explanation. For example, in both 1985 and 1990 the Gallup organization asked representative national samples, "Which is more often to blame if a person is poor—lack of effort on his own part, or circumstances beyond his control?" The percentage answering "lack of effort" was nearly the same in both years (33% in 1985 and 35% in 1990), but the percentage answering "circumstances beyond his control" increased considerably from 1985 to 1990 (from 34% to 45%; Gallup, 1986, 1991).[22] This suggests that the predominance of structural responses Hunt (1996) found in a 1993 southern California sample and the predominance of structural responses I found in 1990 in my Rhode Island sample may reflect a national trend. (See also Hochschild, 1995.) For example, this trend could be the result of increasing public concern about corporate "downsizing."[23] K. Newman (1993, p. 44) noted that between 1978 and 1990 the percentage of U.S. households with a middle-class income declined 20%, with a particularly steep decline between 1986 and 1990. Whether the trend toward increasing structural explanations will continue or reverse under more favorable economic conditions is an open question.

It is important to keep in mind that all of my interviewees were Euro-Americans and, with the exception of Hilda Grafstein, none was a first-generation immigrant. It would be interesting to see if the psychological dominance of individualism shown in this study would be found for Asian Americans, African Americans, or Latinos (cf. Greenfield & Cocking, 1994).

---

[21]Proportions of Individual Effort and Choices versus Social Forces for the 1990 responses minus these two women were .32 and .38, respectively, totaled over all questions.

[22]It would be interesting to see whether the percentage of "lack of effort" answers has remained more nearly constant over all the years this question has been asked than the percentage of "circumstances beyond his control" answers. Longitudinal consistency of this sort might be another mark of dominant ideas.

[23]Herbert Saltzstein (personal communication, November 27, 1988) suggested this possibility to me.

It would also be interesting to see whether the psychological dominance of individualism extends to other areas of thought and behavior beyond explanations for class standing. In my earlier research I found that whereas most of the working-class interviewees in this sample voiced the same economic individualist ideologies as my middle-class interviewees, their behaviors differed. The male working-class interviewees, more often than their middle-class counterparts, made choices of where to live and work that rejected opportunities to get ahead if taking a new job would harm relationships with partners, relatives, or friends (Strauss, 1992).

CONCLUSIONS

Although this research can be suggestive only, its implications are interesting. On the one hand, it lends partial support to advocates of the Individualism-Collectivism (I/C) thesis and the mainstream of U.S. culture research by showing that, in 1985 at least, individualist attributions for class standing were psychologically dominant in my sample: Not only were they predominant overall, but they were voiced ahead of structural and other external attributions, and their rates of expression were more similar between members of dominant and subordinate groups than was the case for structural attributions. In 1990, even though structural attributions were predominant, they were still less frequently represented among first mentions overall, and there was still greater cross-class consistency in individualist than structural attributions. Methodologically, this suggests that advocates of the I/C thesis should look beyond predominance as the measure of "cultural syndromes." Predominance is only one, and not necessarily the best, indicator of psychological dominance.

Yet this research also raises several concerns about the I/C thesis and studies of the United States that emphasize individualism to the exclusion of alternative ideas and practices. As attribution researchers have established (Weiner, 1986) and I/C advocates are beginning to realize, the categories of individualism and collectivism are too broad. Teaching children that they have fixed dispositions (Fixed Nature) is different from teaching them that at any time they can remake their lives (Effort and Choices), even though both of these are individualist models;[24] similarly, it surely makes a difference whether children grow up believing the relevant situationally features are stable structures (Social Forces) rather than random events (Chance), even though both of these are collectivist. Furthermore,

---

[24]Moffatt (1989) argued, however, that these are linked: Because of U.S. Americans' dominant individualism, if they cannot explain why people make the choices they do, they tend to fall back on essentialist fixed nature models.

the basic I/C, internal/external divide overlooks attributions that include elements of both (Involuntary Psychological States, Upbringing Determines Dispositions, and Dispositions Interact With Social Forces). Although these mixed models were infrequently represented in my interviewees' explanations for who gets ahead and why, Involuntary Psychological States and Upbringing Determines Dispositions frequently can be heard both in expert discourse and in everyday talk in the United States.[25]

Finally, to talk about dominant ideas rather than cultural syndromes is to shift the field of discourse considerably about the relation between culture and psychology. The language of cultural syndromes implies that there is a single thing (U.S. culture) with relatively fixed typical traits and predictable modal psychological effects. Although dominant ideas and practices do tend to be stable, they are not completely so (Strauss & Quinn, 1997; see also Greenfield, chap. 10, this volume). Furthermore, political power tends to be downplayed in I/C discourse. (See Turiel, 1997, for a related critique.) By contrast, if cultures are not single things but rather consist of patterns of regularities in shared practices and ideas, there is room for thinking about the way power relations affect which models become widespread and salient and how political battles can affect the dominance of practices and beliefs.

ACKNOWLEDGMENTS

I am grateful for helpful comments from Joan Miller, Larry Nucci, Naomi Quinn, Herbert Saltzstein, Elliot Turiel, and members of the audience at the Piaget Symposium, the City University of New York Graduate Center Psychology Department, and the University of Michigan Culture and Cognition Seminar. A conversation with Roy D'Andrade about the fallacy of dividing attributions into opposing internal/external alternatives helped me to notice some of the mixed models presented here. A Duke University Research Council grant funded the 1990 transcriptions.

REFERENCES

Alipuria, L. L. (1997). *Cultural values research and issues illustrated with the Asian Indian population.* Unpublished manuscript, Claremont Graduate School. Claremont, California.

Allison, A. (1996). *Permitted and prohibited desires: Mothers, comics, and censorship in Japan.* Boulder, CO: Westview Press.

---

[25]In interviews conducted in 1995 with a diverse sample of 16 Rhode Islanders, I found that Upbringing Determines Dispositions (or a Social Learning model) was very widely invoked to explain why people are on welfare. This, of course, is the causal attribution that underlies a culture of poverty model.

Appadurai, A. (1990). Disjuncture and difference in the global cultural economy. *Public Culture, 2*(2), 1–24.

Bakhtin, M. M. (1981). Discourse in the novel. In M. Holquist (Ed.), *The dialogic imagination: Four essays by M. M. Bakhtin* (C. Emerson & M. Holquist, Trans.; pp. 259–422). Austin: University of Texas Press.

Boas, F. (1938). *The mind of primitive man* (Rev. ed.). New York: The Free Press. (Original work published 1911)

Bobo, L. (1991). Social responsibility, individualism, and redistributive policies. *Sociological Forum, 6,* 71–92.

Bourdieu, P. (1977). *Outline of a theory of practice* (R. Nice, Trans.). Cambridge, England: Cambridge University Press. (Original work published 1972)

Brown, D. E. (1991). *Human universals.* New York: McGraw-Hill.

Chen, C. C., Meindl, J. R., & Hunt, R. G. (1997). Testing the effects of vertical and horizontal collectivism: A study of reward allocation preferences in China. *Journal of Cross-Cultural Psychology, 28,* 44–70.

Clifford, J. (1988). *The predicament of culture: Twentieth-century ethnography, literature, and art.* Cambridge, MA: Harvard University Press.

D'Andrade, R. G. (1995). *The development of cognitive anthropology.* Cambridge, England: Cambridge University Press.

Dumont, L. (1970). *Homo hierarchicus: The caste system and its implications* (M. Sainsbury, Trans.). Chicago: University of Chicago Press. (Original work published 1966)

Durkheim, E. (1933). *The division of labor in society* (G. Simpson, Trans.). New York: The Free Press. (Original work published 1893)

Elvin, M. (1985). Between the earth and heaven: Conceptions of the self in China. In M. Carrithers, S. Collins, & S. Lukes (Eds.), *The category of the person* (pp. 156–189). Cambridge, England: Cambridge University Press.

Ewing, K. (1991). Can psychoanalytic theories explain the Pakistani woman? Intrapsychic autonomy and interpersonal engagement in the extended family. *Ethos, 19,* 131–160.

Feagin, J. (1972). When it comes to poverty, it's still, 'God helps those who help themselves.' *Psychology Today, 6,* 101–29.

Feldman, S., & Zaller, J. (1992). The political culture of ambivalence: Ideological responses to the welfare state. *American Journal of Political Science, 36,* 268–307.

Fletcher, G. J. O., & Ward, C. (1988). Attribution theory and processes: A cross-cultural perspective. In M. H. Bond (Ed.), *Cross-cultural research and methodology: Vol. 11. The cross-cultural challenge to social psychology* (pp. 230–244). Newbury Park, CA: Sage.

Foucault, M. (1972). *The archaeology of knowledge and the discourse on language* (R. Swyer, Trans.). New York: Pantheon. (Original work published 1969)

Gallup, G. (1986). *The Gallup poll: Public opinion 1985.* Wilmington, DE: Scholarly Resources.

Gallup, G. (1991). *The Gallup poll: Public opinion 1990.* Wilmington, DE: Scholarly Resources.

Geertz, C. (1973). Thick description: Toward an interpretive theory of culture. In C. Geertz, *The interpretation of cultures* (pp. 3–30). New York: Basic Books.

Geertz, C. (1994, April 7). Life on the edge. *New York Review of Books,* 3–4.

Gilligan, C. (1982). *In a different voice.* Cambridge, MA: Harvard University Press.

Goodwyn, L. (1978). *The populist moment.* Oxford, England: Oxford University Press.

Gramsci, A. (1971). *Selections from the prison notebooks of Antonio Gramsci* (Q. Hoare & G. Nowell Smith, Eds. & Trans.). New York: International Publishers.

Greenfield, P. M. (1994). Independence and interdependence as developmental scripts: Implications for theory, research, and practice. In P. M. Greenfield & R. R. Cocking (Eds.), *Cross-cultural roots of minority child development* (pp. 1–37). Hillsdale, NJ: Lawrence Erlbaum Associates.

Greenfield, P. M., & Cocking, R. R. (Eds.). (1994). *Cross-cultural roots of minority child development.* Hillsdale, NJ: Lawrence Erlbaum Associates.

Harkness, S., Raeff, C., & Super, C. M. (Eds.). (2000). W. Damon (Series Ed.), *New directions for child development, Number 87. Variability in the social construction of the child.* San Francisco: Jossey-Bass.

Hochschild, J. L. (1981). *What's fair?* Cambridge, MA: Harvard University Press.

Hochschild, J. L. (1995). *Facing up to the American dream: Race, class, and the soul of the nation.* Princeton, NJ: Princeton University Press.

Hofstede, G. (1980). *Culture's consequences: International differences in work-related values.* Beverly Hills, CA: Sage.

Hofstede, G. (1991). *Cultures and organizations: Software of the mind.* London: McGraw-Hill.

Hollan, D. (1992). Cross-cultural differences in the self. *Journal of Anthropological Research, 48,* 283–300.

Holland, D., & Kipnis, A. (1994). Metaphors for embarrassment and stories of exposure: The not-so-egocentric self in American culture. *Ethos, 22,* 316–342.

Huber, J., & Form, W. H. (1973). *Income and ideology.* New York: The Free Press.

Hunt, M. O. (1996). The individual, society, or both? A comparison of Black, Latino, and White beliefs about the causes of poverty. *Social Forces, 75,* 293–322.

Kagitcibasi, C. (1996). *Family and human development across cultures: A view from the other side.* Mahwah, NJ: Lawrence Erlbaum Associates.

Kashima, Y., Yamaguchi, S., Kim, U., Choi, S.-C., Gelfand, M. J., & Yuki, M. (1995). Culture, gender, and self: A perspective from individualism-collectivism research. *Journal of Personality and Social Psychology, 69,* 925–937.

Kazin, M. (1994). *The populist persuasion: An American history.* New York: Basic Books.

Kelly, W. W. (1991). Directions in the anthropology of contemporary Japan. *Annual Review of Anthropology, 20,* 395–431.

Killen, M., & Wainryb, C. (2000). Independence and interdependence in diverse cultural contexts. In W. Damon (Series Ed.) & S. Harkness, C. Raeff, & C. M. Super (Vol. Eds.), *New directions for child development, Number 87. Variability in the social construction of the child.* San Francisco: Jossey-Bass.

Kim, U., Triandis, H. C., Kagitcibasi, C., Choi, S.-C., & Yoon, G. (1994). *Individualism and collectivism: Theory, methods and application.* Thousand Oaks, CA: Sage.

Kluegel, J. R., & Smith, E. R. (1986). *Beliefs about inequality: Americans' views of what is and what ought to be.* New York: Aldine deGruyter.

Kurtz, S. (1992). *All the mothers are one: Hindu India and the cultural reshaping of psychoanalysis.* New York: Columbia University Press.

Kusserow, A. (1999) De-homogenizing American individualism: Socializing hard and soft individualism in Manhattan and Queens. *Ethos, 27,* 210–234.

Kuwayama, T. (1992). The reference other orientation. In N. R. Rosenberger (Ed.), *Japanese sense of self* (pp. 121–151). Cambridge, England: Cambridge University Press.

Lamb, K. (1974). *As Orange goes: Twelve California families and the future of American politics.* New York: Norton.

Lane, R. E. (1962). *Political ideology: Why the American common man believes what he does.* New York: The Free Press.

Lebra, T. S. (1994). Mother and child in Japanese socialization: A Japan-U.S. comparison. In P. M. Greenfield & R. R. Cocking (Eds.), *Cross-cultural roots of minority child development* (pp. 259–274). Hillsdale, NJ: Lawrence Erlbaum Associates.

LeVine, R. A. (1982). *Culture, behavior, and personality: An introduction to the comparative study of psychosocial adaptation* (2nd ed.). New York: Aldine.

Linde, C. (1993). *Life stories: The creation of coherence.* New York: Oxford University Press.

Lindholm, C. (1997). Does the sociocentric self exist? Reflections on Markus and Kitayama's "Culture and the Self." *Journal of Anthropological Research, 53,* 405–422.

Lipset, S. M. (1996). *American exceptionalism: A double-edged sword.* New York: Norton.

Maine, H. (1864). *Ancient law* (1st American ed. from 2nd London ed.) New York: Scribner's.

Malinowski, B. (1961). *Argonauts of the western Pacific*. New York: Dutton. (Original work published 1922)

Mann, M. (1970). The social cohesion of liberal democracy. *American Sociological Review, 35,* 423–439.

Markus, H. R., & Kitayama, S. (1991). Culture and the self: Implications for cognition, emotion, and motivation. *Psychological Review, 98,* 224–253.

Marsella, A., DeVos, G., & Hsu, F. (Eds.). (1985). *Culture and self: Asian and Western perspectives*. New York: Tavistock.

McHugh, E. (1989). Concepts of the person among the Gurungs of Nepal. *American Ethnologist, 16,* 75–86.

Mead, M. (1965). *And keep your powder dry: An anthropologist looks at America*. New York: Morrow.

Miller, J. G. (1984). Culture and the development of everyday social explanation. *Journal of Personality and Social Psychology, 46,* 961–978.

Miller, J. G. (1987). Cultural influences on the development of conceptual differentiation in person description. *British Journal of Developmental Psychology, 5,* 309–319.

Miller, J. G. (1997). Cultural conceptions of duty: Implications for motivation and morality. In D. Munro, J. F. Schumaker, & S. C. Carr (Eds.), *Motivation and culture* (pp. 178–192). New York: Routledge.

Mills, C. W. (1956). *White collar: The American middle class*. New York: Oxford University Press.

Mines, M. (1988). Conceptualizing the person: Hierarchical society and individual autonomy in India. *American Anthropologist, 90,* 568–579.

Moffatt, M. (1989). *Coming of age in New Jersey: College and American culture*. New Brunswick, NJ: Rutgers University Press.

Moffatt, M. (1992). Ethnographic writing about American culture. *Annual Review of Anthropology, 21,* 205–229.

Morris, M. W., & Peng, K. (1994). Culture and cause: American and Chinese attributions for social and physical events. *Journal of Personality and Social Psychology, 67,* 949–971.

Newman, K. (1993). *Declining fortunes: The withering of the American dream*. New York: Basic Books.

Newman, L. S. (1993). How individualists interpret behavior: Idiocentrism and spontaneous trait inference. *Social Cognition, 11,* 243–269.

Norback, C. (Ed.). (1980). *The complete book of American surveys*. New York: New American Library.

Noricks, J. S., Agler, L. H., Bartholomew, M., Howarth-Smith, S., Martin, D., Pyles, S., & Shapiro, W. (1987). Age, abstract thinking, and the American concept of person. *American Anthropologist, 89,* 667–675.

Nucci, L. (1997). Culture, universals, and the personal. In W. Damon (Series Ed.) & H. D. Saltzstein (Vol. Ed.), *New directions for child development: Number 76. Culture as a context for moral development: New perspectives on the particular and the universal* (pp. 5–22). San Francisco: Jossey-Bass.

Nuckolls, C. W. (1996). *The cultural dialectics of knowledge and desire*. Madison: University of Wisconsin Press.

Omvedt, G. (1980). *We will smash this prison! Indian women in struggle*. London: Zed Press.

Oxfeld, E. (1992). Individualism, holism, and the market mentality: Notes on the recollections of a Chinese entrepreneur. *Cultural Anthropology, 7,* 267–300.

Parish, S. M. (1994). *Moral knowing in a Hindu sacred city: An exploration of mind, emotion, and self*. New York: Columbia University Press.

Pettigrew, T. F. (1979). The ultimate attribution error: Extending Allport's cognitive analysis of prejudice. *Personality and Social Psychology Bulletin, 5,* 461–476.

Quinn, N. (1996). Culture and contradiction: The case of Americans reasoning about marriage. *Ethos, 24*(3), 391–425.

Redfield, R. (1953). *The primitive world and its transformations*. Ithaca, NY: Cornell University Press.

Reisman, D., Glazer, N., & Denney, R. (1953). *The lonely crowd: A study of the changing American character*. New York: Doubleday.

Roberts, J. M. (1961). The Zuni. In F. R. Kluckhohn & F. L. Strodtbeck (Eds.), *Variations in value orientations* (pp. 285–316). Evanston, IL: Row, Peterson.

Rosenberger, N. R. (1992). Introduction. In N. R. Rosenberger (Ed.), *Japanese sense of self* (pp. 1–20). Cambridge, England: Cambridge University Press.

Ross, L. (1977). The intuitive psychologist and his shortcomings: Distortions in the attribution process. In L. Berkowitz (Ed.), *Advances in experimental social psychology: Vol. 10* (pp. 173–220). New York: Academic Press.

Ross, L., & Nisbett, R. E. (1991). *The person and the situation: Perspectives of social psychology*. Philadelphia: Temple University Press.

Said, E. (1978). *Orientalism*. New York: Vintage Books.

Seymour, S. (1983). Household structure and status and expressions of affect in India. *Ethos, 11*, 263–277.

Shore, B. (1996). *Culture in mind: Meaning construction and cultural cognition*. New York: Oxford University Press.

Shweder, R. A., & Bourne, E. J. (1984). Does the concept of the person vary cross-culturally? In R. A. Shweder & R. A. LeVine (Eds.), *Culture theory: Essays on mind, self, and emotion* (pp. 158–199). Cambridge, England: Cambridge University Press.

Shweder, R. A., Mahapatra, M., & Miller, J. G. (1990). Culture and moral development. In J. W. Stigler, R. A. Shweder, & G. Herdt (Eds.), *Cultural psychology: Essays on comparative human development* (pp. 130–204). Cambridge, England: Cambridge University Press.

Sperber, D. (1985). Anthropology and psychology: Towards an epidemiology of representations. *Man, 20*, 73–87.

Spiro, M. E. (1987). Collective representations and mental representations in religious symbol systems. In B. Kilborne & L. L. Langness (Eds.), *Culture and human nature: Theoretical papers of Melford E. Spiro* (pp. 161–184). Chicago: University of Chicago Press. (Original work published 1982)

Spiro, M. E. (1993). Is the Western conception of the self "peculiar" within the context of the world cultures? *Ethos, 21*, 107–153.

Stack, C. (1974). *All our kin*. New York: Harper & Row.

Stack, C. (1996). *Call to home: African Americans reclaim the rural South*. New York: Basic Books.

Strauss, C. (1990). Who gets ahead? Cognitive responses to heteroglossia in American political culture. *American Ethnologist, 17*(2), 312–328.

Strauss, C. (1992). What makes Tony run? Schemas as motives reconsidered. In R. G. D'Andrade & C. Strauss (Eds.), *Human motives and cultural models* (pp. 191–224). Cambridge, England: Cambridge University Press.

Strauss, C. (1997). Partly fragmented, partly integrated: An anthropological examination of 'postmodern fragmented subjects'. *Cultural Anthropology, 12*, 362–404.

Strauss, C., & Quinn, N. (1997). *A cognitive theory of cultural meaning*. Cambridge, England: Cambridge University Press.

Tobin, J. J., Wu, D. Y. H., & Davidson, D. H. (1989). *Preschool in three cultures*. New Haven, CT: Yale University Press.

Tocqueville, A. de (1956). *Democracy in America* (abridged ed.). R. D. Heffner (Ed.). New York: Mentor Books. (Original work published 1835/1840)

Triandis, H. C. (1995). *Individualism & collectivism*. Boulder, CO: Westview Press.

Turiel, E. (1996). Equality and hierarchy: Conflict in values. In E. S. Reed, E. Turiel, & T. Brown (Eds.), *Values and knowledge* (pp. 75–101). Mahwah, NJ: Lawrence Erlbaum Associates.

Turiel, E. (1997). Beyond particular and universal ways: Contexts for morality. In W. Damon (Series Ed.) & H. D. Saltzstein (Vol. Ed.), *New directions for child development, Number 76. Culture as a context for moral development: New perspectives on the particular and the universal* (pp. 87–105). San Francisco: Jossey-Bass.

Wainryb, C. (1997). The mismeasure of diversity: Reflections on the study of cross-cultural differences. In W. Damon (Series Ed.) & H. D. Saltzstein (Vol. Ed.), *New directions for child development, Number 76. Culture as a context for moral development: New perspectives on the particular and the universal* (pp. 51–65). San Francisco: Jossey-Bass.

Wallace, A. F. C. (1970). Introduction. In *Culture and personality* (2nd ed.; pp. 3–38). New York: Random House.

Weber, M. (1958). *The Protestant ethic and the spirit of capitalism* (T. Parsons, Trans.). New York: Scribner's. (Original work published 1904–1905)

Weiner, B. (1986). *An attribution theory of motivation and emotion.* New York: Springer-Verlag.

Whyte, W. H. (1956). *The organization man.* New York: Simon & Schuster.

Wikan, U. (1987). Public grace and private fears: Gaiety, offense, and sorcery in Northern Bali. *Ethos, 15,* 337–365.

Williams, R. (1977). *Marxism and literature.* Oxford, England: Oxford University Press.

Wolf, E. (1982). *Europe and the people without history.* Berkeley: University of California Press.

Zucker, G. S., & Weiner, B. (1993). Conservatism and perceptions of poverty: An attributional analysis. *Journal of Applied Social Psychology, 23,* 925–943.

Chapter 6

The Moral and the Personal: Sources of Social Conflicts

Larry P. Nucci
The University of Illinois at Chicago

Elliot Turiel
University of California, Berkeley

It seems that people like to listen to music and to dance! Although we have no means for documenting with numbers or other data that this is true the world over (a cross-cultural universal?), we presume that most would agree. The unassailable fact that people worldwide like to listen to music and dance, in itself, is not so interesting with regard to considerations of culture, thought, and development. It becomes quite interesting for the topics of this volume, we believe, if we consider two examples that reveal the extent people go to to listen to music and to dance in certain social contexts.

The first example comes from the recollections told by Fatima Mernissi (1994) of her childhood life, during the 1940s, in a harem in Morocco. The specific context for a tale told by Mernissi in *Dreams of Trespass* is that the women of the harem, in the absence of the men, were prohibited from listening to a "huge cabinet radio" kept under lock and key in the men's salon. Yet, the women listened to that radio while the men were away at work—often listening to music and dancing to the tunes. The women were found out when the children happened to be asked by Fatima's father what they had done that day. Fatima and her cousin (both then 9 years old) said that they had listened to the radio. The result was 2 days of interrogation of the women to determine how they had obtained the "unlawful" key. The men got nowhere in their quest. Subsequently, the mothers castigated their children for revealing the secret. The perplexed children defended themselves saying that they were only speaking the

115

truth. In return, the mothers lectured that "what you keep secret has nothing to do with truth and lies" (Mernissi, 1994, p. 8).

A second example stems from political events in Iran during the 1990s. The Islamic revolution of 1979 resulted in a variety of restrictions on people's activities, including their dress, many forms of entertainment, use of alcohol, reading materials, and fraternization between males and females. In the aftermath of the presidential election of 1997, there surfaced several journalistic accounts of ongoing hidden activities in violation of many of these restrictions. Included in these reports was that people danced in spite of governmental and religious bans on it. As put by a woman who was interviewed for a newspaper article ("Beating the System," 1997): "We live a double-life in this country. My children know that when their school teacher asks whether we drink at home, they have to say no. If they are asked whether we dance or play cards, they have to say no. But the fact is that we do drink, dance, and play cards, and the kids know it. So they are growing up liars, knowing that their parents are also liars and knowing that to survive in this country we have to lie. That's a terrible thing, and I want to change it."

Embedded in these two stories, one from harem life in Morocco of the 1940s, the second from life in Iran in the 1990s, is much that bears on culture, thought, and development. That people like to listen to music and dance involves personal preferences for activities that are sometimes done by oneself (especially listening to music), but they are also often part of social interactions and normative practices. In the two examples, we can also see how activities that are both individual and social can be part of a tension with the social—conflicts with and resistances to cultural practices, and cultural arrangements of power relations, status distinctions, and positions of relative dominance and subordination. We propose that the desire to listen to music and dance is an example of activities in the personal sphere—a fundamental domain of social development. The lengths to which the women of the harem and people in Iran went to fulfill their desires to listen to music and dance in the context of institutionalized taboos and sanctions for their violation reflects another fundamental domain of social development—moral judgments about fairness and rights. Restrictions of personal activities that are judged to be arbitrary or based on inequality of groups of people or to the benefit of one group vis-à-vis another are linked to claims of personal and civil rights.

In this regard, it is important to point out that our two examples actually go well beyond the assertion of the wish to listen to music and dance. The women of the harem in Mernissi's childhood were unhappy with many other restrictions imposed upon them by the men and, more generally, felt that the rules and practices were unfair and violated their rights. The women wished for themselves a life beyond the gate of the harem and had aspirations for different kinds of lives for their daughters. In Iran, it was hoped by many that the election of a president who appeared more moderate than previous ones would result in greater freedoms ("Many Iranians," 1997). Indeed, the people's hidden activities included much more than music and dancing—ranging from recreational activities to relationships between the sexes and politics.

THE PERSONAL AND CONCEPTIONS
OF FAIRNESS AND RIGHTS

The force of the resistance observed in the examples comes, then, from a linkage between the desire to maintain equity in social relations and the need for an area of personal expression, discretion, and privacy. In one of our examples, men, but not women, are accorded such personal freedoms. The *personal* refers to the set of actions that the individual considers to be outside of the area of justifiable social regulation. These actions make up the private aspect of one's life; they are subject not to considerations of right and wrong, but to preferences and choice (Nucci, 1977, 1996). Although particular actions, such as dancing or listening to the radio, may not seem important in and of themselves, individuals seek to control such actions within the personal domain in order to instantiate their subjective experience of agency.

The experience of agency has two aspects. At one level, agency is experienced as an awareness of oneself as the initiator of action. At a second, more fundamental level, agency is experienced as the sense of oneself as having a unique, bounded social identity. Thus, individuals endeavor to control areas of conduct that permit them opportunities to engage in self-expression, personal growth, selection of intimates, and zones of privacy.

If we look to the social sciences for evidence of a general psychological quality of personal agency, we find that there is convergence within contemporary studies of human development around the view that persons experience themselves as agents capable of decision making and the initiation of action (Crapanzano, 1990; Geertz, 1984; Stern, 1985). But, this view of agency is in and of itself rather empty. Although it recognizes that aspect of self as the subjective initiator of action, what James referred to as the "I", it says nothing about elements of the self that compose one's identity. For agency to have meaning, the agent (I) must have a sense of self as having a personal identity distinguishable from others. Some culture theorists do not extend the individual's sense of agency to include a sense of self as a discrete social being with a bounded personal identity. Indeed, the view of self as individual has been characterized as a peculiar Western construction (Geertz, 1984), reflecting a particular set of political beliefs and values (Cushman, 1991). In these social constructivist positions it is proposed that personhood and the individual are cultural variants rather than expressions of some underlying set of psychological realities. Geertz's well-known proposition that in many non-Western cultures conceptions are not held of bounded, discrete selves (persons are unbounded in the sense that they are part of selves blended into social relationships) has been extended to concepts of both self (or persons) and morality around the general distinction between individualistic and collectivistic cultures. Individualistic cultures entail egocentric or independent conceptions of persons (Shweder & Bourne, 1982; Markus & Kitayama, 1991) with a corresponding moral system revolving around equality, individual autonomy, and rights (Shweder, Mahapatra, & Miller, 1987). Collectivistic cultures entail sociocentric or interdependent conceptions of persons, with a corresponding moral system revolving around duties, role obligations in the social hierarchy, and maintenance of the existing social order. It has been argued, therefore, that whereas Western societies and Western morality focus upon moral equivalencies among people, traditional societies place greater emphasis upon differences among people, such as age, gender, and class, which lead to differential rather than equal moral status among people. For example, in most of the world's cultures, men are accorded greater social power and personal freedom than women. Descriptions of such cultures tend to portray members as viewing their lot within the social system as fixed and appropriate. That is to say that the kinds of claims to personal freedom and conflicts around cultural arrangements discussed in this chapter are not presumed to be salient for members of traditional cultural groups. Instead, an orientation toward group goals and a morality based on respect for authority and hierarchy is said to prevail (Haidt, Koller, & Dias, 1994; Shweder, 1990).

Efforts at placing personhood and morality into particularistic cultural constructions have been seen to stem from an overreaching and overextension of analyses of culture as accounts of the psychology and cognitions of individuals (Spiro, 1993; Turiel, 1994, 1996). Spiro (1993), for example, in his overview of anthropological accounts concluded that although notions of *self* are culturally variable, cultures contain some differentiated view of the self, and members of cultures appear to hold conceptions of selves as distinct persons with needs and interests. In particular, Spiro takes issue, on the basis of anthropological evidence, with Geertz's (1984) distinction between culturally based conceptions of bounded and unbounded selves. Spiro also takes issues with efforts to apply Geertz's notion to particular Western and non-Western cultures through distinction between egocentric and sociocentric selves (Shweder & Bourne, 1982) or independent and interdependent selves (Markus & Kitayama, 1991). In line with Spiro's (1993) observations, the position we advance is that individuals maintain a differentiated personal identity—a discrete and unique definition of the self—to instantiate their subjective experience of agency. In order to do so, people lay claim to areas of behavioral discretion and privacy (Nucci, 1996; Nucci & Lee, 1993). The domain of the personal sphere coexists with the moral domain. As shown by numerous studies, at a relatively early age children in Western and non-Western cultures form judgments about moral issues based on considerations of welfare and justice (Smetana, 1995; Tisak, 1995; Turiel, 1998). With regard to moral issues, actions are judged to be justifiably regulated, and preferences are subordinated to promoting welfare and fairness. Research has also shown that moral judgments are applied by children and adolescents to their everyday activities (Turiel, in press). Moreover, studies have begun to document that concepts of rights are part of moral reasoning, not only in Western societies (Helwig, 1995), but also in non-Western ones (Turiel & Wainryb, 1998).

Our hypothesis is that conceptions of a personal domain constitute the psychological source of the general claim to rights to freedom (Gewirth, 1982). At the level of the individual, the bounds of this general claim to freedom are framed by conceptions of the boundaries of the personal domain in relation to the individual's understandings of interpersonal moral obligation and social conventional and legal regulation (Nucci, 1977; Turiel, 1983). The dynamics at work may be seen in the course of individual development and in the tensions within cultural systems. In both cases equilibrium between personal freedoms and social constraints (moral and societal) result in variations in the particular content and expression of the personal.

The balance between individual preferences and the needs of others is coordinated by moral conceptions of fair reciprocity. In such a case, we may speak of moral conceptions of rights. These interrelations with personal freedom as maintained by social and cultural systems, however, may or may not in fact correspond in a simple and direct way to what is required by moral reciprocity, but instead may employ differential characteristics among people, such as intelligence or gender, to establish what Gewirth (1982) referred to as inequalities in which classes of people (e.g., women) are accorded fewer rights than others (e.g., men). In these cases, we may speak of systems of privilege in which a dominant class of persons is accorded freedoms perceived as rights, while a subordinate class is accorded corresponding duties. Baumrind (1998), writing from a perspective different from our own, argued against the notion that such systems of inequalities should be viewed solely from within their own cultural vantage point and be, therefore, immune to external scrutiny. Her argument is that to do so is to ignore the potential claims that could be made by persons in subordinate positions. Baumrind's view, as the one we develop here, assumes that there are multiple ways in which to perceive a culture and its norms and that multiple perspectives exist within cultural systems. Our central thesis is that such internal contradictions and multiple viewpoints result from interactions among conceptions of morality, societal convention, and personal freedom maintained by individuals in reciprocal interaction with corresponding elements within cultural systems. In turn, the existence of multiple viewpoints implies that cultural systems themselves are multifaceted, embodying a coexistence of the components often assigned to one culture (e.g., individualism and independence, collectivism and interdependence) rather than another.

CONFLICTS AND TENSIONS IN SOCIAL DEVELOPMENT

The idea that there are conflicts and tensions in social relationships is not new, although analyses of culture have emphasized shared elements and social harmony. Traditionally, explanations of social and moral development have been based on the idea that young children are in conflict with social expectations until they come to internalize the norms and values of society. The process of socialization was seen as involving a transformation of the child's orientations to their needs and desires into an orientation to the needs and welfare of others and the community. Psychoanalytic theory provides the clearest example of conflicts and tensions of this sort in that it is posited that there is a great struggle in childhood due to the inevitable clash of biological needs or desires and society (Freud, 1930). The struggle continues internally (and sometimes unconsciously) beyond childhood and often makes for pathological symptoms.

Another common set of approaches, based not on the contrast of biology and society, also explains social and moral development as involving periods of struggle between the individual and social expectations (e.g., Kohlberg, 1969, 1984; Loevinger, 1966; Peck & Havighurst, 1960). In these theoretical approaches, it is proposed that there are different phases in development in ways of relating to the social world. An illustrative example can be seen in Kohlberg's (1984) formulation of stages of moral judgment, with progress from the preconventional to the conventional to the postconventional. Initially, the conflicts are between a set of conceptions maintained by children based on the morality of personal needs and self-interests and the constraints and controls imposed on the child by parents, rules, laws, and society. From the perspective of the child, the struggle is either to avoid the restrictions and act upon interests and desires or to act in accord with social expectations in order to avoid punishment, disapproval, and other forms of censure from others. From the viewpoint of society (and parents), the struggle is to avoid the negative consequences of the acts of the young and to direct them to understand the grounds for rules, law, and authority in society.

In Kohlberg's formulation, the next developmental achievement is an understanding of the requirements of societal life. At this 'conventional' phase, there is concordance between individual and society in that individuals come to think in ways that are in accord with societal rules, laws, and authority. Insofar as there is struggle, it is with regard to those who do not accept society's ways. With further development to a postconventional (and most advanced) phase, insofar as there is conflict it is between conceptions of morality and the ways of society. In a sense, the relations of the first phase are reversed. Often, the individual struggles to change the ways of society to make them in greater accord with moral concepts of the welfare of persons, justice, and rights and to change norms, practices, and even laws. From the perspective of society, sometimes the struggle is to maintain the existing social order against criticism.

Our position regarding both development and cultural conflict differs from the traditional socialization approaches and stage-related views (e.g., Kohlberg). Our position is that individuals are, at once, connected to their social or cultural networks and in conflict with aspects of cultural arrangements. Resistance and critique of cultural arrangements and social practices are not tied to a particular way of making moral judgments that represents an advanced way of thinking. People generally are capable of applying their moral judgments in critical evaluations of existing laws, authority, and social practices. Part of such a critical standpoint involves assertion of the importance of maintaining areas of personal jurisdiction.

SOCIAL INTERACTIONS AND THE DEVELOPMENT OF THE PERSONAL IN CHILDHOOD

The dynamics of acceptance of and opposition to social expectations are evident in early childhood—but in different ways from adolescence and adulthood. A body of research shows that young children act in prosocial ways and express emotions of sympathy and empathy toward others (Dunn, 1987; Eisenberg & Strayer, 1987; Hoffman, 1991; Radke-Yarrow, Zahn-Waxler, & Chapman, 1983). Although these findings have been interpreted to show that young children are mainly socially oriented and concerned with the well-being of others (Wilson, 1993), it is also the case that young children often display opposition to others, show increasing interest in engaging in acts that are socially prohibited, engage in disputes and arguments with parents, and act in aggressive ways (Dunn, 1987; Dunn, Brown, & Maguire, 1995; Dunn & Munn, 1987). The coexistence of these different emotions and actions is consistent with the proposition that children develop distinct domains of judgment, including judgments regarding the personal sphere.

Again, the examples from the Moroccan harem and Iran illustrate that social life is not always harmonious and that cultural arrangements or practices are not shared by all. We also propose that the different strands of development (e.g., the personal and moral domains) make for a heterogeneity of social orientations of acceptance and rejection of cultural practices in institutionalized arrangements and in communications from authorities (parental and governmental). Our examples illustrate that what is communicated to children is far from straightforward. In each example, adults gave different types of messages about expected or correct behaviors regarding truth-telling and adherence to others' expectations. Children's social experiences, we propose, are multifaceted and linked to the personal, social, and moral judgments they begin to develop at a fairly young age.

A set of observational studies shows that children's social interactions vary systematically around moral and conventional issues (Nucci & Nucci, 1982a, 1982b; Nucci & Turiel, 1978; Nucci, Turiel, & Encarnacion-Gawrych, 1983). These studies, which were conducted in preschools, elementary schools, and playgrounds, focused on interactions among children and between children and teachers. Observational research also has been conducted in homes in the United States and has examined preschool-age children's interactions with their mothers with regard to areas of personal choice as well as moral, social, and prudential issues (Nucci & Weber, 1995). The study shows that mothers respond differently to children as a function of whether the issues in question are ones within the child's personal domain or in other domains. This differential overall response pattern was carried through in mothers' tendencies to negotiate in response to children's resistance to the mothers' behavioral requests for a given social action. Mothers almost never negotiated with children regarding moral, conventional, or prudential forms of conduct, yet fairly often (nearly one fourth of the interactions) negotiated and made concessions around personal issues. Moreover, negotiations took place (about 50% of the time) in the context of mixed events involving overlaps between the personal and other issues (more than 90% of the observed mixed events involved overlap between issues of convention or prudence with the personal domain).

The study also provides evidence that children play an active role in relation to their mothers, and that they provide feedback in the form of requests and resistances to their mothers that afford mothers information regarding the child's claims to areas of personal control. This feedback is not simply a generalized resistance to adult authority (Brehm & Brehm,

1981; Kuczinski, Kochanska, Radke-Yarrow, & Girnius-Brown, 1987), but a delimited set of claims to choice over a personal sphere. This is most evident in cases of mixed events and suggests that mothers open to their children's feedback have direct access to information about their own children's needs for a personal domain.

Related to children's efforts to differentiate the personal from what is under adult control are instances where personal choice is in conflict with the welfare of others. The prototypical case is the inherent tension between individual property rights and distributive justice. Developmental studies of concepts of distributive justice (Damon, 1977) generally show that prior to the age of 6, children typically have difficulty sharing their property with others. Research (Smetana, 1981) revealed that although prior to age 6 children believe it is wrong for one child to have all of the goods (e.g., toys) common to a classroom, a child is not thought to be obligated to share his or her own personal possessions with others— even in situations of scarcity. On the contrary, young children maintain that it is up to an individual whether he or she wishes to share his or her toys or candy with someone else. Although observations of young children have provided evidence of children's spontaneous helping behavior (Eisenberg, 1982), sharing behavior is a very rare occurrence among children under the age of 6 (Murphy, 1937; Bronson, 1981). The usual explanation for this lack of sharing is that young children are egocentric and incapable of taking others' points of view into account. This view, however, seems at variance with findings that children as young as 3 years of age evaluate an individual's appropriation of all public goods to be wrong (Smetana, 1981), and take strong stands against children who do not engage in turn-taking (e.g., with swings; Nucci & Turiel, 1978). An alternative explanation for this phenomenon regarding the sharing of personal goods is that young children view it as their right not to share their private property. Only after they have constructed a sense of fairness as entailing just reciprocity do children evaluate sharing of personal goods as morally obligatory and then only under conditions of relative scarcity (e.g., if theirs is the only toy available).

The observations of interactions between U.S. mothers and their 4-year-old children (Nucci & Weber, 1995) provided some evidence that U.S. children receive mixed social messages about sharing personal property. Although this aspect of the observational data was not systematically analyzed, it was observed that mothers would sometimes intervene in disputes between children where one child wished to play with a toy owned by another by asking the owner to share. (Much & Shweder, 1978, report similar sharing social messages in U.S. preschools.) However, mothers were inconsistent in these sharing messages because at other times they would intervene by saying that it was up to the owner to decide whether to share and that the child asking to play with the toy did not have a right to expect the other child to share. Similar inconsistencies occurred concerning the sharing of food. The ambivalence and inconsistency shown in the mothers' interventions stem from the ambiguity entailed by the need to respect rights to personal property and the interpersonal moral concerns for welfare and fairness.

Damon (1977) reported shifts in children's judgments about distributive justice from an egocentric perspective of preschool-age children to a view of fairness in terms of direct reciprocity at age 8, followed by concerns for equity at around age 10, and the coordination of equality and equity considerations by age 12. Daniel Patrick Moynihan, writing in the 1960s, noted that societal concerns for distributive justice within the United States seemed to break down into two ideological camps with one group (conservatives) emphasizing equality and another group (liberals) emphasizing equity. The availability at a societal level of both perspectives of distributive justice evident in the course of development indicates that views of fairness with respect to the distribution of goods and respect for individual property are resolved in more than one way. There is evidence that conceptions of personal choice and interpersonal obligation do vary by cultural setting (Miller & Bersoff, 1992; Miller, Bersoff, & Harwood, 1990; Miller & Luthar, 1989), indicating that the coordination of personal rights to freedom with concerns for interpersonal welfare and fairness takes varying forms. Evidence of such variation, however, is also evidence for the universality of the claim to a general human right to freedom rather than the reverse.

CONFLICTS AND RESISTANCES BEYOND CHILDHOOD

A part of the interpersonal negotiation associated with children's autonomy is comprised of a give-and-take over the child's capacity to carry out activity in ways that do not pose undo risks for the child's health and safety. Given such negotiations and that children develop judgments in the domain of the personal, we would expect that in adolescence there are continued and perhaps increased assertions of personal choices and assertions of greater authority for decision making about one's actions. We would also expect, in most instances, periods of adolescent–parent conflicts insofar as parents do not share the adolescent's perspective on his or her readiness for autonomy. However, an alternative set of expectations would hold if development in adolescence involved the types of shifts proposed by Kohlberg (1984) and others. As noted earlier, in those views moral and social development proceeds from judgments based on prudence and self-interest to judgments based on a societal perspective embracing the general validity of rules, laws, and authority.

As we read the evidence, adolescence involves increased assertion of personal jurisdiction and concomitant conflicts with parents. As a domain distinct from the personal, judgments in the moral domain based on concepts of welfare and justice do not involve the same types of conflicts. It has been found that, in general, adolescents and their parents do not have persistent disagreements over moral issues (Smetana, 1989b; Smetana, Braeges, & Yau, 1990; Smetana, Yau, Restrepot, & Braeges, 1991). The relative lack of conflict is due to the commonality of perspectives on moral judgments on the part of adolescents and parents. Accordingly, adolescents are likely to accept moral directives from parents. Younger adolescents also typically hold the view that parents can legitimately regulate conventions within the family (Smetana & Asquith, 1994). However, the endorsement of adherence to convention appears to decline with age, and conflicts do arise in the context of these areas of change. The conflicts are over issues that parents perceive as important to conventions that serve to structure family and household organization but that adolescents see as interfering in their personal lives (issues of this sort in U.S. families include preferences for music, bedtime and curfew schedules, spending decisions, and cleaning up one's room).

The general pattern that emerges from research on adolescent–parent relations is that there is a gradual increase in the range of issues that adolescents assume as matters of personal choice rather than subject to parental authority. Parents generally lag behind temporally in their acceptance of areas within which adolescents should make decisions, but nonetheless accord adolescents a wider degree of freedom than they give to younger children (Nucci, Camino, & Sapiro, 1996; Smetana & Asquith, 1994). This shift is also accompanied by a degree of adolescent–parent conflict, as reported by Smetana (1998), on the basis of data pooled from a series of studies (with more than 300 families, including Chinese adolescents and parents in Hong Kong). In addition, anthropological accounts of adolescent–parent conflicts in 160 cultures provide evidence that such conflicts are widespread (Schlegel & Barry, 1991, as reported in Smetana, 1998).

Nevertheless, the timing and types of conflicts do vary by social situational contexts. In our view, parents' interpretations of their children's risks, vulnerabilities, and competencies influence when and the extent to which they grant autonomy. In the first place, parents from different cultures and social classes are more likely to grant increased autonomy as their children become older. However, the evidence indicates that middle-class children assert realms of personal jurisdiction at earlier ages than children from lower social classes. For instance, in Brazil (Nucci et al.,

1996) middle-class children tend to claim an area of behavioral discretion at an earlier age than lower class children. By adolescence (ages 14 to 16), however, there were no social class differences in judgments of items that should be up to the children to control.

In turn, Nucci and Milnitsky Sapiro (1995) found variations in accord with social class in mothers' judgments regarding matters that should be left to their children's discretion. Mothers of middle-class background from both the southern (modern) and northeastern (traditional) regions of the country thought that their children or adolescents should make decisions about a range of matters (similarly to middle-class mothers from the United States, as found by Nucci & Smetana, 1996). However, mothers of a lower class background from both regions thought, to a greater extent than middle-class mothers, that their children should not make their own choices. Lower class mothers, however, thought that their adolescents should make independent decisions. Among all these groups, therefore, lower class mothers of children (ages 6 to 8) imposed more restrictions than the others. The reasons given by those mothers for restricting their children's decision-making discretion are informative. They judged that freedom of choice for their children would be impractical, posing risks and dangers for them. It appears, therefore, that mothers from lower socioeconomic classes perceive (no doubt with a good degree of accuracy) the world to pose greater pitfalls than do middle-class mothers. This was the case whether the mothers were from the northeastern region of Brazil (a traditional and presumably collectivistic culture) or from the southern region (a modern and presumably individualistic culture). It also appears that the lower class mothers are willing to grant autonomy and decision-making discretion by the time their offspring reach adolescence. Moreover, in judging that children should have choices, Brazilian mothers spontaneously listed activities similar to those listed by mothers from the United States (Smetana & Asquith, 1994).

The study (Nucci & Milnitsky Sapiro, 1995) with Brazilian mothers demonstrated that beliefs about children's personal choice are not confined to mothers from so-called individualistic cultures. Across social classes and geographic regions, the Brazilian mothers expressed beliefs that children require areas of choice for their personal growth. The manner in which these beliefs were expressed, however, varied as a function of the mothers' underlying assumptions about their children's needs and capacities. Middle-class mothers, particularly from the southern modern region of the country held views of young children essentially similar to those of middle-class mothers from the United States. According to their view, young children are to be treated as individuals and given opportunities to exercise choice to enhance their talents and personalities. That view was at variance with those of the lower class mothers, who viewed the limited cognitive capacity of young children as indicative that they were not yet to be accorded the same discretionary authority granted to adolescents and adults. Nonetheless, the lower class mothers valued the emergence of individuality and agency in adolescence and distinguished the adolescent's rights to personal behavioral control from those moral or conventional zones of behavior that are the shared responsibility of parents and others.

The research suggests that conflicts between parents and adolescents reflect individuals' resistances to control over a personal sphere of actions. If it is the case that the personal sphere is a basic domain of development, then we would expect to find evidence of psychological impact when there is excessive control of adolescents' personal sphere by their parents. Indeed, there is a well established literature indicating that parental dominance and intrusiveness is associated with depression and expressions of hostility on the part of adolescents (Kobak, Sudler, & Gamble, 1991). These expressions of pathology are not limited to children in Western households. For example, there is an emerging literature documenting the relation between parental control and eating disorders among Asian adolescent girls (Ahmad, Waller, & Verduyn, 1994; McCourt & Waller, 1995). Most clinical studies, however, use global indexes of parental involvement rather than distinguishing among different arenas of activities. The research we have considered suggests that adolescents and parents both expect and accept parental control over actions that entail matters of morality, convention, and prudence, but reject parental intrusion into adolescent behaviors that constitute personal issues. We would expect, therefore, that clinical problems are more likely to be associated with control in the personal realm than in the other domains (although specific personal issues involved may vary culturally). Some evidence for these propositions was obtained in a cross-national study of large numbers of adolescents in Japan and the United States (the study was part of a more general investigation of psychological abuse; Hasebe, 1999). Two measures were used. One was a questionnaire (Nucci, Hasebe, & Nucci, 1999) designed to elicit adolescents' judgments as to who should control various aspects of their behavior, themselves or their parents. The questionnaire contains items describing behaviors that fit domain definitions of personal, conventional, and prudential issues (as well as some items that overlap the personal with prudence and convention). For each item, respondents were asked to provide their idealized view of who should control their behavior and to evaluate each item in terms of who actually would make the decision. The second measure was a brief inventory of elements of psychopathology (Derogatis & Spencer, 1982).

Japanese and U.S. adolescents responded somewhat differently to a few of the items on the questionnaire. In particular, Japanese adolescents were more likely to accept parental input into their choice of friends than U.S.

adolescents. However, adolescents in both nations treated personal items as ones that they, rather than their parents, should control. They also viewed it as more appropriate for parents to have input or control over actions that comprised matters of prudence or convention. There was also a tendency with age for adolescents in both nations to report that parents exerted less control over their conduct. For the idealized views of who should control activities, there were no significant correlations with the assessments of psychopathology in either nation. This means that variations in individual adolescents' claims to control over their behaviors is not associated with psychopathology. However, for adolescents of both countries there was a significant set of correlations between self-reports of perceived parental intrusion in the personal domain and self-reports of symptoms of anxiety, interpersonal sensitivity, paranoia, psychoticism, and overall symptomatology. For the adolescents from the United States, there were no associations found between psychological symptoms and parental control over issues involving a mixture of personal and conventional or prudential issues. For Japanese adolescents, there were positive associations between the overlapping domain mixtures and symptoms of anxiety, interpersonal sensitivity, paranoia, psychoticism, and general symptomatology. As with the sample from the United States, there were no associations between psychological symptoms and parental control over conventional and prudential behaviors.

FAIRNESS AND PERSONAL JURISDICTION IN CULTURAL CONTEXTS

The findings from the study with Japanese and U.S. adolescents are consistent with patterns obtained in the research on conflicts between adolescents and their parents. It is activities people place in the sphere of personal jurisdiction that were associated with indexes of psychopathology and that were associated with conflicts. It is not our view, however, that psychopathology is the only—or even the main—consequence of parental or other forms of control over the personal sphere. Rather, we propose that part of social life includes conflicts, discontents, and efforts to resist and subvert control exerted by some (e.g., parents, husbands) on others (e.g., adolescents, wives) and institutionalized in certain social norms and cultural practices. Social norms and cultural practices are not solely to be seen as prescriptions dictating how people are expected to act in particular social settings. They also are to be seen in relational terms. That is, they prescribe a complex set of relationships among people. Often, norms and cultural practices pertain to relationships between people in different positions in the social hierarchy (between people in dominant and subordinate positions). As a consequence, social norms and practices may serve to restrict the activities of one group toward the benefit or preservation of the personal entitlements of others. In such cases, the needs, interests, and desires of individuals (the personal domain) can be implicated in issues of fairness, rights, and social justice (the moral domain).

The dynamics of social relationships, which play out in concerns with and negotiations over the personal and moral, are not in our view restricted to childhood. In contrast with traditional socialization perspectives (e.g., Freud, 1930) and some developmental formulations, we propose that the personal realm is of central concern from childhood to adulthood and is to be coordinated with moral considerations. Particular cultural arrangements would not be absent of social conflicts and discontents with norms and practices. The two examples from the Moroccan harem and Iran that we presented at the outset reflect such conflicts and discontents. Personal freedoms and rights in connection to cultural arrangements are at the core of each. As we noted already, in each case the discontents with the social arrangements went well beyond the desires to listen to music and dance to desires for greater freedom and rights. In the case of the women of the Moroccan harem, the restrictions placed on them by the men were judged unfair and oppressive to the point that they were willing to engage in acts of deception and to communicate the necessity of doing so to children. Often enough through history there have been social and political movements aimed at transforming what were considered oppressive conditions. Martin Luther King, Jr., the moral and political leader of the civil rights movement of the 1960s in the United States, identified freedom and rights as primary motivators when he stated that (1963) "Oppressed people cannot remain oppressed forever. The urge for freedom will eventually come. This is what happened to the American Negro."

It is not only an urge for freedom that Martin Luther King thought was key to the civil rights movement. He thought the urge for freedom among oppressed people was connected also to fairness and rights insofar as one group (oppressors) relied on cultural arrangements to dominate another group (the oppressed). These features, we propose, are present in social interactions, given the heterogeneity of social judgments that individuals develop. Furthermore, these features are not necessarily manifested in political movements aimed at transforming the social system. Often, they are played out in social interactions in everyday life. Accordingly, social life has elements of harmony and conflict, of the shared and contested. We are, therefore, in agreement with Nussbaum's contention:

"cultures are not monoliths; people are not stamped out like coins by the power machine of social convention. They are constrained by social norms, but norms are plural and people devious. Even in societies that nourish

problematic roles for men and women, real men and women can find spaces
in which to subvert those conventions, resourcefully creating possibilities of
love and joy." (1999, p. 14)

Nussbaum's contention that cultures are not monoliths is consistent
with the views of several anthropologists who argue for the need to alter
commonly held conceptions of culture (e.g., Abu-Lughod, 1991; Appadurai, 1988; Spiro, 1993; Strauss, 1992; Wikan, 1991). Those commonly
held conceptions have been characterized in somewhat different terms.
For instance, Abu-Lughod (1991) put it in terms of homogeneity, coherence, and timelessness and proposed instead that within cultures people
make choices, struggle with each other, and engage in disagreements and
arguments. Wikan (1991) put it in terms of a concept of culture as a
"seamless whole" and argued instead that within cultures there is human
misery and dissenting voices. The propositions that cultures are not
monoliths, homogeneous, or seamless wholes is applicable to the ways cultures are sometimes characterized as either oriented to individualism and
independence or to collectivism and interdependence (Turiel, 1996,
1997; Wainryb, 1997). In these characterizations, an emphasis on equality and individual autonomy is presumed to exist in modern, "rights-
based" societies, whereas traditional collectivistic societies with stratified
social systems are said to place greater emphasis on duty and fulfilling
roles in the social hierarchy (without objections, conflicts, or resistance).

The heterogeneity of social judgments that includes the moral (entailing not only rights but connectedness in the form of concerns with welfare
and fairness) and personal domains suggests that cultures, indeed, would
entail a mixture of features associated with individualism and collectivism.
Moreover, we have proposed that there are sufficient contextual variations
with regard to autonomy and connectedness within cultures that, in most
instances, it is not feasible to characterize cultures as tending toward one
type or the other. As demonstrated by research conducted in traditional
cultures (Neff, 1997; Wainryb & Turiel, 1994), patterns of judgments
about independence and interdependence are connected to positions on
the constituted social hierarchy. Research among Druze Arabs, who maintain a patriarchal social structure, examined judgments about relative
decision-making power of males and females in family contexts (Wainryb
& Turiel, 1994). It was found that men and boys are accorded (by males
and females) autonomy and decision-making power and that males view
themselves as possessing entitlements to personal choices. Males also saw
females' roles as concordant with their gender-prescribed duties and
roles. Similar findings regarding gender relations within families were
reported by Neff (1997) among Hindu women in India. Several other
studies in non-Western and Western cultures show that people judge and

act in ways that include features attributed to both individualism and collectivism (Ewing, 1990; Helwig, 1995; Hollan, 1992; McClosky & Brill, 1983; Mines, 1988; Mistra & Giri, 1995; Sinha & Tripathi, 1994; Spiro, 1993; Turiel & Wainryb, 1998).

Those who have critiqued the views of culture as homogeneous or a seamless whole have also maintained that such views, in part, stem from a failure to consider the perspectives of people who are not in dominant positions in the social hierarchy. They have called for greater attention to those who see things from the "bottom" (Strauss, 1992) to those who are further "down the social ladder" (Wikan, 1991) to "relatively silent voices, and voices that cannot speak at all in the public space" (Nussbaum, 1999). These are different ways of saying the same thing: That people in subordinate positions in the social hierarchy do not necessarily share understandings about all cultural practices with those in dominant positions and that they may be in conflict with aspects of the cultural arrangements. Martin Luther King, Jr. made a similar point when he addressed the annual convention of the American Psychological Association in 1967 (see "King's challenge to . . . ," 1999). He urged psychologists to use the concept of maladjustment selectively and to recognize that adjustment to society is not always positive:

> "There are some things concerning which we must always be maladjusted if we are to be people of good will. We must never adjust ourselves to social discrimination and racial segregation. We must never adjust ourselves to religious bigotry. We must never adjust ourselves to economic conditions that take necessities from the many to give luxuries to the few." (pp. 26–29)

Take the example of the research with the Druze. It can be asked if the women are adjusted to the cultural practices of patriarchy by which greater power is accorded to men in decision making within the family. There is a sense in which it appears that they are adjusted to it. Females judged that when husbands and wives disagree as to choices of activities it is husbands who can decide and that wives should acquiesce. In addition, females tended to judge the actions of wives with notions of duties and role obligations, whereas they linked the actions of males to autonomy, independence, and personal discretion. In spite of this type of acceptance of the cultural arrangements, the Druze women were not entirely adjusted to the existing social order. This was evident in two ways. One is that the women often stated that females should acquiesce to the wishes of males for pragmatic reasons—to avoid serious consequences to their well-being. Second, the large majority of females considered unfair the existing social arrangements that subordinate women's autonomy to that of males. Additional research showed that Druze females (and males) assert the legitimacy of individual rights (Turiel & Wainryb, 1998).

The Druze women's evaluations of the unfairness of aspects of their cultural practices may well represent the types of "maladjustment" that Martin Luther King, Jr. thought necessary. The actions of the women of the Moroccan harem and people in Iran are, of course, examples of this kind of lack of adjustment and a willingness to act upon one's moral evaluations in subversive ways. Further documentation of subversive activities comes from Abu-Lughod's (1993) research with Bedouin women in Egypt. Abu-Lughod finds that the Bedouin women regard as unfair many practices that benefit men at the expense of the freedoms and needs of women. Moreover, the women engage in overt and covert acts to circumvent the restrictions placed upon them (e.g., with regard to practices such as arranged marriages and polygamy as well as restrictions on their educational opportunities). It is important to stress, however, that conflicts, discontents, and subversive activities occur among people who are also part of the culture. The multifaceted nature of people's connections to the social system includes acceptance in conjunction with critical scrutiny.

Contrary to the distinction between rights-based cultures on the one hand and duty-based cultures on the other, the claims to individual freedom and need for collective responsibility appear to be present in human societies. The variations that emerge would appear to reflect more or less equilibrated systems for bringing both collective norms and duties and individual claims to freedom into harmony. Cultural systems of equilibrium, however, are not static and contain within them contradictions and sources of tension that may generate overt and covert acts of resistance and subversion as individuals and groups interpret their own position in relation to the system of norms, rights, and duties.

In 1999, two years after the election of a moderate president, great tensions still exist in Iran—tensions that have involved demonstrations sometimes turning violent. The tensions in Iran still include listening to music and dancing. As put by Ali, an 18-year-old from the slums of Teheran (quoted in "Letter from Iran," 1999, p. 22): "I'm tired of high prices. I'm tired of all this unemployment. I'm tired of someone telling me I can't dance or can't read this book or watch that movie. It's gone too far, and I'm ready to fight back." Ali and his friends acted upon their resolve to fight back, in one instance, by asserting their right to dance ("Letter from Iran"):

> In a public park during a massive outdoor picnic celebrating a pre-Islamic Zoroastrian holiday, Ali and his friends sang banned Iranian pop songs from Los Angeles, widely available on the Teheran black market, and invited giggling girls to dance with them.
> "O beautiful girl, like a flower, please come to my side," Ali crooned, mimicking one of those songs, much to the delight of a large crowd that encircled him, clapping their hands to the beat. "One girl to dance with,

that's all we need," Ali exhorted continuing to push the bounds of "propriety" and, indeed, law, in the severe Islamic Republic of Iran, which punishes such public displays of gaiety. Finally, one brave young girl, her brown scarf displaying dangerously large amounts of her chestnut-colored hair, accepted Ali's exhortations and joined the circle of boys dancing. It was a defiant moment, its importance not underestimated by the crowd, who gave the girl a rousing cheer for her courage. After all, Iran's morals police, the Komiteh, could punish the offending dancers harshly for the sin of dancing in public and mixing with members of the opposite sex. (1999, p. 23)

Indeed, it seems that people like to listen to music and dance and will go to great extent to do so in certain social contexts.

REFERENCES

Abu-Lughod, L. (1991). Writing against culture. In R. E. Fox (Ed.), *Recapturing anthropology: Working in the present* (pp. 137–162). Santa Fe, New Mexico: School of American Research Press.

Abu-Lughod, L. (1993). *Writing women's worlds: Bedouin stories*. Berkeley: University of California Press.

Ahmad, S., Waller, G., & Verduyn, C. (1994). Eating attitudes among Asian schoolgirls: The role of perceived parental control. *International Journal of Eating Disorders, 15*, 91–97.

APA Monitor. (1999, January). "King's challenge to the nation's social scientists," pp. 26–29.

Appadurai, A. (1988). Putting hierarchy in its place. *Cultural Anthropology, 3*, 36–49.

Baumrind, D. (1998). From ought to is: A neo-Marxist perspective on the use and misuse of the culture construct. *Human Development, 41*, 145–165.

Beating the system with brakes and the big lie. (1997, May). *New York Times*, p. A4.

Brehm, S. S., & Brehm, J. W. (1981). *Psychological reaction: A theory of freedom and control*. New York: Academic Press.

Bronson, W. (1981). *Toddlers' behavior with agemates: Issues of interaction, cognition, and affect*. Norwood, NJ: Ablex.

Crapanzano, V. (1990). On self characterization. In J. W. Stigler, R. A. Shweder, & G. Herdt (Eds.), *Cultural psychology: Essays on comparative human development* (pp. 401–426). Cambridge, England: Cambridge University Press.

Cushman, P. (1991). Ideology obscured: Political uses of the self in Daniel Stern's infant. *American Psychologist, 46*, 206–220.

Damon, W. (1977). *The social world of the child*. San Francisco: Jossey-Bass.

Derogatis, L. R., & Spencer, P. M. (1982). *The Brief Symptom Inventory: Administration, scoring, and procedures Manual I*. Baltimore: Clinical Biometric Research.

Dunn, J. (1987). The beginnings of moral understanding: Development in the second year. In J. Kagan & S. Lamb (Eds.), *The emergence of morality in young children* (pp. 91–112). Chicago: University of Chicago Press.

Dunn, J., & Munn, P. (1987). Development of justification in disputes with mother and sibling. *Developmental Psychology, 23*, 791–798.

Dunn, J., Brown, J. R., & Maguire, M. (1995). The development of children's moral sensibility: Individual differences and emotion understanding. *Developmental Psychology, 31*, 649–659.

Eisenberg, N. (1982). *The development of prosocial behavior*. New York: Academic Press.

Eisenberg, N., & Strayer, J. (Eds.). (1987). *Empathy and its development*. New York: Cambridge University Press.

Ewing, K. P. (1990). The illusion of wholeness: Culture, self, and the experience of inconsistency. *Ethos, 18*, 251–278.

Freud, S. (1930). *Civilization and its discontents*. New York: Norton.

Geertz, C. (1984). From the natives' point of view: On the nature of anthropological understanding. In R. A. Shweder & R. Levine (Eds.), *Culture theory* (pp. 123–136). Cambridge, England: Cambridge University Press.

Gewirth, A. (1982). *Human rights: Essays on justification and application*. Chicago: University of Chicago Press.

Haidt, J., Koller, S. H., & Dias, M. G. (1994). Affect, culture, and the morality of harmless offenses. *Journal of Personality and Social Psychology, 65*, 613–629.

Hasebe, Y. (1999). *Parental psychological abuse and adolescent psychopathology: Its relevance to parental control in the U.S. and Japan*. Unpublished doctoral dissertation, University of Illinois at Chicago.

Helwig, C. C. (1995). Adolescents' and young adults' conceptions of civil liberties: Freedom of speech and religion. *Child Development, 66*, 152–166.

Hoffman, M. L. (1991). Empathy, social cognition, and moral action. In W. M. Kurtines & J. L. Gewirtz (Eds.), *Handbook of moral behavior and development, Vol. 1: Theory* (pp. 275–301). Hillsdale, NJ: Lawrence Erlbaum Associates.

Hollan, D. (1992). Cross-cultural differences in the self. *Journal of Anthropological Research, 48*, 283–300.

King, M. L., Jr. (1963, April). Letter from a Birmingham city jail. Nyack, NY: Fellowship Reconciliation.

Kobak, R. R., Sudler, N., & Gamble, W. (1991). Attachment and depressive symptoms during adolescence: A developmental pathways analysis. *Development and Psychopathology, 3*, 461–474.

Kohlberg, L. (1969). Stage and sequence: The cognitive-developmental approach to socialization. In D. Goslin (Ed.), *Handbook of socialization theory and research* (pp. 347–480). Chicago: Rand McNally.

Kohlberg, L. (1984). *Essays on moral development: The psychology of moral development*. San Francisco: Harper & Row.

Kuczinski, L., Kochanska, G., Radke-Yarrow, M., & Girnius-Brown, O. (1987). A developmental interpretation of young children's non-compliance. *Developmental Psychology, 23*, 799–806.

Letter from Iran. (1999, July 19). *The Nation*, pp. 22–24.

Loevinger, J. (1966). The meaning and measurement of ego development. *American Psychologist, 21*, 195–217.

Markus, H. R., & Kitayama, S. (1991). Culture and the self: Implications for cognition, emotion, and motivation. *Psychological Review, 98*, 224–253.

Many Iranians hope moderate brings change. (1997, May 26). *New York Times*, pp. A1–A4.

McClosky, M., & Brill, A. (1983). *Dimensions of tolerance: What Americans believe about civil liberties*. New York: Russell Sage.

McCourt, J., & Waller, G. (1995). Developmental role of perceived parental control in the eating pathology of Asian and Caucasian schoolgirls. *International Journal of Eating Disorders, 17*, 277–282.

Mernissi, F. (1994). *Dreams of trespass: Tales of a harem childhood*. Reading, MA: Addison-Wesley.

Miller, J., & Bersoff, D. M. (1992). Culture and moral judgment: How are conflicts between justice and interpersonal responsibilities resolved? *Journal of Personality and Social Psychology, 62*, 541–554.

Miller, J., Bersoff, D., & Harwood, R. (1990). Perceptions of social responsibilities in India and the United States: Moral imperatives or personal decisions? *Journal of Personality and Social Psychology, 58,* 33–47.

Miller, J., & Luthar, S. (1989). Issues of interpersonal responsibility and accountability: A comparison of Indians' and Americans' moral judgments. *Social Cognition, 7,* 237–261.

Mines, M. (1988). Conceptualizing the person: Hierarchical society and individual autonomy in India. *American Anthropologist, 90,* 568–579.

Misra, G., & Giri, R. (1995). Is Indian self predominantly interdependent? *Journal of Indian Psychology, 13,* 16–29.

Much, N., & Shweder, R. A. (1978). Speaking of rules: The analysis of culture in breach. In W. Damon (Ed.), *New directions for child development. Vol. 2. Moral development.* San Francisco: Jossey-Bass.

Murphy, L. (1937). *Social behavior and child personality.* New York: Columbia University Press.

Neff, K. (1997). *Reasoning about rights and duties in the context of Indian family life.* Unpublished doctoral dissertation, University of California, Berkeley.

Nucci, L. (1977). *Social development: Personal, conventional, and moral concepts.* Unpublished doctoral dissertation, University of California, Santa Cruz.

Nucci, L. (1996). Morality and personal freedom. In E. Reed, E. Turiel, & T. Brown (Eds.), *Knowledge and values* (pp. 41–60). Mahwah, NJ: Lawrence Erlbaum Associates.

Nucci, L. Camino, C., & Sapiro, C. (1996). Social class effects on Northeastern Brazilian children's conceptions of areas of personal choice and social regulation. *Child Development, 67,* 1223–1242.

Nucci, L., Hasebe, Y., & Nucci, M. S. (1999, April). *Parental overcontrol of the personal domain and adolescent psychopathology.* Paper presented at the biennial meetings of the Society for Research in Child Development, Albuquerque, NM.

Nucci, L., & Lee, J. Y. (1993). Morality and personal autonomy. In G. Noam & T. Wren (Eds.), *The moral self* (pp. 123–148). Cambridge, MA: MIT Press.

Nucci, L., & Milnitsky Sapiro, C. (1995). *The impact of region and social class on Brazilian mothers' conceptions of children's areas of personal choice.* Unpublished manuscript, University of Illinois at Chicago.

Nucci, L., & Nucci, M. S. (1982a). Children's responses to moral and social-conventional transgressions in free-play settings. *Child Development, 53,* 1337–1342.

Nucci, L., & Nucci M. S. (1982b). Children's social interactions in the context of moral and conventional transgressions. *Child Development, 53,* 403–412.

Nucci, L., & Smetana, J. (1996). Mothers' concepts of young children's areas of personal freedom. *Child Development, 67,* 1870–1886.

Nucci, L., & Turiel, E. (1978). Social interactions and the development of social concepts in pre-school children. *Child Development, 49,* 400–407.

Nucci, L., Turiel, E., & Encarnacion-Gawrych, G. (1983). Children's social interactions and social concepts in the Virgin Islands. *Journal of Cross-Cultural Psychology, 14,* 469–487.

Nucci, L., & Weber, E. K. (1995). Social interactions in the home and the development of young children's conceptions within the personal domain. *Child Development, 66,* 1438–1452.

Nussbaum, M. C. (1999). *Sex and social justice.* New York: Oxford University Press.

Peck, R. F., & Havighurst, R. J. (1960). *The psychology of character development.* New York: Wiley.

Radke-Yarrow, M., Zahn-Waxler, C., & Chapman, M. (1983). Children's prosocial dispositions and behavior. In P. Mussen (Series Ed.) & E. M. Hetherington (Vol. Ed.), *Handbook of child psychology: Vol. 4. Socialization, personality, and social development* (4th ed., pp. 469–545). New York: Wiley.

Schlegel, A., & Barry, H., 3rd. (1991). *Adolescence: An anthropological inquiry.* New York: The Free Press.

Shweder, R. A. (1990). In defense of moral realism: Reply to Gabennesch. *Child Development,* *61,* 2060–2067.

Shweder, R. A., & Bourne, E. J. (1982). Does the concept of person vary cross-culturally? In A. J. Marsella & G. M. White (Eds.), *Cultural conceptions of mental health and therapy* (pp. 97–137). Boston: Reidel.

Shweder, R. A., Mahapatra, M., & Miller, J. G. (1987). Culture and moral development. In J. Kagan & S. Lamb (Eds.), *The emergence of morality in young children* (pp. 1–83). Chicago: University of Chicago Press.

Sinha, D., & Tripathi, R. C. (1994). Individualism in a collectivistic culture: A case of coexistence of opposites. In U. Kim, H. Triandis, C. Kagitcibasi, S. Choi, & G. Yoon (Eds.), *Individualism and collectivism: Theory, method, and applications* (pp. 123–136). London: Sage.

Smetena, J. (1981). Preschool children's conceptions of moral and social rules. *Child Development, 52,* 1333–1336.

Smetana, J. (1989). Adolescents' and parents' reasoning about actual family conflict. *Child Development, 60,* 1052–1067.

Smetana, J. (1995). Morality in context: Abstractions, ambiguities, and applications. In R. Vasta (Ed.), *Annals of child development* (Vol. 10, pp. 83–130). London: Jessica Kingsley.

Smetana, J. (1998). Conflict and coordination in adolescent-parent relationships. In S. Shulman (Ed.), *Close relationships and socioemotional development.* Norwood, NJ: Ablex.

Smetana, J., & Asquith, P. (1994). Adolescents' and parents' conceptions of parental authority and adolescent autonomy. *Child Development, 65,* 1143–1158.

Smetana, J., Braeges, J. L., & Yau, J. (1991). Doing what you say and saying what you do: Reasoning about adolescent-parent conflict in interviews and interactions. *Journal of Adolescent Research, 6,* 276–295.

Smetana, J. G., Yau, J., Restrepo, A., & Braeges, J. (1991). Adolescent-parent conflict in married and divorced families. *Developmental Psychology, 27,* 1000–1010.

Spiro, M. (1993). Is the Western conception of the self "peculiar" within the context of the world cultures? *Ethos, 21,* 107–153.

Stern, D. (1985). *The interpersonal world of the infant: A view from psychoanalysis and developmental psychology.* New York: Basic Books.

Strauss, C. (1992). Models and motives. In R. G. Díandrade & C. Strauss (Eds.), *Human motives and cultural models* (pp. 1–20). Cambridge, England: Cambridge University Press.

Tisak, M. (1995). Domains of social reasoning and beyond. In R. Vasta (Ed.), *Annals of child development, Vol. 11* (pp. 95–130). London: Jessica Kingsley.

Turiel, E. (1983). *The development of social knowledge: Morality and convention.* Cambridge, England: Cambridge University Press.

Turiel, E. (1994). Morality, authoritarianism, and personal agency. In R. J. Stenberg & P. Ruzgis (Eds.), *Personality and intelligence* (pp. 271–299). Cambridge, England: Cambridge University Press.

Turiel, E. (1996). Equality and hierarchy: Conflict in values. In E. S. Reed, E. Turiel, & T. Brown (Eds.), *Values and knowledge* (pp. 71–102). Mahwah, NJ: Lawrence Erlbaum Associates.

Turiel, E. (1997). Beyond particular and universal ways: Contexts for morality. In H. Saltzstein (Ed.), *Moral development in culture: Particulars and universals. New Directions for Child Development* (pp. 87–105). San Francisco: Jossey-Bass.

Turiel, E. (1998). The development of morality. In W. Damon (Series Ed.) & N. Eisenberg (Vol. Ed.), *Handbook of child psychology,* Vol. 3. *Social, emotional, and personality development* (5th ed., pp. 863–932). New York: Wiley.

Turiel, E. (in press). The development of moral and personal judgments and cultural arrangements. In G. Dux (Ed.), *Moral und recht en diskurs der modern.* Germany: Leske and Burdich.

Turiel, E., & Wainryb, C. (1998). Concepts of freedoms and rights in a traditional hierarchically organized society. *British Journal of Developmental Psychology, 16*, 375–395.

Wainryb, C. (1997). The mismeasure of diversity: Reflections on the study of cross-cultural differences. In H. D. Saltzstein (Ed.), *Culture as a context for moral development. New perspectives on the particular and universal. New Directions for Child Development* (pp. 51–65). San Francisco: Jossey-Bass.

Wainryb, C., & Turiel, E. (1994). Dominance, subordination, and concepts of personal entitlements in cultural contexts. *Child Development, 65*, 1701–1722.

Wikan, U. (1991). Toward an experience—near anthropology. *Cultural Anthropology, 6*, 285–305.

Wilson, J. Q. (1993). *The moral sense*. New York: The Free Press.

Part III

THE DEVELOPMENT OF
PHYSICAL AND SPATIAL
KNOWLEDGE

Chapter 7

Does the Mind Know the Difference Between the Physical and Social Worlds?

Andrea A. diSessa
University of California, Berkeley

In the 1990s, there has been a surge of interest in domain-specific competence and "modularity of mind." In oversimplified terms, is human cognition largely general, flexible, and homogeneous, or does it consist of modules that may be highly specific, possibly "hard-wired" (innate), and independent in the sense of not interacting much with each other? A Piaget-relevant example is whether one views conservation an indicator and component of a global shift in human logic (homogeneous, domain general), or just "learning a little physics" (domain specific). One of the attractive features of modularity is that it might help solve the learning problem—how do people miraculously learn the things they evidently do? Modularity helps with the learning problem particularly if some (modular) competence is present at birth. Another general attractiveness of modularity and domain specificity is that these help deal with empirical complexities that always seem to arise in homogeneous views of human development—phenomena such as horizontal *décalage*, where stage characteristics do not appear across all domains at the same time. Similarly, assumptions about independent competencies have been proposed to help explain apparent complexities in what might otherwise be viewed as global capacities, such as intelligence (Gardner, 1993). Modularity may also explain why learning some things is hard—if those things contradict the relevant congenital module. A good reference on domain specificity and modularity is Hirschfeld and Gelman (1994).

The two domains that I investigate in this chapter are, very roughly, the physical world and the social world. Simply put, is there any intersection between the knowledge and competence that human beings exhibit in these two domains, or is this an issue of distinct domains or modules?

There is a distinct asymmetry in the way that the literature has treated these two domains. On the one hand, physical competence is almost always treated as a single domain and is frequently hypothesized to constitute a module, usually called *naive physics*. On the other hand, the social world is probably too broad to constitute a single module, and defining what module or modules are involved varies considerably from researcher to researcher. In order to avoid complexities that I do not believe bear critically on the arguments that I make, I am inclusive on the social side. In particular, I include both social and cultural competence even if, under some circumstances, these should have separate treatments. This explains my use of the term *sociocultural* in place of *social* on occasion, usually to emphasize that cross-cultural differences might be implicated. On occasion I broaden *social* even more to include knowledge and competence concerning human psychology. Thus, I am really contrasting competence with what philosophers and cognitive scientists call intentional phenomena with competence concerning the inanimate, physical world. Naive psychology, naive sociology, and morality have all been proposed as candidate modules concerned with intentional phenomena.[1] Technically, I discuss whether an independent physics module exists and whether it overlaps with any competence or module for dealing with intentional phenomena. For simplicity, accessibility, and relevance to this volume, I emphasize what most people would call *social competence* within the intentional domain.

A secondary aim of this chapter is to comment on an issue of scientific tradition. In the 1990s, a visible rift appeared between sociocultural approaches to cognition and cognitivist approaches. Sociocultural approaches have concentrated on social phenomena, and cognitive approaches have similarly concentrated primarily on more individual human activities, such as individual problem solving. Such specialization is, in my view, unproblematic in that (a) I assume that it is important to understand how individuals think and how groups of people interact and work together and (b) understanding one of these probably does not (and certainly does not necessarily and obviously) mean understanding the other. What is more problematic is the assumption that these are incommensurable points of view, that one must choose between them, or that one approach "owns" sociocultural issues and the other individual issues. A good example of the rift is the continuing debate between situated cognition and ordinary cognitive studies. (See Anderson,

---

[1]See, for example, Sperber (pp. 42, 54), Hirschfeld (pp. 201–202), Hirschfeld and Gelman (especially, pp. 12–15), Boyer (cultural invariance of the intuitive psychology module, e.g., p. 404) and others in Hirschfeld and Gelman (1994).

Reder, & Simon, 1996 and 1997; Greeno, 1996.) One of the threads in this debate is whether one can think at all about learning as an individual phenomenon, or whether both learning and competence are irreducibly social phenomena, which are impossible to localize in people's heads. Is learning acquiring appropriate concepts, or is it a process of becoming a member of a group (Lave & Wenger, 1991)? Another indicator of the divide is whether one can cite Piaget approvingly (thus being identified as a cognitivist) or, in contrast, must one systematically take a position identified as Vygotsky's (thus marking oneself as a socioculturalist) that—even if all knowledge is not irreducibly social—all the best knowledge originates in social interaction.

After considering modules and domains, I come back to see what my conclusions may have to say about the sociocultural/cognitivist divide.

SETTING THE SCENE: BASIC CLAIMS

The central question is: How does knowledge of the physical world relate to social knowledge?[2]

By physical and social knowledge, I do not mean schooled or professional knowledge, but the everyday competence that allows one to act reasonably and sometimes fluidly in particular circumstances, as in moving objects and oneself around or reacting appropriately in social circumstances.

I argue (in rough terms, to be elaborated later):

• There is every reason to believe that physical and social knowledge, or at least significant components of each, operate with the same mental machinery. There is no reason to believe different brain parts account for physical and social competence. Within a computational metaphor, this is, very roughly, a claim that there may be common hardware.

• The overlap between particular physical and social knowledge is at least nontrivial and perhaps quite substantial. That is, there are actually common knowledge elements across these domains. Within a computational metaphor, this claim asserts that, in addition to common machinery, these domains may share software.

• Ontogenetically, there is every reason to believe that the interaction of physical and social knowledge is at least nontrivial and perhaps quite substantial. The developmental and learning processes that

---

[2]Whether all competence can be explained as the result of knowledge is a complex semantic issue I hope to suppress. My inclination is, roughly, to define *knowledge* as that which explains competence, which alleviates the issue. However, such a definition stretches the meaning most people have for knowledge.

result in particular knowledge involve interaction across domains. This claim extends the first two, which dealt with use or operation, to a claim about genesis.

TWO DISTINCTIONS

I need two distinctions to organize my discussion. The first is between *specific knowledge* and *mechanism*. Specific knowledge (which I frequently gloss as *knowledge*) has a focus on a particular range of objects, attributes, and relations. Disciplinary knowledge, biology, physics, and so forth, might be a good prototype. In contrast, mechanism should be construed as architectural and usually more general. Whether it is the case or not, most people probably believe physicists do not think very differently than biologists: "They just know different things." Mechanisms might be general reasoning or learning processes, logic, and, for professional scientific practice, mathematical reasoning or modeling. Frequently mechanism is construed as built-in and unchangeable, but that may not be true. In any case, the division into knowledge and mechanism requires a relatively stable layer (mechanism) into which more particular variations of competence may be poured, or which can be used with a range of more particular competencies.[3] It is helpful to remember that, in principle, there may be several levels of mechanism. For example, using a particular fact may involve both memory and reasoning mechanisms, which might, in turn, be implemented with different patterns of shared neuronal mechanisms.

Here are some metaphors or, possibly, examples. First, natural language has a relatively stable syntax and grammar, but its lexicon may change significantly from one domain to another. In this case, physicists and biologists share a mechanism-like layer but vary significantly at the knowledge level: their technical lexicons contain different words that concern different objects and relations. Second, a computer language or machine architecture defines a mechanism, and particular software may be likened to knowledge. One can implement many programs concerning different things with the same basic mechanisms.

Sometimes researchers call the level of mechanism *structure* (similar to Piagetian structures) and presume thereby its invariance or its pervasive influence if it does change. Other times the term *form* is used quite simi-

---

[3]Mechanism might be assumed to implement specific knowledge. This is an appropriate sense for much of my discussion. However, for the main issue, mechanism as invariant structure that may be used with various specific knowledge pools, regardless of their implementations, serves the same function. Mathematical thinking counts as mechanism in this latter sense.

larly to structure and *content* is used to contrast, as in "the content may vary, but the form is the same."

The second distinction is simpler. The *operation* of any system (mechanical, cognitive, social) is conceptually distinct from its *genesis*, the processes that led to its existence and particular form. Although it should be obvious, it is important to be clear on whether one is talking about processes of genesis or operation, and the answers one gives to questions such as "Are these systems similar?" might depend on whether one is asking about one or the other.[4]

Together, these distinctions create a two-by-two matrix of categories, which I use systematically in the analyses that follow. Table 7.1 demonstrates use of these categories, although not in a way that is integral to the following discussion. The table provides sometimes obvious, sometimes very speculative answers to questions concerning cognition. Answers that are particularly characteristic of sociocultural approaches appear in italics. In general, I have not been careful to be uniform or explicit about paradigms from which these answers are drawn, and I note that the whole knowledge/mechanism distinction seems less salient in sociocultural theory.

INTUITIVE PHYSICS

Let us start with the knowledge people have about the physical world. If it is not completely obvious, a great deal of evidence shows that humans have a lot of uninstructed understanding of physics. Studies of infants show that at extraordinarily early stages, babies respond with apparent surprise to nonphysical events such as two solid objects passing through each other (Leslie, 1988), or, at a slightly later age, a released and unsupported object hanging in the air without falling (Spelke, 1991). Piagetian research uncovered substantial development, including such landmark accomplishments as object permanence and conservation of volume and mass. On the educational side, a huge ruckus has been made about intuitive misconceptions that persist well into instruction and appear to interfere with learning real physics (Confrey, 1990). Few people, if any, dispute the existence of this knowledge of the physical world, but its nature and, consequently, educational remedial strategies are strongly contested. The following is an abbreviated account of a theory of intuitive knowledge in physics that I have developed (diSessa, 1993), and which I take as a reference point to begin comparing social knowledge. As an advance organizer, consider Table 7.2.

---

[4]It is entirely possible that the processes that account for normal operation of a cognitive system also account for changes in it. In fact, I believe this is a good assumption. However, development and change are still not the same things as operation.

TABLE 7.1
Profiles (Temporal, Spatial, Ontological, and Developmental) of Knowledge and Mechanism

	Operation	Genesis
Time scale		
Knowledge	A fraction to several seconds	Months
Mechanism	Same as knowledge	Biological evolutionary time scales *Cultural evolutionary time scales*
Spatial location		
Knowledge	Individual's head, body *Relation between person and environment*	Sociophysical locus (surrounding the individual) *(surrounding the social group, probably excluding the head)*
Mechanism	Individual's head, body *Relation between person and environment*	Historical evolutionary line *Historical cultural line (excluding the head)*
Ontology		
Knowledge	Particular facts, concepts, p-prims *Participation, practices, literacies*	Learning, memorizing, shifting priorities *Appropriation, becoming a member*
Mechanism	Recall, recognition, the categories of fact, concept, p-prim	Evolution in functional brain structure
Principles of stabilization/innovation		
Knowledge	Brain structure, reinforcement/Failure at goals *Cultural reproduction/Contradictions*	Memory/Disequilibration *Cultural reproduction/Contradictions*
Mechanism	Brain structure, genes/None	Natural selection/Mutation

The central theoretical entity of intuitive knowledge I call a *phenomenological primitive*, or *p-prim* for short. P-prims are fairly simple knowledge elements with few parts. They are evoked as units and serve their primary function as self-explanatory descriptions. That is, when you recognize a p-prim in a situation, your attitude is one of complacency or naturalness—"That's the way things should happen." P-prims also engender feelings of surprise if they are violated.

P-prims account for commonsense and intuitive explanations of the physical world. This does not mean that p-prims appear explicitly in explanations. Far from it. In fact, the relation of p-prims to language is problematic. No words pick out particular p-prim meanings, and in gen-

TABLE 7.2
Intuitive Knowledge of Physics

	Operation	Genesis
Knowledge	Hundreds or thousands of elements, called p-prims	Reorganization: Shifting "priorities" (preconditions)
	Elements are "small" and simple	Occasional new p-prims (Simple descriptions "knighted" as explanatory)
		New functions
Mechanism	Recognition	
	Feelings of naturalness, surprise	Biological evolution?
	Expectations	
	Function as explanatorily primitive	

eral it is difficult to describe a p-prim in language. Instead, p-prims are more experiential, prototypically (but not exclusively) involving kinesthetically encoded relations of personal bodily experience. So in saying that p-prims account for intuitive explanations, I really mean they are not said, but constitute implicit assumptions that account for why some descriptions and explanations "feel right," and others do not.

To define a p-prim, it helps to describe the mechanisms by which p-prims work. Recognition is a good metaphor for the mechanism of activation of p-prims. This activation is contingent on aspects of the situation or aspects of the prior mental state of the individual. I describe these contingencies in terms of priorities. For example, an important p-prim will have high priority in many situations. That means it will likely come to mind in situations where one has learned it is likely to be of use. High priority of a p-prim also means that one may prefer an explanatory description relying on that p-prim, compared to less "strong" p-prims. As there are hundreds, at least, and probably thousands of p-prims, nuance is important. Thus, priorities (which determine when it is used) are absolutely critical in describing a p-prim and its meaning. I describe the collection of p-prims as a *sense of mechanism*, that is, people's intuitive understanding of how things like the physical world work. The sense of mechanism should not be confused with the mental mechanisms by which p-prims work. Common folks have no sense of p-prims' mechanism; how p-prims work is exclusively an analyst concern. But common folks do have a sense of mechanism concerning many other things. In particular, people have a sense of mechanism concerning the physical world.[5]

The sense of physical mechanism is not unstructured. Some p-prims are much more important than others; there are clusters and types of p-prims. However, given their status as inarticulate, bottom-up descriptions in a large vocabulary of such, characterizing them as "theories" or even "beliefs" is both unlikely and misleading, implying too much structure, more systematicity, and more articulate access than is possible. Empirical data that undermine considering the sense of mechanism as a theory include: (a) evidence of partial and incomplete construction of putative "theories" rather than full-blown and constant presence; (b) "data fluidity," that switching or changing contexts can bring other ways of thinking—other p-prims—to the fore; (c) incompleteness—proposed accounts for the intuitive sense of mechanism as a theory never encompass the full range of physical expectations that are evident in subjects; and (d) lack of well articulated descriptions of the processes that can result in the construction of intuitive theories (especially given the nonlinguistic nature of these expectations). See diSessa (1993) for an elaboration of these arguments.

The development of the sense of mechanism occurs in the following ways. First, the origins of p-prims are not terribly problematic. They are frequently, in essence, simple descriptions of common phenomena. However, not any description is a p-prim, but only ones that have been learned to constitute "the way things generally work." I describe p-prims sometimes as "knighted (as explanatory) descriptions." Again, the contexts in which a p-prim is considered to work are critical to defining it, and a long process of sorting and prioritizing is implicated in the development of the sense of mechanism.

Because p-prims supply people with their sense of how things work and what explanations are adequate, they are critical in learning school physics. Basically, one must learn new situation-specific sensibilities of explanation. However, perhaps surprisingly, changes in the sense of mechanism are more a reorganization than a replacement. Many or even most p-prims remain in more expert understanding, but they are connected to different situations and work differently. For example, a particular p-prim may make one think of conservation of energy, so it serves the function of heuristic cue. Other p-prims may still be considered explanatory, but only in rough approximation. If an expert is queried about why something happens, or he or she just troubles to think more carefully, he or she will refine or even put aside a p-prim in favor of explanation using sanctioned physical principles, such as Newton's laws or the conservation of energy.

_____

[5]The term *intuitive causal sense* might be used in place of sense of mechanism to avoid confusion with cognitive mechanism. But for consistency with other treatments (e.g., diSessa, 1993), I continue to use sense of mechanism.

I do not have a strong and empirically founded position on which p-prims are genetically determined and on how those relate to the learned set. Research on infants suggests, as mentioned, that babies do have built-in, p-prim-like expectations. However, I do feel that there is strong evidence that the naive sense of mechanism is substantially malleable. Indeed, it must change in learning physics if students are ever to consider what they learn to be sensible. I interpret misconceptions studies that show the effect of naive ideas well into instruction as demonstrating the influence of the naive sense of mechanism and that instruction frequently does not deal well with it (Smith, diSessa, & Roschelle, 1993).

Here is a sample list of p-prims:

1. Ohm's p-prim. A central and important p-prim, called Ohm's p-prim, has a tripartite structure. First, an *agency* or *impetus* is driving some process. The *effect* of that driving force is a second part. The third part is a *resistance* that moderates the effect of the impetus on the effect. When one recognizes a situation in which Ohm's p-prim applies, one expects a collection of qualitative relations to apply. A greater impetus begets a greater effect; a lesser impetus begets less effect; more resistance implies (other things equal) less effect; and so on. Applications of Ohm's p-prim are widespread. Anytime you struggle to move an object, you interpret the consequences of your actions in terms of it. If you are failing to achieve a desired result, you "work harder," or you try to lessen the resistance. Resistance can be intrinsic, such as the weight of an object (about which one can do little), or imposed, such as the presence of an interfering force or quality, for example, gravity or friction.

2. Force as mover. Force as a mover is essentially an abstraction of a toss. You apply a directed burst of effort, and the object of your efforts moves in the direction you push it. Unfortunately, Newtonian physics frequently does not work exactly this way. Pushing on an object adds to existing momentum, resulting in a compromise movement between the push and existing motion. This mismatch between force as a mover and schooled physics is a well-documented misconception, which appears in difficulties learning physics (diSessa, 1982).

Humans seem sensitive to the distinction between rapid and forceful ("violent") interactions and quasi-static, steady ones. For steady state situations, even at speeds similar to those involved in a toss, the "continued motion in absence of the initiating impetus" phenomenon (which physicists call momentum) is much less salient, and people may feel motion will disappear immediately subsequent to cessation of the driving force (McCloskey, 1983).

3. Force as a spinner. Pushing an object off center causes it to turn, rather than move, in the obvious way.

4. Motion dies away. People expect that non-self-generated movement or actions that do not have a source of sustaining impetus naturally just die away. A thrown ball comes to a stop, and the sound of a struck bell fades. Sometimes people have learned that technical "excuses," such as dissipation of energy or friction, may be given to account for this dying away. But under many circumstances that unsustained action just dies away is considered primitive.

5. Balance and overcoming. Humans have a rich sense of balance and imbalance, which they consider explanatory. These p-prims are seldom aligned well with principles of physics. For example, if something is "in balance," people expect stability and lack of motion. In contrast, stability needs particular explanation to a physicist; balance is insufficient by itself. Balanced forces, according to Newton's second law, may perfectly well result in constant, continuing motion. *"Conflict"* is a salient attribute involved in many balancing situations. Furthermore, changing patterns in the magnitude of strength or "effort" of conflicting partners beget characteristic patterns in result. An impetus' becoming stronger in the context of a balance, or the other's becoming weaker, results in *overcoming*; outcomes emerge consistent with the stronger's "wishes."

6. Blocking. It is a common primitive of physical experience that big, heavy, immobile, "strong" objects can simply stop or prevent motion that might otherwise have occurred. A table is interpreted merely to block the fall that would otherwise have taken place by an object resting on top of it. Again, this has been noted as a learning difficulty. A proper physical analysis requires something other than blocking; it requires what is immensely implausible for many naive physicists, that is, that the table is actually exerting an upward force on the object it supports (Minstrell, 1982).

Now I begin to look to see what this analysis of naive physics might have to do with social competence.

MECHANISM

For clarity, I first abstract a description of the cognitive mechanism of p-prims from the more general discussion of p-prims. First, we have a selected set of schemata that embody a person's causal sense of how a class of phenomena work. The second and third components of mechanism are the processes that result in activation of a p-prim, and the results of that activation. Technically, the priority structure of a p-prim determines when it is activated and how securely one feels one's judgment must apply. A p-prim's activation in a situation where its entailments are met results in a feeling of naturalness. Activation with a misfit—say, the p-prim's results do not match what one sees in the situation—produces surprise and puzzlement. In terms of learning, priorities are amenable to change with experience. In addition, people can generate new p-prims by selecting descriptions of phenomena that effectively serve an explanatory role.

As far as I know, there is every reason to expect that this mechanism is built-in for humans. In a series of arguments, I attempt to show that at least a part of social knowledge works just like people's sense of physical phenomena.

Argument 1

The description of mechanism makes no commitment to domain or content of the knowledge elements. There is no reason the same mechanism should not operate to develop and utilize p-prims that deal with other classes of phenomenology, including socially and culturally based interaction. In fact, except for some ancillary conditions, some of which are treated later, the existence of such a mechanism implies that a social sense of mechanism should develop. If it does not exist, some serious rethinking would be needed concerning my theory of intuitive knowledge in physics.

Argument 2

The function of a physical sense of mechanism and that of a parallel social sense seem remarkably aligned. They are about causality in different domains. Spelling this out a bit, the physical and social senses of mechanism are both about how human beings develop and encode a sensitivity to regularities in their experienced world. These sensitivities explain, in part, what one attends to in patterns of activity and how one takes sensible actions that have intended effects.

Argument 3

In order to bootstrap one's sense of mechanism, that is, a set of p-prims, an agent (e.g., a child) must have a sufficient sensitivity to relevant phenomenology. People do not develop a sense of mechanism for atomic interactions on the basis of their everyday experience for the simple reason that their senses do not report relevantly textured experience and because they cannot effectively manipulate atomic circumstances to have effects of value to them. In contrast, I believe a very strong prima facie argument exists that the phenomenology of social interaction is as rich as physical phenomenology. Watching young children gradually becoming attuned to social interaction, for example learning social graces, implicates significant sensitivity and consequent development. This bootstrapping of a sense of social mechanism is similar to physical play and experimental interaction that children, and even babies, perform. Indeed, social interaction may be intrinsically richer in terms of its phenomenology because of the diversity of affective reports—fear, shame, pleasure, possibly "belonging," affection, and so forth—in comparison to relatively impoverished parallels for the physical world, which would be something like surprise, or a sense of natural and appropriate causality.

Argument 4

Both the physical and social domains show evident human competence that needs explaining. Humans do navigate everyday social and physical situations with considerable ease, and we need to explain the origins and nature of this competence. I put forward the p-prims story about intuitive knowledge in physics as one reasonably well-thought-out and empirically backed explanation of a slice of physical competence. The projection of the same mechanism working on social phenomena, I argue, might hold. Not only does one see competencies that appear to have similar properties, but also variation in competence among humans seems comparable between the two domains. Within the physical domain, one encounters a range of competence between an athlete or a watchmaker—with exquisite sensitivity and control over physical phenomena with which most humans will be incompetent—and a "klutz" or clumsy individual. Similarly, intuitive social competence ranges from suave or socially sophisticated individuals to social bumpkins. The vast majority of people get by reasonably in both domains.

Argument 5

Physical and social phenomena have a similar presence in language. I mentioned that the physical sense of mechanism relates problematically to language. But, this does not mean there is no relation at all. People can report their judgments about plausibility of physical events and about the plausibility of various explanations of those events. Furthermore, natural language is full of words that relate—not directly, but at least tangentially—to p-prims. One speaks of force, balance, overcoming, fading, and so on. Compare:

Friendly, antagonistic, prideful, proper, insulting, stronger (personality).

Push, pull, twist, leverage, fading away, stronger (force).

Furthermore, people seem adept at reading a linguistic description of an event in order to render judgments of the plausibility and explanatory basis of the event. No one has trouble with, "Are heavier things harder to push than light ones?" Although predictions and explanations from verbal description may not always be aligned with those one would make in a situation of participation or observation, still, they are frequently enough surprisingly similar. In any case, people usually feel they can make judgments based on verbal descriptions.

Limitations of verbal descriptions of phenomenology also seem similar between physical and social knowledge. People frequently try to explain to each other how they believe things work—explicating their p-prims—but this certainly does not always convey either a relevant p-prim in any degree of precision or the feeling of naturalness that is the hallmark of having a p-prim. Telling a child "you should feel embarrassed" frequently has no effect in engendering such feelings. Again, language seems connected but substantially incomplete with respect to communicating both senses of how the physical world works and of how people behave.

Argument 6

Another important quality of the physical and social senses of mechanism is their limitations in comparison to scientific theories that cover the same domains. In addition to limitations in articulateness, discussed earlier, important limits in systematicity exist. Instead of a few principles of Newtonian mechanics, there are hundreds of p-prims, and these do not fall into simple hierarchical or other strict systematic patterns. I do not believe any compelling accounts of social competence exist that reduce it to a few principles. But, of course, I am open to argument against this (in the case of the physical sense of mechanism as well as the social!).

In both physical and social cases, people recognize causal patterns when they see them. They are not very good at articulating exactly when those causal patterns appear, and they may change their minds with subtle changes in the situation. "I know one when I see one." "That's just different." In other cases, people cannot decide what should happen; neither the physical nor social sense of mechanism is exhaustive, articulately precise, or definitive.

So far, I have made the claims summarized in Table 7.3.

The case for the similarities in genesis compared to the arguments about operation is, at this point, more circumstantial and indirect. But, genesis is difficult to see in any case, and competing arguments to mine are probably similarly weak with respect to it. In addition, I take up the question of genesis more seriously at the knowledge level, later.

KNOWLEDGE

I now make a stronger move. Not only may social knowledge of a certain sort work with the same cognitive mechanism as intuitive physics, but there are substantial overlaps at the level of specific knowledge. Sharing

TABLE 7.3
Relations Between Physical and Social Knowledge

	Operation	*Genesis*
Knowledge	Similar in its structural characteristics (richness, heterarchy, data fluidity, . . .	Similar in its structural characteristics (origins as knighted descriptions, development via priority sorting)
Mechanism	Identical (at least for some aspects of each)	Presumably the same

content, given my description of intuitive physics, comes down to sharing p-prims (and descriptive vocabulary implicated in p-prims). On the first pass, I emphasize mostly similarity; later, I return to discuss some issues concerning whether these are rough parallels, "merely metaphorical," or if they implicate genuine overlap.

The first-mentioned p-prim, Ohm's p-prim, is central in intuitive physics. It happens to work just as well concerning human interaction. In fact, Ohm's p-prim seems to have a prominent position of very wide scope, including the physical world, the personal intentional world, and the social world. People influence each other according to the effort they put into it, and inversely with the resistance offered. When I wished my children to do something and they did not do it, I would raise my voice and in other ways escalate the impetus toward their action. Persuasion and rational argument, not just bluster and threat, are interpreted according to Ohm's p-prim. One must *try harder* to develop a *stronger* argument to *overcome* an adversary. Intrapersonal dynamics follow the same patterns. I *try harder* to overcome my own laziness, or I *resist* internal or external pressure, for example, peer pressure. See Talmy (1988), especially concerning "the divided self."

Balance and characteristic shifts in balance are just as common in thinking about interacting human beings as they are in thinking about the physical world. In the social or personal intentional worlds, just as in the physical, any balancing relationship where one of the forces or agents has variable strength leads to the possibility of *overcoming*. Furthermore, the same default assumptions about balance exist in the social and intrapersonal worlds as in the physical world. That is, balance implies stability, unlike instructed physics. So, a balance of power between social groups is interpreted to mean a relatively static and quiescent state, until the balance is altered.

Within the same cluster of physical ideas, conflict is one of the most salient relationships between influences (Talmy, 1988). Indeed, one of the significant changes that takes place when students learn physics is a drop in priority for conflict—where there are simply winners and losers—in favor of more compositional relationships. Vector addition, interpreted initially and qualitatively as compromise, replaces pure competition or interference between forces. Similarly, conflict and competition are extremely salient attributes of relationships in the social world. In fact, the social world apparently owns most of the linguistic forms for expressing this relationship. The words *conflict* and *helping* are prototypically social, yet they organize our experience and interventions just as well in the physical world. Perhaps paralleling the early dominance of competition and conflict in intuitive physical reasoning, it well may be that helping, coordination, compromise, and negotiation are less prominent early in social development. Instead, the nonconflictual cluster becomes more central and highly refined later. Children's natural first presumption is that winners (the stronger) simply prevail. On the other hand, both less strong forces and failed social movements have noticeable consequences that adults attend to.

Blocking, as I observed, applies as an explanatorily primitive idea in physical situations. It also applies to interpret and explain social interaction. A group may block the efforts of another, passively or actively.

In all of these, strength and power are intuitive attributes that mediate an individual's or group's influence in social relations. These are the salient properties of individuals in interaction (and objects and forces) viewed through Ohm's p-prim.

Because it adds to my argument to look at characterizations of intrinsically social knowledge that come from well outside my own perspective, I want to continue by considering a view on the development of moral thought put forward by Premack and Premack (1994). Premack and Premack admit that there are some connections between moral thinking and other knowledge about intentional or social processes. However, their line of attack is fundamentally a modular one. They say, "Judgments concerning [morality] are sui generis, and cannot be derived from concepts belonging to other parts of social competence" (p. 150). From the context and content of their arguments, I think it would be a fair extension of their intent to say, "Morality cannot be derived even from concepts belonging to other parts of social competence and certainly does not come from physical competence."

In the following, I go through a portion of the bases for the development of moral knowledge that Premack and Premack list, looking for structures that are at least similar, if not identical, to physical p-prims. I do this in the order that Premack and Premack use. I intend to show that the overlap between physical and moral reasoning, if one looks at the level of p-prims, is surprising.

Premack and Premack begin by noting that morality is about judging actions to be either positive (right) or negative (wrong). They then observe some basic indexes for these judgments. One of the earliest is the distinction between soft or weak motions (positive) and strong or hard ones (negative). But I already observed that this distinction, violent or gentle actions, is also the basis of determining the sort of causality that applies to objects in physical interaction. A common attribute, violence, appears to be a fundamental bifurcation of both physical and moral reasoning.

The second index noted by Premack and Premack is helping versus hurting. In this regard, I have already noted that especially conflict but also coordination appear in intuitive thinking about physics. Aligned influences cooperate, whereas opposed or simply unaligned influences conflict or interfere. In this interpretation, morally relevant helping and hurting are coordination or conflict that happen to be intentional. One individual puts him- or herself in the position of conflicting or coordinating. Although not identical, the basis for an important distinction in moral and physical domains is similar enough that it is easy to imagine either distinction serving as a model or prototype for the other. Individuals have goals, and two individuals may be aligned or not in their goals. Similarly, inanimate forces such as gravity have outcomes they will achieve in the case there is no blockage, or no opposing or interfering other force.[6] In both physical and moral situations, conflicting or interfering situations lead to a competition of strength, leverage, or other relevant determiner.

Premack and Premack believe that possession fundamentally extends and modifies moral relationships. In the first instance, acts against the possessions of others may be interpreted morally, whereas acts against nonintentional objects generally are not. In addition, the relationship of parent to child is interpreted as one of possession. As a consequence, reciprocation—the normal requirement that return acts should preserve valence—is abrogated. Children are not expected to thank their parents or return "good deeds," such as being fed, with similar good deeds.

Possession sounds like a necessarily intentional, social phenomenon. However, Premack and Premack note a strongly physical basis. In its most basic form, possession is contact with an object and mutual movement. "The relation between parent and child offers a perfect example of possession. When a child and parent moves together, the parent carries the child, . . . one way or another controlling its movement" (Premack &

---

[6]This very goal-like property of any physical influence, namely, that its prototypical (even defining) effects may not be achieved in the presence of other influences, undermines the strength of the argument that goal-like behavior fundamentally transcends physical analysis. See, for example, Leslie (1994).

Premack, 1994, p. 156). It is striking that possession of exactly this sort appears to be a fundamental distinction that alters physical presumptions about objects. When an object moves with a "possessing" object—say, a block moves with a wagon in which it lies—the motion of the focal object (the block) is taken to be unproblematic. "Contact conveys motion" is a gloss of this p-prim. (See the "bringing the paper with it" section in diSessa & Sherin, 1998.) Thus, one need not ask about the force of intervention by which the wagon causes the block to move, and the block is not felt to have its own motion. That is, the momentum that one might attribute to a thrown block is much less salient, and many will reject its existence, in the case of a carried ("possessed") block. Adult physics students, not just children, make these attributions. "I wouldn't think that the block (carried or possessed object) *has its own motion.*" Not only does possession alter causality, but also causality is described in terms of possession, "having its own motion."

Power, control, and overcoming are more general aspects of possession and intergroup moral relations, according to Premack and Premack. In parallel, Ohm's p-prim, balance, blocking, overcoming, and similar physical relations come down to strength, power, and control.

There are two aspects of this discussion of morality to which I need to draw attention. First, I am not claiming that physical causality is the same as intentional causality, which is the same as moral description. Adults can certainly muster the resources to make important distinctions like these— whether something is a moral or physical issue—at least in common and less problematic situations. Neither do I doubt that there is some distinctive knowledge associated with these domains. But what is the architecture and infrastructure of thinking about these domains? This is an issue about which intuition is suspect. Even if people can distinguish, for example, "*is* from *ought,*" we cannot rely on that as an indicator that there is no common knowledge used in these domains. I argue that there is both structural similarity, and even quite a bit of common knowledge, at the level of p-prims. Especially when one finds so much in common, so close to the heart of each domain,[7] one must question the basis for a distinction that seems so natural.

The second point is that my arguments about content are of the form "very similar schemata account for important reasoning in multiple domains." There is nothing, a priori, to prevent a situation where each domain has its own dedicated versions of what might be, in an important sense, identical schemata. Say, there is a social Ohm's p-prim that works with social knowledge, and a physical one that works with other mechan-

---

[7]Premack and Premack, for example, are looking at the developmentally constitutive structures of morality, not all the refined filigrees of moral thinking in all of its diversity.

ical knowledge. My arguments here do not systematically reach that level of precision. But arguments from use of common mechanisms (previous section), from parsimony, from apparent use of identical cues (e.g., soft versus hard motion), and from development (following section) undercut such a possibility.

STORIES ABOUT DEVELOPMENT

Development brings an important new dimension of data and argument into the discussion. As with other sections, I must be satisfied with collecting plausibility arguments rather than reviewing decisive argument. Development, in general, is particularly hard to make definitive statements about. But, my judgment is—especially on the basis of my theoretical orientation and empirical studies—that partial merging and mutual influence is by far the most plausible relationship between physical and social knowledge.

I want particularly to be clear that my position is not that physical and bodily experience and knowledge are the foundation of all human understanding.[8] The neutral model of mechanism I use makes no provision for claims of priority or even distinctiveness of physical knowledge, and I do not feel the necessity to add ancillary assumptions that split or select preferred domains.

On the other hand, I find it implausible that personally developed understanding of the physical world does not propagate to other domains. The general principle is that any knowledge, particularly strong and well-developed knowledge, will be appropriated into understanding domains where that knowledge fits, at least somewhat independently of the domain of genesis.

Ohm's p-prim makes a good place to start because, at least in adult thinking, it appears to travel effortlessly among physical, personal intentional, and social phenomena. What can we say about the development of such a knowledge element? Perhaps the most secure statement is that its prominence is, at least in part, due to the breath of its power and use. Good ideas become good default guesses exactly because one has learned they are frequently useful. One might expect the most central and powerful intuitive ideas to have exactly this property of extending beyond narrow domains of application. In fact, one should be quite sure that pure domain ownership is muted more and more as an element of wide scope

---

[8]This is a misinterpretation of my prior work that I have found common, even though I have systematically and explicitly rejected it. I believe the misperception is because I happen to have chosen physical understanding as my focus and because I find important and powerful ideas in physical intuitions.

matures. In the absence of detailed, empirically based traces of the development of such ideas, it may not be worth speculating on the real origins of important domain-crossing schemata like Ohm's p-prim. Even after such studies one may find that an idea develops before the child systematically distinguishes—in the critical sense of using different reasoning for—domains adults intuitively distinguish.

On the other hand, there are cases where significant understanding of the course of development, even if these are still contested, exists. The basic attribute of agency is, I believe, one of these cases.

Piaget was one of the first and most convincing writers about the projection of the child's personal sense of agency to the physical world. He emphasized the limits of this projection in describing "adherences" that limited mechanically causal understanding (Piaget, 1927). Children anthropomorphize, they see participation, purpose, and intention in many corners of experience where adults see only "physics."

In my view, Piaget very much underestimated the productive value of these "mistakes." Moving objects may not be alive, but they are more alive than objects at rest, particularly in their ability to animate other objects. Extending the attribute "living" to moving objects is a good transitional move before one develops a finer classification scheme.

In my own work, I see that fundamental intuitive schematization, which I call *causal syntax*, becomes deeply entrenched in understanding the physical world. Causal syntax is tripartite, involving an agent, a sanctioned interaction, and patient. For example, *agents* are the initiators of motion; *patients* are the locus of effect where agents' goals or tendencies are realized; and the patient's reciprocal effect on agent is highly backgrounded. (For a detailed exposition on the logic and empirical basis of this argument, see diSessa, 1993.) The results of this appropriation of the intentional world into thinking about the physical world are profound. The most visible manifestation, perhaps, is in the immensely counterintuitive nature of Newton's third law, where every patient must push back exactly the same amount as the agent pushes. Let me detail implication of the importation of agency into mechanics precisely with regard to action and reaction.

If agency figures in judgments of physical interaction, then one must expect features related to agency to become involved. Because agents are the originators of interactions and because their "intentions'" passing to the patient is the central issue, seeing the patient as necessarily coequal in interactions is a difficult and extended accomplishment in learning physics. This is precisely what one finds (Brown & Clement, 1987). Furthermore, Minstrell (1992) produced wonderful data about how changing the animacy characteristics of agent and patient (is it alive?, is it "active"?, is it big (strong)?, is it "trying hard"?) can systematically shift judgments of who is exerting what force on whom.

Again, however, there is a positive aspect of importing agency into the physical world. It actually provides quite a good basis for organizing Newtonian mechanics, excepting Newton's third law. The tradition of physics instruction has, in fact, evolved a way of teaching mechanics that more or less explicitly evokes agency by placing the notion of force (as the sanctioned interaction between agent and patient) at the center of the theory. Historically, some notable physicists and philosophers, Ernst Mach and Heinrich Hertz among them, have felt that the notion of force was a superstitious importation of human agency into the physical world and should be eliminated.[9] Hertz wrote a treatise on mechanics specifically to eliminate the notion of force from mechanics. In diSessa (1980), I show another way of eliminating or suppressing force and agency in mechanics and discuss the epistemological ramifications. Unlike Hertz and Mach, I do not believe agency (force) "is mere superstition" in its application to the physical world, but that it is one choice among several for beginning with existing intuitive ideas, ideas which (a) might seem to belong to one domain, but actually can travel pretty well into another, and (b) have both advantages and disadvantages in terms of the ultimate "expert understanding" and the path to expertise when chosen as an educational stepping-stone.

I want to spend some time now discussing how another prototypically nonphysical idea travels, many times productively, into thinking about the physical world. This is the idea of knowing, or, more generally, the concept of information. In the course of studying young children's intuitive understanding of physics, we (the work was done jointly with Tamar Globerson) returned to the Piagetian sling task, which also has been used systematically in the study of older students' intuitive understanding of physics. If an object is spun in a circle, for example, a ball is spun around on the end of a string, and the restraining tie (the string) breaks, what is the continuing trajectory of the object? Whereas older students gave us answers that are familiar from "misconceptions" studies (e.g., McCloskey, Caramazza, & Green, 1980), younger students, age 5 and younger, often had quite different things to say. One is that an object would simply stop "because it wouldn't know which way to go."[10] On many other occasions, children would appeal to knowledge or lack of it to explain what an object does.

Although this seems quaint and possibly silly, reflection and other data reveal it to be part of a very profitable if difficult step—figuring out how to think about the physical world in terms of knowledge and information. To begin, at least several of the young students who gave such explanations

---

[9]See, for example, Jammer (1962), pp. 221–229.

[10]Another charming response is that the object will move either in the direction it was going before, or perpendicular to that (outward, in the direction defined by the string) "because that is the way it is facing." Presumably, things, like people, follow their noses.

showed sensitivity to the metaphorical nature of these descriptions. When queried about this "knowing," they would remark that, of course, the object does not really know. It is not a person, or even alive. But then they would resume contemplating what the object knows or does not know.

The knowing idea may not work particularly well for helping young children decide what happens with the sling, but it is genuinely productive at other points in the development of physical understanding. For example, I have initiated discussions with physics students concerning what an object remembers of its prior motion at any point in time. Students come with various intuitions about this, and very frequently find the Newtonian fact—that objects "remember" only and exactly their position and velocity—extremely counterintuitive. For example, it seems more plausible that an object remembers something about the "curviness" of its past motion so that, if it is going in a circle, at least some degree of curving is preserved.

Now, of course, the literal version of the presumption of such a discussion, that objects know or remember anything at all about their histories, is absurd. But there is real substance to the discussion. For some purposes, it might be worth pruning intuitions and refining terms so that all aspects of anthropomorphism are eliminated. We might speak more neutrally of information, or perhaps better, simply of "informational support" for (our!) extrapolating future trajectory. But, in fact, this is pedantic and overkill in instruction. Students know objects do not "know" or "remember," but they instinctively understand that such ideas can apply productively to the physical world.

Here is a similar example. I mentioned before that novices have difficulty believing that a table pushes up on a book that it supports. One of the intuitive arguments against the table's pushing is "how could it *know* that it should push." This turns out not to be a mistake or problem, but a very productive move. Almost every physicist would consider this a very reasonable question and would go on to answer by noting that the table is compressed by the book, so its state is different when the book is on top of it in exactly the right way to cause an upward force. Again, information and knowing can be productive ideas in exploring the inanimate world.

I could give more examples of the productive use of manifestly intentional ideas in physics, but I hope the main point is made. Ideas from one domain may always find productive use in another. When that happens, of course, the ideas are typically extended and refined for that new domain—perhaps even to the point that the new domain is what one feels instinctively is the real home for the idea. Force seems, certainly to most physicists, fundamentally about the physical world, whereas it may have started, I suggest (along with Mach, Hertz, and possibly Piaget), in senses of personal agency.

Let me close with a very speculative possibility that, nonetheless, shows some of the interesting intertwining between domains that may regularly occur. I discussed the possibility that personal agency may be the critical seed for learning physics via instruction focusing on force as a central conceptual component. This strategy might be particularly adapted to instruction in Western cultures, with their emphasis on individual agency and conflict. Some provocative research suggests that Asian cultures may have more collaborative and dialectical epistemologies, where mutual constitution, mutual definition, and coordination dominate typically Western concerns of differentiation and conflict (and possibly directed agent–patient causality as represented in, for example, an orientation toward persuasion rather than neutral dialog). This cultural distinction seems to propagate at least as far as graduate students of the natural sciences (Peng & Nisbett, 1999). In dialectical cultures, might agent and force-centered physics best give way to more culturally appropriate conceptions? Maintaining a sense of physics as a domain of directed imperatives might even be difficult. Instead, born of a cultural instinct to define things reciprocally, Newton's action and reaction might seem more sensible, obvious, and fundamental. Other aspects of Newton's mechanics would then take the position of peripheral and hard to understand.

TWO CAVEATS

Aside from the general empirical uncertainty, which underlines appropriate caution in drawing definitive conclusions, it is only fair to raise two particular caveats about how the distinctiveness of physical, intentional, and social understanding might be more pronounced than in the picture I have painted. The first has to do with the representational form of schemata. It might in principle be that modules do not interact for the simple reason that their encoding is different. One does not mistakenly believe one has heard something in attending visually to a scene partly because visual codes simply cannot be understood within auditory processing (at least, this is a sufficient reason for modularity). Are intentional, social, or cultural codes distinct from physical codes? Many of the arguments and data referred to suggest at least an overlap. Recall, as an example, that violent motion enters into physical and moral judgments. In addition, there are interesting data concerning cross-modal schemata in infant cognition (Flavell, Miller, & Miller, 1993, pp. 39–46), for example, specifically with respect to number (Starkey, Spelke, & Gelman, 1990). Spelke (1991) summarized similar research with respect to physical causality as suggesting it is amodal. But I do not believe contemporary science has these issues particularly well settled.

The second modularity issue arises if, after all, human beings have innate modules directed separately at these domains. As I pointed out earlier, this is a popular speculation. But it is speculation, not fact. Even if there are such modules at birth, developmental studies and my own studies of conceptual development suggest that learning might well blur, combine, and change such modules to the point that their original domain specificity becomes much less relevant, if it is discernible at all. Interspersed in my arguments are specific cases where, from an epistemological point of view, strict modularity would seem extremely counterproductive. If children are strictly bound not to see agency in the physical world, perhaps they could not learn as much about it, and they might find instruction in terms of agentive concepts such as force immensely implausible. Similarly, if "knowing" is strictly a human phenomenon, then important discussions about what the physical world can or does know might be ruled out. On the reverse side, how unparsimonious would it be to think about psychological or social interaction (effort, result, overcoming, blocking, etc.) in terms that are nearly isomorphic to the physical case, but which are modularly distinct? Of course, evolution makes "mistakes," but developing this modularity seems a pretty serious one, and a particularly silly one as far as I have seen the commonalities of important ways of thinking about the physical and social worlds.

REVIEW AND CONCLUSION

In order to consider the intrinsic separation of physical and social worlds, I have introduced two levels (that of specific knowledge or content and that of underlying mechanism), and two modes (the normal operation and the genesis of the structure in question). For reference, I used a theory I have developed concerning intuitive physical knowledge. The theory entails a particular underlying cognitive mechanism—basically a recognition architecture that operates with a selected set of "things to recognize." In terms of genesis and development, certain simple descriptions are gradually picked out as more broadly explanatory, and they are linked to descriptions of circumstances where they are found to be apt.

Such an architecture makes a good basis for developing an explanatory sense in many domains. In particular, I argued that there is no evident reason the same architecture cannot account for social competence—for learning, thinking, and acting in socioculturally adapted ways. It is specific knowledge, at best, not the nature of the mind itself that distinguishes the social from physical worlds. Instead, making the distinction regularly and effectively, when necessary, is one of the accomplishments of learning.

Beyond mechanism, I considered both the specific content of thinking about physical and social worlds, and how it might have developed. Drawing from my own work and even on work that presumes modular distinctions between physical, psychological, and moral thinking, I find a remarkable parallelism in some central ways of thinking about these disparate domains. I argued that developmental data suggest a great deal of intertwining in learning about distinct domains.

Presumptions of modularity, in this discussion, fare rather poorly. Of course physical and social worlds are somewhat different (professional theories of them do not intersect much), and it would be highly counterproductive if humans never developed an understanding of the distinction. But the intuitive feeling of confidence that these are just different matters must give way to careful consideration of how one actually does think about these domains, both in microstructure (acknowledging that one can distinguish, if asked), and in the long developmental path to competence. Modules may bootstrap a quick start, but modules that do not have substantial flexibility during development would surely miss important possibilities for reusing and extending abilities from one domain into another. In any case, domains and their interaction in development are empirically tractible, and the considerations I develop here strongly favor significant overlap and intertwining lines of development into adult competence.

How do these arguments bear on the rift between cognitive and sociocultural approaches? First, I have intended to build a fairly sturdy, if still tentative, bridge across cognitivist and sociocultural interests: A theory of intuitive knowledge in the cognitivist tradition shows good signs of being applicable to understanding human social competence. Social knowledge compared to knowledge of the physical world may be understood to exhibit many of the same phenomena of richness, stability, or instability, and even similar developmental trajectories (in terms of origins and gradual shifting in priority)—and for the same reasons. For example, the theory suggests that the social sense of mechanism cannot reduce to a few very general principles.

With the theory also come empirical and analytic techniques to understand sociocultural issues. For example, one of the more exciting possibilities is a more precise accounting of cultural commonalties and differences. These may be locatable in the distribution of social p-prims and their relative priorities across cultures.

My theory of intuitive physical knowledge is accountable to concerns that are more typical of sociocultural approaches. For example, the nuanced connection of p-prims to physical contexts addresses one primary commitment of situated approaches—dealing with material situatedness of knowledge.[11] In addition, the theory does not draw a firm line

---

[11]An extension of the present theory (Sherin, 1996) describes how intuitive knowledge becomes involved with symbol systems in learning technical fields. That extension thus provides a cognitive analysis of how cultural artifacts affect thinking.

between material and intentional phenomena. So, for example, conceptions of agency and even of knowledge seem implicated in the development of the physical sense of mechanism.

The empirically determined overlap between physical and social competence and the presumed mutual influence during development bring to light still other possibilities that may have important implications. For example, the influence of physical ideas on the formation of social thought may provide a relatively invariant core across cultures. On the other hand, carefully determining both physical and intentional patterns of thinking may reveal more than might be expected influence of culture on conceptions of the physical world. Cultural diversity or homogeneity is not a built-in theoretical assumption. Instead, the theory suggests possibilities such as a partially overlapping set of schemata and developmental intertwining, and it also provides a methodological approach to evaluating them.

To sum up, the considerations of this chapter strongly undermine presumptions about incommensurability of social and cognitivist views of cognition. Instead, they suggest a great value in pursuing a common agenda.

ACKNOWLEDGMENTS

I gratefully acknowledge the support of the Spencer Foundation, grant number B-1393. The work accomplished under that grant contributed significantly to what is recorded here. The final analysis and writing of this chapter was conducted while the author was a Fellow at the Center for Advanced Study in the Behavioral Sciences. Financial support for the CASBS Fellowship was also provided by the Spencer Foundation, grant number 19940032.

REFERENCES

Anderson, J. R., Reder, L. M., & Simon, H. A. (1996). Situated learning in education. *Educational Researcher, 25*, 5–11.

Anderson, J. R., Reder, L. M., & Simon, H. A. (1997). Situative versus cognitive perspectives: Form versus content. *Educational Researcher, 26*, 18–21.

Brown, D. & Clement, J. (1987). Misconceptions concerning Newton's law of action and reaction: The underestimated importance of the Third Law. In J. D. Novak (Ed.), *Proceedings of the Second International Seminar: Misconceptions and Educational Strategies in Science and Mathematics* (Vol. 3, pp. 39–53). Ithaca, NY: Cornell University.

Confrey, J. (1990). A review of the research on student conceptions in mathematics, science and programming. In C. Cazden (Ed.), *Review of research in education* (Vol. 16, pp. 3–56). Washington, DC: American Educational Research Association.

diSessa, A. A. (1980). Momentum flow as an alternative perspective in elementary mechanics. *American Journal of Physics, 48*, 365–369.

diSessa, A. A. (1982). Unlearning Aristotelian physics: A study of knowledge-based learning. *Cognitive Science, 6,* 37–75.

diSessa, A. A. (1993). Toward an epistemology of physics. *Cognition and Instruction, 10* (2–3), 105–225; Responses to commentary, 261–280. (*Cognition and Instruction,* Monograph No. 1.)

diSessa, A. A. & Sherin, B. (1998). What changes in conceptual change? *International Journal of Science Education, 20*(10), 1155–1191.

Flavell, J. H., Miller, P. H., & Miller, S. A. (1993). *Cognitive development.* Englewood Cliffs, NJ: Prentice-Hall.

Gardner, H. (1993). *Multiple intelligences: The theory in practice.* New York: Basic Books.

Greeno, J. G. (1997). On claims that answer the wrong questions. *Educational Researcher, 26,* 5–17.

Hirschfeld, L. A., & Gelman, S. (1994). *Mapping the mind: Domain specificity in cognition and culture.* Cambridge, England: Cambridge University Press.

Jammer, M. (1962). *Concepts of force.* New York: Harper & Brothers.

Lave, J., & Wenger, E. (1991). *Situated learning: Legitimate peripheral participation.* Cambridge, England: Cambridge University Press.

Leslie, A. M. (1988). The necessity of illusion: Perception and thought in infancy. In L. Weiskrantz (Ed.), *Thought without language* (pp. 185–210). Oxford, England: Clarendon.

Leslie, A. M. (1994). ToMM, ToBy, and Agency. In L. Hirschfeld & S. Gelman (Eds.), *Mapping the mind: Domain specificity in cognition and culture* (pp. 119–148). Cambridge, England: Cambridge University Press.

McCloskey, M. (1983). Naive theories of motion. In D. Gentner & A. Stevens (Eds.), *Mental Models* (pp. 299–324). Hillsdale, NJ: Lawrence Erlbaum Associates.

McCloskey, M. Caramazza, A., & Green, B. (1980). Curvilinear motion in the absence of external forces: Naive beliefs about the motion of objects. *Science, 210,* 1139–1141.

Minstrell, J. (1982). Explaining the "at rest" condition of an object. *The Physics Teacher, 20,* 10–14.

Minstrell, J. (1992, April). *Facets of students' knowledge and relevant instruction.* Unpublished paper presented at the Annual Meeting of the American Educational Research Association, San Francisco.

Peng, K., & Nisbett, R. E. (1999). Culture, dialectics, and reasoning about contradiction. *American Psychologist, 54,* 741–754.

Premack, D., & Premack, A. J. (1994). Moral belief: Form versus content. In L. Hirschfeld & S. Gelman (Eds.), *Mapping the mind: Domain specificity in cognition and culture* (pp. 149–168). Cambridge, England: Cambridge University Press.

Piaget, J. (1927). *The child's concept of causality* (M. Gabain Trans.). London: Routledge & Kegan Paul.

Sherin, B. L. (1996). *The symbolic basis of physical intuition: A study of two symbol systems in physics instruction.* Unpublished doctoral dissertation, University of California, Berkeley.

Smith, J. P., diSessa, A. A., & Roschelle, J. (1993). Misconceptions reconceived: A Constructivist analysis of knowledge in transition. *Journal of the Learning Sciences, 3*(2), 115–163.

Spelke, E. (1991). Physical knowledge in infancy: Reflections on Piaget's theory. In S. Carey & R. Gelman (Eds.), *The epigenesis of mind* (pp. 133–169). Hillsdale, NJ: Lawrence Erlbaum Associates.

Starkey, P., Spelke, E., & Gelman, R. (1990). Numerical abstraction by human infants. *Cognition, 36,* 97–127.

Talmy, L. (1988). Force dynamics in language and cognition. *Cognitive Science, 12,* 49–100.

Chapter 8

Frames of Spatial Reference and Their Acquisition in Tenejapan Tzeltal

Penelope Brown
Stephen C. Levinson
Max Planck Institute for Psycholinguistics

GOALS OF THIS CHAPTER

In this chapter, we describe a line of research, essentially independent of the Piagetian tradition, which, nevertheless, bears on some of the central tenets of Piagetian thinking. We describe some specific results concerning language learning in a Mayan Indian community in southern Mexico, where the essential spatial discriminations in language and cognition employ Euclidean rather than topological or projective concepts and where these linguistic terms—despite their apparent complexity—seem to be learned very early by children.

It may be helpful to summarize our argument in advance, but we return to elaborate each of the points. Many languages utilize one or more of three basic frames of reference in reckoning spatial relationships: *Relative* (using the speaker's viewpoint to calculate spatial relations, like the familiar 'left'/'right'/'front'/'back' systems of European languages); *absolute* (using fixed angles extrinsic to the objects whose spatial relation is being described, like the cardinal direction systems of many Australian Aboriginal languages); and *intrinsic* (relying on intrinsic properties of objects being spatially related, e.g., parts and shapes of the Ground or landmark object) to reckon spatial relations, as in the body part systems of many languages. In the Mayan language Tzeltal, as spoken in the southern Mexico community of Tenejapa, the predominant

emphasis is on the intrinsic and absolute frames of reference. Longitudinal speech data from Tzeltal children ages 1;6 to 4;0 suggest that the
acquisition of spatial systems may run counter to the Piagetian ordering
of cognitive stages—topological prior to projective. The children use
and understand the rudiments of the absolute 'uphill/downhill' system,
which requires them to project coordinates based on the prevailing slope
of the landscape to spatially related objects, before the grammatically
analogous intrinsic systems (body parts, relational nouns), which encode
topological relations such as containment, surface support, and immediate proximity. Older Tzeltal children can extend the absolute system
productively to the novel context of a referential matching task by age 6
to 7;8, well before many Western children can use their relative
'left/right' in similar tasks. This evidence for both unexpectedly early
acquisition of language-specific spatial categories and the early ability to
use these in novel tasks motivates a reassessment of theories that attribute developmental priority to universal cognitive categories over cultural categories and insist on a universal sequence of cognitive development uninfluenced by culture and language input.

This study is part of a much larger cross-cultural survey of the relationship between language and spatial thinking conducted at the Max
Planck Institute for Psycholinguistics.[1] That larger study suggests the following four theses:

1. Languages differ, sometimes fundamentally, in the spatial concepts
   they encode.
2. Spatial concepts in a specific language correlate with the kinds of
   spatial coding used in nonlinguistic thinking in the community that
   speaks that language.
3. Language appears to play a causal role in that correlation.
4. Consequently, language- and culture-specific concepts play a role in
   the conceptual development of the child, and, specifically, they may
   affect the order or rate of development of particular concepts in
   "representational thought."

The implication for the Piagetian tradition is that the child's development
must be relativized to the local adult norms toward which development is
directed. The course of development likewise has no ineluctable direc-
tionality, but may be influenced by the nature of the requirements that
learning the local language places on children.

---

[1] See Pederson et al., 1998, for some results of this research program; see also the Max
Planck Institute for Psycholinguistics Annual Reports 1992–1996.

BACKGROUND

Cross-Cultural Studies of Adult Spatial Language and Cognition

Our research team has been preoccupied with a large cross-cultural investigation, over more than 20 cultures, into the relationship between spatial language and spatial cognition. One of our findings is that the language for describing spatial locations and directions on the horizontal dimension[2] differs systematically across cultures. In fact, as mentioned earlier, there appear to be just three major types of frame of reference or coordinate system usable in small-scale local space: absolute, in which locations are specified by reference to fixed bearings (as in 'The boy is west of the tree'); relative, in which locations are specified by reference to the body-planes of the viewer (as in 'The boy is to the left of/behind the tree'); and intrinsic, in which locations of one object are specified by reference to a landmark or 'Ground' object's parts (as in 'The boy is to the rear of the truck').

The background concepts here are actually quite complex, and the details within each category can differ significantly across languages,[3] but what is shared among the three systems is a way to express an angular relation between a landmark object or place L, and the object to be located, O. One can do so by saying, for example, that O is 'west' of L (absolute), O is 'left' of L (relative), or O is at the 'front' of L (intrinsic; where L is, for example, a car or other object with an inherent front).

Not all languages employ all of these systems, at least in colloquial parlance. Some languages use only absolute coordinates, some use absolute plus intrinsic, some use all three, and so on. In a language that uses only absolute, or only absolute and intrinsic coordinates, one cannot, for example, say 'The ball is to the left of the tree'; one must instead say something like 'The ball is south of the tree.' The same holds even for small-scale space, including the description of things immediately in front of one. We may illustrate the uneven distribution of frames of reference across languages with a selection from our cross-linguistic sample (see Pederson et al., 1998):

---

[2]By "language for describing spatial locations on the horizontal dimension," we intend the language dedicated to specifying precise angles (directions) on the horizontal (words glossing as 'left/right,' 'front/back,' 'north/south/east/west,' 'uphill/downhill/across,' 'upwind/downwind,' 'seawards/landwards', etc.). Deictic expressions that simply indicate relative distance from the speaker ('here/there', 'this/that') without indicating a particular direction are not considered here.

[3]See Levinson, 1996 for discussion.

<1> Distribution of Frames of Reference.

INTRINSIC	INTRINSIC RELATIVE	INTRINSIC RELATIVE ABSOLUTE	ABSOLUTE	ABSOLUTE INTRINSIC
Mopan	Japanese Dutch	Kalagadi Yucatec Maya	Guugu-Yimithirr	Tzeltal Hai//om

The generalization is clear: any frame of reference (coordinate system) can appear alone or in combination with any other, except that the use of a relative system implies the presence of an intrinsic one. Note that Tzeltal, the language focused on here, has intrinsic and absolute but no relative frames of reference.

Our large-scale project has been interested in correlations between linguistic frames of reference and nonlinguistic thinking, for example, coding of spatial arrays for memory or inference. We therefore have carried out independent but parallel investigations in many cultures, testing language use under many conditions, on the one hand, and testing memory and inference under many conditions, on the other. To test nonlinguistic cognition one must devise tasks of a kind that have no essential reliance on linguistic instructions. We trained subjects to do tasks such as memorize arrays of objects, and then rotated the subjects 180 degrees and got them to reconstruct the arrays. An egocentric or relative coding (in terms of notions such as left/right/front/back) should result in subjects reconstructing the array rotated 180 degrees from the stimulus, whereas an absolute coding should result in no such rotation. The general finding over a range of cultures whose members use absolute or relative coordinates but not both when describing small-scale spatial arrays is that in nonlinguistic tasks the type of coding for memory matches the linguistic coding. More specifically, the following prediction seems to hold:[4]

<2> Isomorphism in Adult Cognition.

If an adult speaks an absolute language, then he or she will almost certainly code in fixed bearings on a nonlinguistic task.
If an adult speaks a relative language, then he or she will almost certainly code in 'left/right/front/back' concepts on a nonlinguistic task.

This correlation is strong and reliable across cultures where the language is highly restrictive in this manner (one may expect weaker results where a language *prefers*, say, relative over absolute, but where both are colloquially current). We believe that this correlation comes about at least in part

---

[4]See Brown & Levinson, 1993a; Levinson, 1997; and Pederson et al., 1998, for further details of these studies.

because coding for language requires an isomorphic coding in memory and cognition; in general, you cannot speak in terms of 'A is to the north of B' if your coding for memory is in a different coordinate system, for example, 'A is to the left of B.' In order to speak using concepts appropriate to one coordinate system, it seems essential to remember scenes in the same terms (see Levinson, 1996 for detailed arguments). We therefore propose that there is a causal relationship in these cases, as indicated in <3>:

<3> Causal Hypothesis.

If language L specifies a restricted set of frames of reference for spatial description, then this will induce a standardization of nonlinguistic coding in the community that speaks L, using the same frames of reference employed in the language.

Perhaps we should emphasize that this is a neo-Whorfian prediction but for non-Whorfian reasons. The prediction is based not, as Whorf proposed, on the grounds of linguistic habit, but on apparently necessary facts about cognitive architecture: certain linguistic expressions presuppose certain conceptual distinctions, and in many cases those distinctions must be coded in memory at *experience time*, otherwise they will not be available at *speaking time*.

But these findings do not necessarily entail a tabula rasa view of conceptual development. There may be some highly structured innate dispositions on which languages build in divergent ways. Some aspects of these linguistic systems may thus be, in some way to be explicated, "unnatural." For example, little Korean children will need to rapidly learn honorific distinctions that are irrelevant in other societies; they will do so independently of some hypothesized natural course of conceptual development. So is the learning of absolute specifications unnatural in the same sort of way, requiring some overriding of more natural inclinations toward a relative system? Relative concepts of front, back, left, or right, for example, seem independently motivated by the analysis of humans' visual field or by the needs of motor behavior. Consider the "symptoms of natural categories" specified by Landau and Gleitman (1985):

<4> Four Symptoms of Natural Categories in Language Acquisition.

1. Early learning (e.g., in the third year).
2. No alternative construals considered.
3. Universal lexicalization in core vocabulary.
4. Learnable under poor input conditions.

However, in terms of these criteria, it seems clear that both absolute distinctions and relative ones are in some respects "unnatural"; neither, for example, are universally lexicalized in core vocabulary, nor are they fully learned in the third year. Interesting questions then arise about children's acquisition of the vocabulary for such spatial systems:

<5> Is the Vocabulary for Absolute Spatial Systems Delayed?

Question 1: Do children in "absolute speech communities" learn absolute terms later than children in "relative speech communities" learn relative terms?

Question 2: Do children in "absolute speech communities" learn absolute terminology later than alternative intrinsic descriptions of spatial relations?

It is to these questions we now turn.

Consequences for Theories of Conceptual Development

Piaget proposed a sequence of development in spatial reasoning. He believed that children's early spatial reasoning is "topological." Topology is often characterized as "rubber-sheet geometry" (i.e., concerning relations invariant under elastic deformation), but Piaget meant something more specific. For him topological concepts involve only proximity, separation, inclusion, and order (see Piaget & Inhelder, 1967). Children are held to build more complex spatial concepts only slowly from about the age of 4 on, first utilizing their own perspectives (as in sighting along objects to construct a straight line), then understanding other persons' perspectives (as in the famous three mountains task), and finally building (around the age of 11) a more abstract conception of spatial relations independent of perspective. He characterized this progression as from a "topological" to a "projective," and finally to a "Euclidean" model of the spatial world. The projective understanding makes available a fairly rapid transition to the Euclidean level of understanding, but the full transition only takes place in late childhood.

Developmental psychologists and psycholinguists have assumed that there is some resemblance between Piaget's projective and topological schemes and the relative (or "deictic") and intrinsic (or "inherent") systems in language. Take, for example, the linguistic distinction between topological and projective/deictic adpositions, as illustrated by the English prepositions. (In the following description, O is reference object and E is ego or other person.) The English topological prepositions expressing nonoriented two-place spatial relations are *in, at, on,* and also arguably O's *front₁/back₁* (i.e., front/back as inherent body parts of a featured O, as in 'at the car's front'), and E's own inherent *left₁/right₁* (as in 'turn left'). The projective ones (involving at least a three-place relation, projected from E's viewpoint) are *in front₂ of, in back₂ of, to the left₂ of, to the right₂ of.* In this second sense of these same word forms, something is, for example, 'in front of the tree,' if it lies between the viewer and the tree. Despite the fact that there are various different usages of the same words, there is reasonable overlap between the developmental psycholinguistic scheme and the Piagetian categories. The observable order of acquisition in the familiar languages is indeed in the predicted Piagetian order, as shown in and <6> and <7>:

<6> Acquisition Order of Adpositions in Several European Languages (Johnston & Slobin, 1979).

TOPOLOGICAL   PROJECTIVE

$in> on> under> beside> back_1> front_1>$ $back_2> front_2$

Age 2 ⸻⟶ Age 4 ⸻⟶

<7> Piaget's 1928 Data.

$own\ left_1/right_1$ $other's\ left_1/right_1$ $x\ is\ left_2\ of\ y\ for\ ego$

Age ⟶ 6 ⸻⟶ 8 ⸻⟶ Age 11/12

Because of this correspondence between acquisition order and the predicted Piagetian order, it is generally held that *the order of language acquisition is driven by conceptual development*. In other words, the presumption is that language does not facilitate or influence the course of conceptual development but depends on it.

However, some recent developments challenge this story. One is the discovery of absolute languages, where primary or sole emphasis is put on fixed-bearing systems for spatial reference. How are these to be placed in the Piagetian scheme? In fact, the inclusion is simple enough. These systems employ fixed angles ('north,' 'downhill,' etc.) and, as Piaget and Inhelder (1967; p. 30) declared: "It is the analysis of the angle which marks the transition from topological relationships to Euclidean ones."[5] The interesting thing about the angles employed is that they are (in the adult language) entirely abstract concepts: 'north' or 'downhill' defines a conceptual slope across the environment, or, if one likes, a conceptually infinite series of north-pointing parallel arrows across the landscape, as illustrated in Fig. 8.1. These are thus indubitably Euclidean notions, which do not rely on a physical slope; they are used to establish spatial relationships even on completely flat terrain, even in the dark and at night.

To fit the Piagetian conceptual development sequence, the acquisition of these absolute concepts would need to come after the development of topological ones, and should be enabled by prior projective relations. But as we shall see, the Tzeltal language acquisition data do not fit this prediction.

---

[5]See also Piaget, Inhelder, B., & Szeminska, A. (1981) for Piaget's later views on Euclidean thinking.

'He's downhill (north) of the house.'

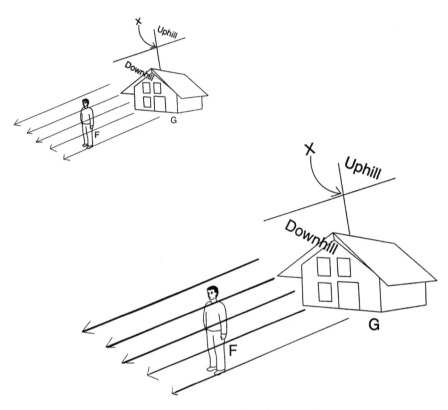

FIG. 8.1.   The geometry of absolute coordinates.

A second basis for doubting the presumption that conceptual development is always prior to and independent of linguistic development comes
from the work of Bowerman. This work shows that, in some respects, conceptual development is led by the linguistic nose, rather than vice versa
(Bowerman 1996, chap. 9, this volume; Bowerman & Choi, 2000; Choi &
Bowerman, 1991). For example, even at 18 months of age, infants can be
shown to have internalized language-specific spatial categories. In addition, there are also reasons to think that some spatial concepts are intrinsically linguistic: for example, *south* is not given by any individual's independent act of cognition, and even if it were, it would have no necessary
collective (communicative) utility. In this respect *north 180 degrees* is just as
culturally arbitrary as feet and inches or other systems of metric distinc-

tion. These kinds of spatial notions, then, are the sort of concepts that may be learned first through language and only later come to play a language-independent role in mental life. They are thus good candidates for where language might promote conceptual development of a sort and at an age unlikely in cultures where the language provides no such concepts in everyday child-relevant contexts.

These developments re-invigorate the old debate between the two titans of developmental psychology, Piaget and Vygotsky. Whereas Piaget held that it is action and nonlinguistic experience that spurs conceptual development (Ginsburg & Opper, 1969, p. 171), Vygotsky held that the internalization of linguistic categories can play a central role in conceptual development (Vygotsky, 1986; Wertsch, 1985). This distinction is shown schematically in <8>:

<8>   The Two Hypotheses.

    A. Conceptual development drives linguistic development (PIAGET).
       Evidence: for example, order of acquisition of Indo-European prepositions matches Piagetian order: topological prior to projective
    B. Language can also drive conceptual development (VYGOTSKY).
       Evidence: (a) language-specific concepts are encoded very early (Bowerman, 1996; Choi & Bowerman, 1991; Bowerman & Choi, 2000)
          (b) Euclidean spatial descriptions emerge at the same time as, or even prior to, topological ones, in absolute communities (possible development described in this chapter)

It is obvious that any investigation of the relation between language and thinking ought to tap linguistic and nonlinguistic data independently. This is precisely what we have tried to do in our large-scale cross-cultural project. But if one is interested in the early stages of language acquisition this is often impractical: trying to get pre- or almost prelinguistic infants to perform on a conceptual (as opposed to a perceptual) task is difficult, especially in cultures where childrearing practices inhibit exploration and manipulation of the environment. Nevertheless, by studying the first two years of language acquisition, much can be learned about the child's cognitive development, providing one subscribes to the following assumption, which we believe needs no justification:

<9>   Semantic Distinctions Presuppose Cognitive Distinctions.

    If the semantics of linguistic expression L presupposes a conceptual distinction D, then evidence that a child/adult *uses L correctly* is prima facie evidence that the child/adult is employing D.

When a large set of related terms in different grammatical categories is correctly used by a child, we can be reasonably certain that the relevant conceptual distinctions are being employed. Note, however, that a few cautions must be observed:

1. The rote-learning problem: Because correct usage could be based on memorized collocations, the child should be observed using novel combinations.
2. The subdomain problem: Because the correct usage in one context alone might be based on rote learning or some partially correct understanding, the child should be observed using L across a wide range of applications, in different contexts, and with syntactic variations.
3. The absence problem: Absence of the use of L does not allow us to infer absence of the distinction D. For that, one needs direct evidence that the child cannot reason using D.
4. The problem of usage versus meaning: It is in principle possible to exhibit apparently correct usage based on incorrect analysis of meaning. However, to the extent that adults themselves converge on identical meanings, they do so through extended use in all domains and contexts. Therefore, child language should ideally be monitored across all relevant contexts.

We return to these caveats when discussing the significance of our results.

We now turn to a study of the first years of spatial language acquisition in the Mayan community of Tenejapa, in southern Mexico. (See Fig. 8.2). In this community, the absolute frame of spatial reference is the single, major adult coordinate system for spatial description except where objects are touching or in close proximity, in which case an intrinsic system is used.

TENEJAPAN TZELTAL: ADULT SPATIAL LANGUAGE AND COGNITION

Let us first describe the relevant properties of the linguistic systems used in each of the two available coordinate systems. We use the term *Ground* to refer to the landmark object with respect to which the location of the *Figure* (the object to be located) is described (Talmy, 1983).

The Intrinsic System: Topological, Object-Centered

Where two objects are contiguous, the exact relation of one of them (the Figure) to the other (the Ground) can be specified by using the name of a part of the Ground, so that one says, in effect, things like 'The axe is at

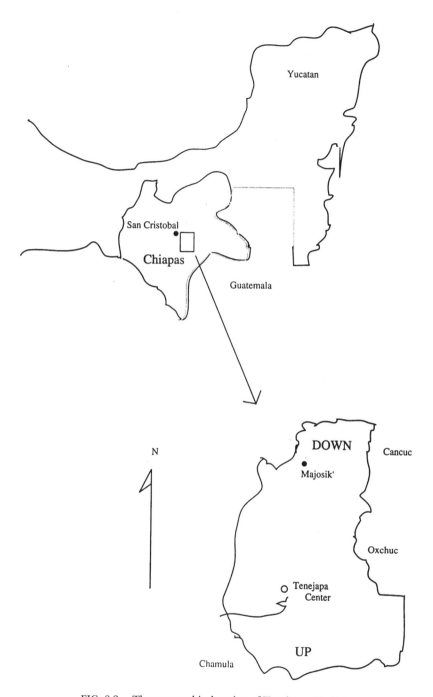

FIG. 8.2.   The geographical setting of Tenejapan Tzeltal.

the mouth of the house.' Tzeltal provides a rich set of part names, based on human and animal prototypes, which can partition any physical object (see Levinson, 1994; Brown, 1994). These part names are used in the possessive (as in 'the mouth of the house'), and are thus grammatically similar to the relational nouns involved in the absolute system described later. Some examples are given in <10>:

<10> *kotol ta sjol karo te tz'i'e.*
'The dog is standing at the "head" of the car' (i.e., directly in front of it, at its front end).

waxal ta xchikin mexa te limete.
'The bottle is standing at the "ear" (i.e., corner) of the table.'

ta yakan xalten ay, te use.
'The fly is at the "leg" (i.e., handle) of the frying pan.'

ta yutil bojch, te mantzanae
'The apple is at the "inside" of the gourd.'

The vocabulary of the intrinsic system is in some respects quite similar to English spatial prepositions like *in, on,* and *under,* which, as we have seen, are among the first spatial words to be learned by English-speaking children. The Tzeltal terms are restricted to situations where objects are directly adjacent; for objects that are further apart, the absolute system comes into play.

The Absolute System: Euclidean/Projective, Geographically Centered

There is no relative 'left'/'right'/'front'/'back' system in Tenejapan Tzeltal. Instead, there is an absolute 'uphill'/'downhill' system based ultimately on the overall general slope of the territory of Tenejapa (downward from high south to low north). This has been abstracted, however, to yield an abstract cardinal direction axis analogous to 'south/north' although systematically skewed from our cartographic axis, as indicated in Fig. 8.3. Together with an orthogonal axis, labeled 'across' at both ends, this provides a system of cardinal directions (see Fig. 8.3). These directions are used to specify locations of both the small scale (e.g., things on a tabletop) and the large scale, and are not restricted to outside space. The cardinal direction system is independent of the actual slope of the terrain, being usable on the flat, and even outside the territory altogether. The system is expressed both in nouns and in verbs of motion (e.g., 'ascend' can mean in effect 'go south'). Because there is no relative system (with notions like 'in front of,' 'to the left of,' etc.), and because the intrinsic body-part system can only be used when objects are contiguous, the absolute system

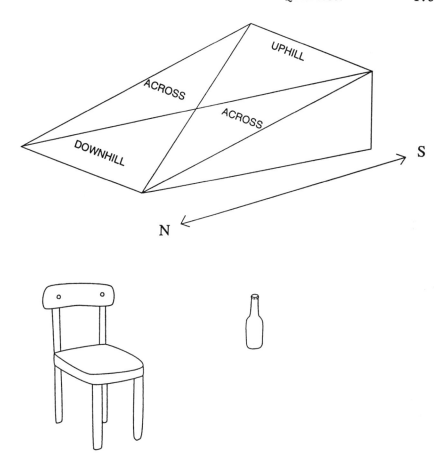

'The bottle is uphill of the chair.'

FIG. 8.3.   The Tzeltal absolute system.

plays a crucial role in linguistic descriptions of location. Thus in Tzeltal one describes spatial relationships as in the following examples:

<11>   *waxal ta yajk'ol bojch te limete.*
        'The bottle is standing "uphillwards" (i.e., southwards) of the bowl.'

        chotol ta yanil amak' te tz'amalte'e.
        'The bench is "beneath" the patio.' (downhillwards/north of)

        ya xmo ta jobel te winike.
        'The man is "ascending" to San Cristobal.'

ya xwil koel mut.
'The bird is flying in a "descending" direction.' (either downhillwards, or straight down)

jelaw ta colonia.
'He "crossed" to Colonia.' (i.e., went across (orthogonal to) the
south-north slope of the land)

tzakben tal machit tey xik'il ta yajk'ol ti'nel.
'Bring me the machete standing "above" (uphillwards of) the door.'

ta alan otzesa.
'Put it (a puzzle piece) in downhillwards (in the downhillwards hole).'

There is a dedicated spatial vocabulary for this purpose, consisting of (a)
intransitive verb roots ('ascend'/'descend'), (b) their transitivized counterparts ('cause it to 'ascend'/'descend'), (c) directional adverbs ('ascending'/'descending') and (d) nouns, which may be unpossessed and hence
only implicitly relational ('uphill'/'downhill') or explicitly relational possessed nouns ('its above-or-uphill-side'/'its underneath-or-downhill-side').
This vocabulary is given in Table 8.1.

There are systematic ambiguities in the usage of the whole set of these
words. First, the vertical axis ('up/down' vertically) is conflated with the
absolute system of spatial reference for calculating angles on the horizontal ('up/down' in relation to the south/north slope of the land). So when
people say the Tzeltal equivalent of 'ascend' or 'descend', they can mean

TABLE 8.1
Dedicated Spatial Vocabulary for the Tzeltal Absolute System

| | MOTION | | STASIS | |
	Verb	*Directional*	*Relational Noun: unpossessed*	*Relational Noun: possessed*
UP	*mo* 'ascend'	*moel* 'ascending	*ajk'ol* or *kajal* 'uphill'	*y-ajk'ol* 'its-above-side' *s-ba* 'its top or uphill side'
DOWN	*ko* 'descend'	*koel* 'descending'	*alan* 'downhill'	*y-anil* 'its underneath or downhill side' *y-e'tal* 'its downhill side'
ACROSS	*jelaw* 'cross'	*jelawel* 'acrossways'	*jejch* 'side'	*s-tz'e'el* 'its side'

either vertically or along a coordinate abstracted from the lay of the land. Secondly, there is yet another ambiguity between the *local* actual gradient as opposed to the global absolute (south-north) slope, because, if the local slope deviates from the absolute slope, it may be used as an additional coordinate for describing local spatial relationships. Thus an utterance glossing 'It is uphill from the house' might mean either 'It is south of the house' (cardinal direction sense) or 'It is up the local slope from the house' (local geographic sense). This is a vocabulary that is therefore not only semantically complex, but also has a range of alternate complex interpretations, which are disambiguated by pragmatic principles (see Brown & Levinson, 1993b, for details). In short, nothing makes this easy for children to learn.

In Piagetian terms, spatial relations describable with the Tzeltal intrinsic system (where an object is spatially related to the named body parts or regions of a reference object), are essentially topological. A two-place relation is at issue: a Figure is said to be '*AT*' some named part or region of a Ground object. The absolute system, in contrast, is Euclidean: the location of objects is described in a coordinate system independent of the scene described, and indeed independent of the perspective of the observer. Because precise directions and angles are involved in using the coordinate system and the system is independent of the objects related, it constitutes an abstract spatial framework at least Euclidean in character, if not Newtonian! At least a ternary relation is involved: 'A is uphill from B' involves A, B, and the direction C, 'uphill.' On first principles, and judging by studies of Western children, we would expect the Tzeltal intrinsic system to be conceptually easier, and therefore earlier learned, than the absolute 'uphill/downhill' system. We might also expect this on the grounds that intrinsic systems seem to be found in nearly all languages and might thus be held to be based on universally available concepts. The very general hypothesis that language encoding cognitively simpler concepts (such as topological spatial concepts) is learned earlier by children than that encoding more complex concepts (such as projective spatial concepts) is generally well-grounded. Moreover, in the domain of spatial language, it is very robustly supported by evidence from the acquisition of European spatial adpositions. As shown in <8> and <9>, children learn topological prepositions ('in', 'on') before intrinsic 'in front'/'behind', and they learn those before projective 'in front'/'behind', and well before 'left'/'right'. As mentioned, this has long been taken as support of the position that conceptual development drives language development.

Yet these studies did not consider languages with absolute systems. These would be expected to develop late, because they have cognitive properties that are considered to be difficult. They are (at least potentially) decentered, making no reference to ego's point of view, and (at least in full-blown adult form) they require an oriented mental map. The first acquisition study of an absolute system (to our knowledge) was conducted by de León (1994), working in another Mayan language, Tzotzil, spoken in a neighboring community, and very similar linguistically to Tzeltal. She found evidence of remarkably early competence of children in the absolute system. In a cross-sectional study, she found competent child use by about age 4 in production and comprehension placement tasks on a tabletop (although full adult-like performance is much later) and concluded that absolute and intrinsic come in together, at about the same age, around age 4.

In this Tzeltal study we build on her work, but we are interested in the very earliest appearance of the absolute system, the form it takes, how it develops, and how it relates to the acquisition of the intrinsic system.

THE CHILD DATA

The Data

The data reported on here are drawn from a longitudinal study of five children in monolingual Tzeltal families, covering the ages of 1;6 to about 4;6 with four to six weekly samples, plus any older siblings or cousins that happen to be present. (The data cover a total of more than 20 children less than 10 years old). The database consists of more than 600 hours of tape-recorded and/or videotaped natural interaction of children, mostly in their own homes, interacting with caregivers, siblings, and/or cousins. This is supplemented by elicited production and "space game" tasks with older children. The data have been transcribed by native speakers in the field and are still in the process of being checked, computerized, and coded by P. Brown.

Questions: Children's Production, Ages 2 to 4

The questions to be addressed here by looking at Tzeltal children's language development are the following:

Q1. Does the intrinsic system appear earlier than the absolute one in children's language production? (Recollect that Tzeltal has both.)

Q2. Within the absolute system, is the vertical sense (being more "natural") learned earlier than the horizontal sense?

Q3. In the horizontal absolute uses, is the local-slope sense (because it is more concrete and visible) learned earlier than the abstract cardinal-direction sense?

Q4. Are absolute systems so complex and "unnatural" that children learn them later than the corresponding relative (left/right/front/back) systems are learned in communities that use relative coordinates?

We take these questions in turn.

Question 1: Is Intrinsic Learned Before Absolute?

Insofar as we can infer from production data alone, the answer is no. Children's production of intrinsic vocabulary in locative expressions is either simultaneous with or actually later than absolute vocabulary. The evidence from longitudinal data of three children[6] is summarized in Table 8.2, which presents the absolute vocabulary, with columns for each major grammatical category in which it is encoded. As Table 8.2 shows, absolute vocabulary first appears in children's speech around the age of 2;0, in some cases when the child is still in the one- or two-word stage. It is fully productive (in contrast sets, in different contexts, in different grammatical constructions, in both possessed and unpossessed forms, etc.) by at least age 3;7.

Intrinsic vocabulary, in locative uses (i.e., not just as names of animate body parts), appears somewhat later in this natural production data, as shown in Table 8.3. The nouns meaning things like 'top,' 'back,' 'middle,' 'inside' in either unpossessed or (explicitly relational) possessed form are extremely rare until age 3;6, and possessed body parts used as locatives are virtually nonexistent in the data even by age 4. On the basis of this production data, then, absolute vocabulary appears to come into use prior to the intrinsic terms.

We consider the Tzeltal dedicated intrinsic system to consist of possessed body parts and in addition certain relational nouns (e.g., indicating 'underneath', 'on top') used as locatives. As can be seen from Table 8.3, this whole vocabulary comes in relatively late. However, topological place relations can also be expressed using the single Tzeltal preposition with little inherent meaning: such expressions of the form 'AT trail,' or 'AT town' for example, without any further spatial discriminations, do appear much earlier, at the two-word stage (around the age of 2;0). But the intrinsic system of body parts and topological relational nouns ('inside,' 'outside,' 'topside,' 'middle,' etc.) is used productively very late. There are no

---

[6]The two other focal children are omitted here as their data are not yet processed sufficiently to analyze. Their performance in terms of absolute and intrinsic vocabulary, however, is consistent with that of these three focal children, as is that of several other children present in the data collected. See Brown, 2000, for details.

TABLE 8.2
Summary of Production, Ages 2 to 4, for Absolute Vocabulary

Age	Verbs ('ascend' 'descend')	Directionals ('ascending' 'descending')	Unpossessed Nouns ('uphill' 'downhill')	Possessed Nouns ('its-uphill', 'its-downhill', 'above it', 'below it')
2;0–2;5	x[a]	x	x	
2;6–3;0	yy[b]	yy	yy	
3;0–3;6				x
3;7–4;0				yy

Note. Sample size is 3.
[a]x = first appearance of terms; [b]yy = Productive use, in contrast sets, with no errors.
From "Learning to Talk about Motion UP and DOWN in Tzeltal: Is there a Language-Specific Bias for Verb Learning?, 2000 by P. Brown, in M. Bowerman and S. C. Levinson (Eds.), *Language Acquisition and Conceptual Development*, Copyright 2000 by Cambridge University Press. Reprinted with permission.

TABLE 8.3
Summary of Production, Ages 2 to 4, for Intrinsic Vocabulary

Age	Unpossessed nouns ('middle', 'top', 'back', etc.)	Possessed Relational Nouns ('its-middle', 'its-inside', 'its-top', 'its-underneath')	Unpossessed Body Parts ('its-head'/'its-foot'/'its-belly'/'its-nose'/'its-ear', etc.)
2;0–2;5			
2;6–3;0			
3;0–3;6			
3;7–4;0	x[a]	x	
4;1–4;6	yy[b]	yy	x ??

Note. Sample size is 3.
[a]x = first appearance of terms; [b]yy = Productive use, in contrast sets, with no errors.

examples of possessed body parts used as locatives—the Tzeltal dedicated intrinsic system—in the three children's speech in the data examined to date (sampling ages 1;6 to 4;0).[7] Children less than 4 years of age do not seem to use these productively as locatives, although they probably understand adult locative uses of them.

---

[7]This is with the exception of a few frozen unpossessed forms that are compound nouns and not productive combinations; for example, *ti'nel* 'door [lit: mouth-house],' *patna* 'back (of) house.' In such cases, saying that something is 'at the *ti'nel*' is equivalent to saying it is 'at the door,' not that it is 'at the mouth/edge of the door.'

Although these nouns constitute the main intrinsic vocabulary, there are other, more indirect ways of expressing topological concepts, for example, through verbs of 'putting in' or 'taking out'. These do appear in children's speech earlier than the intrinsic nouns, some even earlier than the corresponding absolute verbs of 'ascending,' 'descending,' and 'crossing.' The motion verbs 'enter' and 'exit' might also be held to encode topological notions of containment, and they also appear at about the same time as 'ascend'/'descend' (around age 2;0), at around the two-word stage. (These verbal notions also appear in gerundive directional adverbs at about the same age.) There is therefore evidence from language production of early understanding of some topological notions, especially those of containment.

On the basis of this linguistic evidence, we can see that Tzeltal children of 2 years of age do indeed talk about some topological relationships using the single preposition to express location at a place, and verbs to indicate motion in and out of containers. We can therefore infer that they have the corresponding topological concepts, as would be expected on Piagetian grounds. But the children do not seem to use these concepts as the basis for an early acquisition of the more detailed Tzeltal intrinsic body part system, which requires both an analysis of the shape of objects (e.g., an 'arm' is a rigid protrusion) and the use of the parts isolated on the basis of shape to speak about the location of other objects close to those parts. There is evidence that children have mastered many of the basic body part words for humans and animals between the ages of 2;0 and 2;6, suggesting that there is nothing inherently complex in the phonology or constructions. Nevertheless, they do not use the same lexemes as intrinsic spatial relators until much later.

Let us return to the early use of the absolute vocabulary, as shown in Table 8.2. Of course we need to know just how children of ages 2 to 3;6 are *using* their absolute vocabulary. Is it really being used in the abstract, cardinal direction sense that would entail a Euclidean level of conceptual development? To assess this, we must place their usage within the physical and geographical context in which it occurs, which is initially the children's own house compound (consisting minimally of two small houses). Even when the layout of a household compound is relatively flat, children from about age 2;0 use absolute vocabulary to talk about spatial relations within this local household space. They use absolute motion verbs ('ascend'/'descend') to describe movement between the houses, absolute directionals ('ascending'/'descending') to convey the direction of motions and the orientation of positions vis-à-vis the absolute axis, and relational nouns ('uphill'/'downhill') to talk about the spatial relations of objects within this local arena. Thus when playing with toys, they might say 'push the truck uphill here; it's ascending' and so forth, either in the cardinal direction sense, or in the sense of up the local slope. They also use absolute vocabulary for more distant spatial relations: for example, someone who has gone south to the school may be said to have gone 'uphill,' or when coming back may be said to be 'descending.'

Now, there is of course a progression in understanding the system. From production data one can see that, although the terms appear to be used with correct reference from the beginning, children may have some simplified understanding of the meaning. On the basis of limited productivity, one may guess that children's first usage of the 'uphill/downhill' nouns is perhaps much like the use of place names; it is nonprojective and nonrelational, in the kind of examples illustrated in <12>.[8] Verbs of motion encoding correct cardinal directions also occur, as in <13>, but early uses may be constructed by emulated collocation with named places rather than by active construal of the direction:

<12> From Age 2;0 to 2;6: Possibly Nonprojective, Nonrelational Uses of 'Uphill/Downhill' nouns.

'Mrs. (at) uphill.' (the uphill-living Mrs. is the one I mean)
'I come (to) across, that is, I traverse.' (orthogonal to the uphill/downhill axis)
'He's gone (to) downhill.' (down to place where their cornfields are)
'Antun (at) downhill.' (response to 'Who hit Father's foot?')
'He's gone (to) house (of) father downhill.' (response to 'Where's your namesake?')

<13> Age 2 to 2;5: Early Use of Absolute 'Ascend/Descend' Verbs.

'I'm ascending/descending.' (For example, to the other house, either actually up/down the slope of the land, or on the flat but in the direction of the south/north overall slope of land)
'It descended toward here.' (toy car down hillside)
'I'll ascend too.' (to other house, steeply 'uphill')
'Nik is ascending away.' (to his house)

We can only be sure that children have the abstract ternary conceptual relation in mind (e.g., A is in the uphill relation to B) when the ground object (B) is explicitly mentioned. Certainly by age 3;6, some examples of explicitly relational absolute uses are found in the children's data, showing that they are now able to use absolute coordinates to project angles in order to calcu-

---

[8]The examples here are from naturally occurring language production of the children. For reasons of space only the English glosses are given; see Brown, 2000, for many full Tzeltal examples.

late novel spatial relationships of moveable objects in relation to fixed land-marks or reference objects, as illustrated in <14> in English gloss:

<14> By Age 3;6 : Explicitly Relational Uses of Absolute Nominals.
'There it (the ball) is downhill of the mandarin tree.'
'To "its uphill" (uphill side of house) here we come again.'
'We went for injections to uphill-of Alvina's house.'
'It was found below (downhill of) the water tap.'
'He lives downhillwards of the school.'

The complexity of the Tzeltal constructions can be best seen from examples <15> and <16>:

<15> (3;6) *ya ka'y xan tza'nel jo'tik lum a ine ta yanil retrina.*
'We're going again for a shit over below ("downhillwards of ")
the latrine.'

<16> (3;11) *lum ay ta yanil mantarinae.*
'It's below (lit: at-its-downhill) the mandarin tree.'

To return to our initial question, the answer is clear: on the basis of children's linguistic production, the absolute system appears to be produced in its entirety and to be productive (at least in a limited way) well prior to the full appearance of the body part intrinsic system.
We turn now to our second question.

Question 2: Within the Absolute Usages, Are Vertical Uses Earlier Than Horizontal Uses?

The essential answer is no, except for one child. In general, the vertical senses of these up/down words do not seem to necessarily precede the local-slope senses; they appear together (Brown, 2000). This is of course contrary to what one might expect on the grounds that the vertical is universally perceptually given and presumably universally encoded in languages (Clark, 1973), whereas the uphill/downhill distinction is culturally specific. But in the sample, all the children use the uphill/downhill nouns initially in their land slope sense only, even though they sometimes hear adults use them in their vertical sense; in addition some children use the verbs *mo/ko* 'ascend/descend' in the absolute horizontal senses as early as they use them in the vertical sense (as in 'climb a tree'). A clear case of such absolute usage ('ascend' on flat ground) is the following:

<17> Ant is 3;5, Lus is 2;0: [they are playing with a toy car on flat ground outside house]

Ant; *bajt jobel ja' ini, bajt jobel.*
gone San Cristobal it_is this, gone San Cristobal.
'It's gone to S.C., it's gone to S.C.' [toy car]

Lus; *moem bel*
ascend-STAT goDIR
'It has ascended awaywards' [re car mentioned as going to S.C., to the south]

Although utterances like Lus's in <17> are relatively rare at this early age and are certainly outnumbered by utterances using vertical senses for 'ascend/descend' verbs, the children already display, by around age 2, the ability to use them in either sense.

Question 3: In the Horizontal Absolute Uses, Is the Local-Slope Usage Earlier Than the Cardinal Direction Usage?

Here the answer is clearly yes, as one would expect on the grounds that the perceptual support of a local, visible slope with its experiential implications for motor exertion would facilitate the acquisition of the local-slope meanings (e.g., 'up this incline'). These land-slope meanings of the 'up'/'down' vocabulary are at first restricted to a relatively small set of contexts, as de León (1994) found in her Tzotzil data as well. In the Tenejapan village under study, the relationship between local-slope and the cardinal directions (north/south) varies across households, as does the arrangement of houses and relevant other places. Households normally consist of at least two houses, one for sleeping in, one for cooking and eating in. In some households, these houses are uphill/downhill from each other, in others they lie 'acrossways' from another. Where the local-slope deviates markedly from the North/South axis, the language allows utilization of 'uphill/downhill' terms to describe the local slope. In the households where this is the case, both adults and small children use the local-slope for describing the angle of events occurring on the flat patio area between houses. Children are thus not yet forced into the abstract cardinal direction use of the absolute system, because another usage with more perceptual support is available.

To summarize: Tzeltal children start using the absolute vocabulary with both land slope senses and vertical senses at the two-word stage, from about age 2;0. Initially, these terms are used nonrelationally, that is, without explicitly specifying the Ground in relation to which something is up-

or downhill. By at least age 3;0, they have mastered the semantic contrasts for the entire set of absolute terms, and the syntax of possessed nouns is mastered by at least age 3;7 (this syntax is equally relevant for both absolute and intrinsic nominals). They are using the vocabulary in an explicitly relational way by this time, specifying the Grounds where relevant, and sometimes in novel contexts (saying things such as "F is uphillwards of G" for novel F's and G's). At this point in contrast they do not yet seem to be using the intrinsic system productively (although, as mentioned, they know the names for animate body parts and probably understand at least some of the intrinsic usage of adults around them).

Now three important points must be stressed:

1. As mentioned, the vertical senses of these 'up/down' words do not seem to necessarily precede the local-slope senses; they appear together. Thus the universally relevant vertical axis does not seem to give the child a significant lead or way in to the meaning of these terms.

2. The frequency of use in the input language, at least on initial examination, does not seem to explain the priority of absolute over intrinsic frames of reference.[9]

3. Grammatical complexity cannot explain the priority of absolute terms over intrinsic terms, since they occur in the same grammatical constructions. For example, both involve the same possessive construction type, as illustrated in <18>:

<18> Explicitly Relational Absolute and Intrinsic Possessed Nouns.

     ABSOLUTE   *ta y-ajk'ol na*
                 PREP 3E-uphill house
                 'at its-uphill house' [i.e., uphillwards of the house]

     INTRINSIC   *ta s-xujk na*
                 PREP 3E-side house
                 'at its-side house' [i.e., beside the house]
                 ta y-util na
                 PREP 3E-inside house [i.e., inside the house]
                 'at its-inside house'

In the possessed noun construction, absolute nouns ('its-uphill/downhill') are productively used by children at least as early as intrinsic ones.

---

[9]Both are relatively infrequent, at least in comparison with Indo-European spatial language encoded in prepositions (three examples of each appeared in a sample of 368 utterances, in 1.25 hours of natural interaction with a 2-year-old). There are of course difficulties in comparing the frequencies of two *sets* of vocabulary; this is a problem which needs to be further explored.

However, there are of course severe limitations to natural production data. One often cannot know just from the speech children produce how productive these vocabulary items are, because in many cases their linguistic production could in principle be based simply on memorized collocations between absolute expressions and particular locations or landmarks, despite a good range of contexts and named locations.[10] If such child usage is based on rote collocation, it would of course fail to index any of the abstract conceptual grasp of a spatial framework independent of objects and perceptual viewpoints that is the conceptual fundamentals of a real absolute system. We need therefore controlled evidence of use in completely *novel* situations, to which we now turn.

Child Data: Ages 4 to 12, Farm Animal Games.   For this reason a number of referential communication tasks designed as interactional "space games" were carried out with children down to the age of 4;0 (which is about the limit of the method). The farm animal task requires one player, the director, to describe a spatial layout to another, the matcher, who—despite being visually screened from the director's scene—has to recreate the array with a matching set of toys (see Fig. 8.4 for an example of the stimuli). This is one of many kinds of naturalistic experiment devised by members of the Space Project at the Max Planck Institute;[11] in this case, it is a verbal game played between two native speakers, designed to prompt spatial descriptions. Adults describe the scenes depicted by saying things like: 'place the cow uphillwards of the tree,' 'pull the horse downhillwards,' and so forth. We found that some children are able to take the matcher role, to understand and follow the instructions utilizing uphill/downhill spatial relators in these novel tabletop tasks, from as young as age 4, albeit with a lot of repetition by the director. These children are already at age 4;0 using the abstract, cardinal-direction sense of the absolute terms.[12] For production in the same novel tasks—operating as the director—we find adult-like usage ('put the cow uphillwards of the horse, facing acrossways,' for example) in general by age 7;8. (So far there is one precocious child who can do this at the age of 5;8, and four others between 6;5 and 7;8.) By the time children can perform the director role in this game, their uphill/downhill usage is fluent, accurate, and productive and (for at least some) can be used indoors as well as outdoors. There is no doubt that for this novel task, setting up toys in arrangements they

---

[10]Although children by age 3;6 can use this system to spatially relate objects and events to places and people familiar to them, this might amount (as a guess) to 20 or 30 places; just when this extends to *any* place is still unclear.

[11]See Space Stimuli Kit 1.2, 1993, produced by the Cognitive Anthropology Research Group at the Max Planck Institute for Psycholinguistics, Nijmegen, the Netherlands.

[12]The farm animal games of five children ages 4 to 5 have been analyzed so far.

FIG. 8.4.   Farm animal game stimulus.

have never seen before, the children must be using their absolute system as an abstract set of coordinates that can be applied to novel assemblages, to generate the correct application of linguistic labels. That they use the full cardinal-direction abstraction of the system underlines the precocity of this behavior from a Piagetian point of view. There may of course be various ways in which these children still do not have adult mastery of the absolute system. It may still be the case, for example, that children have not learned the pragmatic priorities that effectively disambiguate the various possible senses (cardinal-direction, local-slope, vertical) of the terms. We can expect them to be less good at the dead-reckoning that allows adults to use such a system in the dark, in an unknown town, inside an unfamiliar building. Nor at this stage do we know how much individual variability there is in children's usages, perhaps determined in part by the ecologies of their households and visiting relations with other households.[13] Answers to these questions are being pursued in ongoing research.

Thus, although most children of 8 years of age appear to have mastered the system completely, it may be that their understanding of it is less than fully adult. Nonetheless, we can be confident at this point that there is surprisingly early acquisition of a conceptually complex frame of reference, mastered for local (familiar) situations and tabletop space, indicating at least a limited productivity of these spatial terms by age 7½ or so.

---

[13]There is some suggestion, for example, that the acquisition pattern may not be exactly the same as what de León (1994) described for Tzotzil in the neighboring Tzotzil community of Nabenchauk, raising the possibility that it is influenced by the different north/south slope of the land in these two communities, with a crosscutting east/west 'sunset'/'sunrise' axis in Tenejapa but not in Nabenchauk.

How Do the Children Do It?   There are three points to make about the situation in which Tzeltal children learn their language, which may provide them with the scaffolding allowing them to use this absolute system in novel contexts so early:

1. Perceptual support. Because the absolute system allows one to use the local-slope axis as a basis for the coordinate system, children can get direct perceptual support for some early, more local, uses of the system.

2. *Gesture.* The absolute system is supported by very accurate directional pointing, which typically co-occurs with absolute usage in adult speech, and this may systematically help the child to grasp the conceptual underpinnings of the abstract system (Levinson, in press).

3. *Input.* Although these spatial words are not particularly high frequency items in the input to small children (because caregivers often do not need to be specific about locations, and they can often use deictics), the uphill/downhill terminology is used consistently in particular contexts: (a) for describing vertical motion and vertically aligned static spatial relations, (b) for describing motion and static relations in spatially close proximity using the local-slope coordinates, and (c) for describing motion and static relations across significant distances along the absolute axis.

Absolute descriptions are sometimes also used by caregivers to small children for small-scale location on flat (e.g., tabletop) surfaces, although small children may not spontaneously use it this way (except in the space game tasks).

In the contexts where small children use and hear language, there is thus a very consistent mapping between the 'uphill/downhill' words and particular places, directions, people, and events, which may provide the initial entry to the system. This then can later be used for more moveable objects and more ephemeral spatial relations.

We turn now to our fourth and final question, about the relative acquisition order of absolute and relative systems.

Question 4: What, If Anything, Is Unnatural?
Absolute Versus Relative Systems

On the basis of the "symptoms of natural categories" specified by Landau and Gleitman (1985; summarized in <6>), both absolute and relative systems are in some senses unnatural. What we have presented so far demonstrates that the absolute system is not delayed, in relation to relative 'front/back/left/right' systems. If it is unnatural, it seems to be less unnatural than the left/right part of our own (English/Dutch/German, etc.) projective system. Consider the evidence accumulated about the ages when children speaking European languages learn the spatial pre- or postpositions (already given in <9>), and let us compare it with the ages when Tzeltal children are learning their absolute and intrinsic vocabulary, as summarized in Table 8.4. Thus, the Tzeltal data contrast with evidence from European languages about the relative order of acquisition of intrinsic/topological and Euclidean/projective vocabulary. The same conclusion was reached by de León (1994) in relation to her Tzotzil data which showed absolute appearing at least as early as intrinsic. These Mayan language data suggest that children do not find the learning of an absolute system particularly difficult. Rather than child speakers being delayed, for example, in their 'uphill/downhill' system, in comparison with children who speak relative languages (and learn to use a 'left/right/front/back' system), the Mayan children would seem to be advanced. Tzeltal children understand their absolute system used in novel tasks on flat tabletop space by the age of about 4 to 5; they produce it in such novel tasks fluently, accurately, and productively by at least 7½ years. This

TABLE 8.4
Comparative Data on Age of Absolute/Relative Vocabulary Acquisition

	$in > on > under > beside >$	$back_1 > front_1 >$ [a] ('boy behind truck')	$back_2 > front_2$ ('boy behind tree')
European:	Age 2 ----------------------c. 3;10---------------------->		Age 4 on[b] ---------->
Tzeltal:	Absolute -------------> 3;6 --------->		Intrinsic --------->
European:	*own left$_1$/right$_1$*[c]	*other's left$_1$/right$_1$*[d]	*x left$_2$ of y for ego*[e]
	Age[f] ---------> 6 ----------> 8 ---------->		11/12

Note. Order of language acquisition in Relative languages is summarized from Piaget (1928), Laurendeau & Pinard (1977), Harris (1972), Johnston & Slobin (1979), Tanz (1980), Weissenborn & Stralka (1984).

[a]Johnston & Slobin (1979, p. 538) production data, mean age of acquisition: intrinsic *in front* (English 3;9; Italian 3;10; Serbo-Croatian 3;10; Turkish 3;4), intrinsic *behind* (English 4;4; Italian 2;1 (*n* = 2); Serbo-Croatian 3;9; Turkish 2;10).

[b]Tanz (1980, p. 26) Correct comprehension at 66% of subjects at 4;2, 70% at 4;11 (20% Hausa pattern); Johnston & Slobin (1979) production data suggest few children of 4;4 have both deictic back and front notions.

[c]Comprehension tasks: Piaget (1928): 75% of 5;0s; Galifret-Granjon (1960) 75% of 6;0s.

[d]Comprehension at 75% criterion at 8;0 (Piaget, 1928; Galifret-Granjon, 1960), at 10;0 (Laurendeau & Pinard, 1977).

[e]Comprehension at 75% criteria at 11;0/12;0 (Piaget, 1928; Galifret-Granjon, 1960).

[f]Nearly all this data is comprehension only; Weissenborn & Stralka (1984) production data suggest 11 years for full system.

would seem to contrast favourably with Western children performing on the same sorts of tasks using a left/right system.[14]

CONCLUSION

The acquisition of a Euclidean absolute linguistic system before a topological intrinsic system does not necessarily show anything about the ordering of conceptual development. For although it is not possible to grasp Euclidean semantics without having Euclidean ideas, it is of course possible to have, for example, topological ideas that do not show in a linguistic system. We are thus not arguing that Euclidean/projective thinking is conceptually prior to topological concepts for Mayan children. But the fact that the absolute linguistic system comes in very early in Tzeltal, and apparently at least as early or earlier than the intrinsic system, raises some doubt about the importance of the Piagetian stages as prerequisites for corresponding linguistic developments. If conceptual development is independent of language and must precede it, as Piaget supposed, then the precocity of Mayan children is in serious need of explanation. If however, we admit the Whorfian possibility that language may actually play an active role in conceptual development, then we would have a natural explanation for the precocity: adults all around the Tzeltal children are presuming an absolute coordinate system in thought and action, and this is made accessible to children through language in particular. Language use is among the most highly practiced aspects of skilled human behavior, so that participation in such a linguistic system may push forward the development of a special form of Euclidean reasoning in Tzeltal children. The spatial concepts described here seem to us to be good candidates for where language might promote conceptual development of a sort and at an age that would be unlikely in cultures where no such concepts are available in everyday child-relevant contexts.

The pattern of acquisition of Tzeltal absolute and intrinsic forms seems to provide evidence against a universal course of acquisition for spatial language (based on a scale of cognitive complexity) in favor of a view that children are capable of learning cognitively complex frames of reference remarkably early, if this is what is used and what is useful in their language environment. This provides a challenge to the view of the role of language in cognition influentially promulgated by Piaget, as summarized by Gins-

---

[14]See Weissenborn & Stralka (1984), who found that, on a director/matcher route task, German children ages 6 to 9 cannot solve the problem due to lack of an overall frame of reference, plus left/right problems. Children of 9 to 11 years can mostly solve the problem, but cannot foresee trouble, and those of 11 to 14 years can do it and also control for possible misapprehensions. Other work has also found some evidence for priority of absolute over relative systems (see Wassman & Dasen, 1995, for Balinese and de León, 1995, for the Australian Aboriginal language Guugu Yimithirr).

burg and Opper: (1969, p. 170): "Russian psychologists [e.g., Vygotsky] have proposed that one specific type of factor, namely the child's own language, is vital for the development of behavior. Piaget's view is in strong contrast . . . Piaget feels that logical thinking is primarily non-linguistic and derives from action." Piaget himself is uncompromisingly clear (Piaget, 1974, pp. 109–110): "All this has taught me that there exists a logic of coordination of actions far deeper than the logic related to language and much prior to that of propositions in the strict sense." The work we have reported on here inclines us to a more Vygotskian perspective. Crosslinguistic work (see Bowerman & Levinson, 2000) suggests the reciprocal, mutual influence of language on cognition and vice versa not later than the age 4;0 to 5;0 predicted by Vygotsky.

Why, despite his interactionism, did Piaget reject the influence of language on the child's developing thought? Because, it seems, he held that children can produce appropriate language before they have fully internalized the underlying semantical concepts: ". . . Language is by no means sufficient to assure the transmission of ready-made operatory schemes which the child would thus receive from without by linguistic coercion" (Piaget, 1974, p. 118)—rather the child must be preadapted for them. In this Piaget is no doubt partly right, but he underestimated the extent to which language forms part of the ecology of action. The child's efforts to play a role in the social world demand an understanding of those aspects of language which crucially structure social activities (e.g., 'take this there downhill' or 'bring it across here'), aspects which are also reflected in other behavior, like the consistent gesturing accompanying spatial descriptions. Such an ecological view of the Tenejapan child suggests that there are multiple motivations, and multiple scaffoldings, for acquiring these precocious spatial understandings.

ACKNOWLEDGMENTS

A first version of this paper was presented at The Growing Mind conference in Geneva, September 14-18, 1996, and a revised version at the Biennial Meeting of the American Psychological Anthropology Society in San Diego, California, October 1997. We are grateful to Melissa Bowerman, Suzanne Gaskins, Patricia Greenfield, Paul Kay, and Wolfgang Klein for helpful comments on various versions.

REFERENCES

Bowerman, M. (1996). The origins of children's spatial semantic categories: Cognitive vs. linguistic determinants. In J. J. Gumperz & S. C. Levinson (Eds.), *Rethinking linguistic relativity* (pp. 145–176). Cambridge, England: Cambridge University Press.

Bowerman, M., & Choi, S. (2000). Shaping meanings for language: Universal and language specific in the acquisition of spatial semantic categories. In M. Bowerman & S. C. Levinson (Eds.), *Language acquisition and conceptual development*. Cambridge, England: Cambridge University Press.

Bowerman, M., & Levinson, S. C. (Eds.). (2000). *Language acquisition and conceptual development*. Cambridge, England: Cambridge University Press.

Brown, P. (1994). The INs and ONs of Tzeltal locative expressions: The semantics of static descriptions of location. In J. B. Haviland & S. C. Levinson (Eds.), *Spatial conceptualization in Mayan languages* [Special issue]. *Linguistics, 32*(4/5), 743–790.

Brown, P. (2000). Learning to talk about motion UP and DOWN in Tzeltal: Is there a language-specific bias for verb learning? In M. Bowerman & S. C. Levinson (Eds.), *Language acquisition and conceptual development*. Cambridge, England: Cambridge University Press.

Brown, P., & Levinson, S. C. (1993a). *Linguistic and nonlinguistic coding of spatial arrays: Explorations in Mayan cognition*. Working Paper No. 24. Nijmegen, The Netherlands: Max Planck Institute for Psycholinguistics, Cognitive Anthropology Research Group.

Brown, P., & Levinson, S. C. (1993b). 'Uphill' and 'downhill' in Tzeltal. *Journal of Linguistic Anthropology, 3*(1), 46–74.

Choi, S., & Bowerman, M. (1991). Learning to express motion events in English and Korean: The influence of language-specific lexicalization patterns. *Cognition, 41*, 83–121.

Clark, H. H. (1973). Space, time, semantics and the child. In T. E. Moore (Ed.), *Cognitive development and the acquisition of language* (pp. 28–64). New York: Academic Press.

de León, L. (1994). Exploration in the acquisition of geocentric location by Tzotzil children. In J. B. Haviland & S. C. Levinson (Eds.), *Spatial conceptualization in Mayan languages* [Special issue]. *Linguistics, 32*(4/5), 857–884.

de León, L. (1995). The development of geocentric location in young speakers of Guugu Yimithirr. Working paper No. 32. Nijmegen, The Netherlands: Max Planck Institute for Psycholinguistics, Cognitive Anthropology Research Group.

Galifret-Granjon, N. (1960). Batterie Piaget-Head (tests d'orientation gauche-droite). [Piaget-Head Battery (tests of left/right orientation]. In R. Zazzo (Ed.), *Manuel pour l'examen psychologique de l'enfant*, Fascicule I [Manual for the psychological examination of the child]. (pp. 24–56). Neuchâtel et Paris: Delachaux et Niestlé.

Ginsburg, H., & Opper, S. (1969). *Piaget's theory of intellectual development*. Englewood Cliffs, NJ: Prentice-Hall.

Harris, L. (1972). Discrimination of left and right and development of logic of relationships. *Merrill-Palmer Quarterly, 18*, 307–320.

Johnston, J. R., & Slobin, D. I. (1979). The development of locative expressions in English, Italian, Serbo-Croatian and Turkish. *Journal of Child Language, 6*, 529–545.

Landau, B., & Gleitman, L. (1985). *Language and experience: Evidence from the blind child*. Cambridge, MA: Harvard University Press.

Laurendeau, M., & Pinard, A. (1977/1970). *The development of the concept of space in the child*. New York: International Universities Press.

Levinson, S. C. (1994). Vision, shape, and linguistic description: Tzeltal body-part terminology and object description. In J. B. Haviland & S. C. Levinson (Eds.), *Spatial conceptualization in Mayan languages* [Special issue] *Linguistics, 32*(4/5), 791–855.

Levinson, S. C. (1996). Frames of reference and Molyneux's question: Crosslinguistic evidence. In P. Bloom, M. A. Peterson, L. Nadel, & M. F. Garrett (Eds.), *Language and space* (pp. 109–69). Cambridge, MA: MIT Press.

Levinson, S. C. (1997). Language and cognition: The cognitive consequences of spatial description in Guugu-Yimithirr. *Journal of Linguistic Anthropology, 7*(1), 98–131.

Levinson, S. C. (in press). The body in space: Cultural differences in the use of body-schema for spatial thinking and gesture. In G. Lewis & F. Sigaut (Eds.), *Culture and uses of the body*. Oxford, England: Oxford University Press.

Pederson, E., Danziger, E., Wilkins, D., Levinson, S.C., Kita, S., & Senft, G. (1998). Semantic typology and spatial conceptualization. *Language, 74*, 557–589.

Piaget, J. (1928). *Judgement and reasoning in the child.* London: Routledge.

Piaget, J. (1974). *The child and reality: Problems of genetic psychology.* London: Muller.

Piaget, J., & Inhelder, B. (1967/1948). *The child's conception of space.* New York: Norton.

Piaget, J., Inhelder, B., & Szeminska, A. (1981/1960). *The child's conception of geometry.* New York: Norton.

Talmy, L. (1983). How language structures space. In H. L. Pick & L. P. Acredolo (Eds.), *Spatial orientation: Theory, research, and applications* (pp. 225–282). New York: Plenum.

Tanz, C. (1980). *Studies in the acquisition of deictic terms.* Cambridge, England: Cambridge University Press.

Vygotsky, L. (1986). *Thought and language.* Cambridge, MA: MIT Press.

Wassman, J., & Dasen, P. R. (1995, September). *Balinese spatial orientation: Some empirical evidence for moderate lingusitic relativity.* Paper presented at The Growing Mind Conference, Geneva, Switzerland.

Weissenborn, J., & Stralka, R. (1984). Das Verstehen von Missverständnissen: Eine ontogenetische Studie [The understanding of misunderstandings: An ontogenetic study]. *Zeitschrift für Literaturwissenschaft und Linguistik, 14*(55), 113–134.

Wertsch, J. V. (1985). *Vygotsky and the social formation of mind.* Cambridge, MA: Harvard University Press.

Chapter 9

Where Do Children's Word Meanings Come From? Rethinking the Role of Cognition in Early Semantic Development

Melissa Bowerman
Max Planck Institute for Psycholinguistics

Acquiring a first language is a feat of astonishing complexity and speed. By 2 years of age children have learned many words and can put them together to form simple sentences, and by 4 years they have mastered most of the grammatical machinery of their language. For any theory of language acquisition, the central problem is to explain how this is possible.

Opinions about the underlying mechanisms of language development diverge widely, with some scholars urging that children come equipped with innate, domain-specific knowledge of language structure and others arguing for the power of general-purpose learning procedures. But until recently there has been widespread agreement on one important claim: that in the early stages of language development, children link linguistic forms directly to concepts and categories that they have already established in the course of their nonlinguistic cognitive development.

In this chapter I first sketch how this widely shared view has come about. Then I discuss how it is being challenged by contemporary crosslinguistic research on semantic structure and semantic development. This work suggests that although nonlinguistic cognitive development provides an indispensable foundation for semantic development, its role is less direct than has often been envisioned. Different languages organize meanings in different ways. This means that the semantic organization of a particular language is as much a part of the structure to be mastered as are the language's syntax and morphology. Instead of simply matching words to preexisting concepts, learners draw on their conceptual resources to help them determine how their local language structures the content to be expressed. Children's skill at building semantic categories is in fact remarkable: from their earliest productive language use and at least in some cases even before, the semantic categories children associate with the forms of their language are already language specific.

THE RISE OF THE COGNITIVE APPROACH

The hypothesis that children's nonlinguistic cognitive categories play a central role in language acquisition emerged in the 1970s. Before then, the study of language development was for some time dominated by approaches that paid little attention to meaning; these included behaviorism, with its emphasis on direct modeling, imitation, and reinforcement, and distributional analyses, which focused on the positioning of linguistic forms and restrictions on their co-occurrence.

There were several reasons for the new attention to cognition in language acquisition studies. One was the outcome of the first modern studies comparing children learning different languages. Researchers had initiated these crosslinguistic studies inspired in part by Chomsky's (1959, 1965) arguments that in acquiring a language children are constructing an abstract rule system, and that in doing so they are guided by innate knowledge about the possible form of a human language. At that time, students of language acquisition were beginning to develop a detailed picture of the early speech of children learning English and—drawing on a handful of evidence from other languages—were starting to make proposals about possible universals of language development. By establishing universals, they hoped to make inferences about the nature of the underlying capacity for language acquisition.

Firm crosslinguistic evidence was essential to this enterprise. Without this evidence, it was unclear whether children's observed speech patterns reflected acquisition mechanisms common to all learners, or resulted from exposure to a language with a particular structure. For example, children learning English were found to observe a relatively fixed word order in their early word combinations. But was this because of a bias in the universal capacity for language acquisition (e.g., Slobin, 1966) or because English is a language in which word order is in fact relatively rigid? To untangle what is universal from what is language specific, researchers began to compare children learning structurally diverse languages (cf. Bowerman, 1973 on Finnish; Blount, 1969 on Luo; Kernan, 1969 on Samoan; see R. Brown, 1973 and Slobin, 1973 for overviews).

The most important outcome of these early crosslinguistic comparisons was not—contrary to expectations—a finding about invariants of early syntax, but a finding about meaning. All around the world, children's first sentences were seen to revolve around a restricted set of meanings to do with agency, action, location, possession, and the existence, recurrence, nonexistence, and disappearance of objects (Bowerman, 1976; Braine, 1976; R. Brown, 1973; Slobin, 1970, 1973). As Slobin put it, "If you ignore word order, and read through transcriptions of two-word utterances in the various languages we have studied, the utterances read like direct translations of one another. There is a great similarity of basic vocabulary and basic meanings conveyed by the word combinations" (1970, p. 177).

Where did this surprising convergence on a handful of meanings come from? Piaget's work provided a critical clue. At that time—in the waning days of behaviorism—Piaget's research was only beginning to become widely familiar to U.S. developmentalists. Imagine the click of things falling into place when language acquisition researchers realized that the meanings that figure so heavily in children's early speech were precisely the kinds of meanings that Piaget (e.g., 1954) had stressed in his account of conceptual development in the first 2 years of life. An influential statement of this insight came from R. Brown (1973):

> I think that the first sentences express the construction of reality which is the terminal achievement of sensori-motor intelligence. What has been acquired on the plane of motor intelligence (the permanence of form and substance of immediate objects) and the structure of immediate space and time does not need to be formed all over again on the plan of representation. Representation starts with just those meanings that are most available to it, propositions about action schemas involving agents and objects, assertions of nonexistence, recurrence, location, and so on. . . . (p. 200)

The observed correspondence between nonlinguistic and linguistic meanings gave rise to an important new vision of the nature of language acquisition. According to this view, first language development can be understood as a process of mapping the forms and combinatorial patterns of language onto concepts that have already been established in the course of nonlinguistic cognitive development (L. Bloom, 1970, 1973; Bowerman, 1973; Braine, 1976; R. Brown, 1973; Nelson, 1974; Slobin, 1973; Schlesinger, 1971). For example, constructions like *more X* and *X all-gone* could be linked to nonlinguistic notions of the recurrence or disappearance of an object or event, and word order patterns could be used to express categories of relationships; for example, *mommy hug* or *daddy go* would specify a relation of actor to action, *hug mommy* a relation of action to patient, and *sweater chair* a relation of entity to location.

This view of language acquisition—dubbed the "Cognition Hypothesis" by Cromer (1974)—took hold and spread rapidly during the 1970s.

Its success can be attributed to its incorporation of several attractive features:

1. It provided a plausible account of the apparent universality of the meanings expressed in children's early utterances. The meanings would be universal because they would arise from processes of cognitive development hypothesized to be common to all children.

2. It provided an explanation of productivity—how children go beyond the sentences they have heard to produce and understand an infinite number of novel sentences. Productivity was on researchers' minds because of Chomsky's stress on this important feature of natural languages. Productivity would follow—so the thinking went—from children's reliance on their nonlinguistic concepts to guide their application of words and word order rules. For instance, if children have formulated a simple rule like "first name the actor and then the action," they can use it to produce not only unremarkable strings like *daddy go* but also unusual ones like *spider move* (cf. Braine, 1976, p. 15).

3. The learning procedure posited by the Cognition Hypothesis could easily be hooked up to an appealing developmental "motor": children's presumed desire to communicate their emerging ideas. Many developmentalists had been persuaded by Chomsky's argument that in learning a language, children are mastering an abstract rule system. But they were less willing to accept his proposal that language acquisition is guided by the workings of an innate mental module devoted to grammar. For them, an attractive alternative was that children make progress in language by trying to identify the conventional linguistic devices—words, inflections, word order patterns, and so forth—with which they can communicate their unfolding thoughts about the world. Children would not necessarily be able to express a particular meaning in a conventional way from the moment it emerges, since rate of acquisition also is affected demonstrably by linguistic factors like the formal complexity of the device needed (Slobin, 1973). But the onset of the communicative intent would set the search process in motion.

4. Finally and perhaps most important, the Cognition Hypothesis conformed with the theoretical Zeitgeist of the 1970s, which featured a growing emphasis on universality and constraints in studies of human mental processes. A critical initial impulse for this orientation was Chomsky's (1965) argument that structural variation among languages is more superficial than many had believed, with variation held in check by inborn constraints on the possible structure of language. Initial interest in language universals focused on syntax, but there soon followed studies of semantic structure emphasizing universality and possible biological

determination (e.g., Berlin & Kay, 1969 on color terminology; Allan, 1979 and E. Clark, 1976 on object categorization in numeral classifier systems). Such findings suggested that the semantic categories of language reflect fundamental properties of human perceptual and cognitive organization. If semantic structure follows the contours of nonlinguistic human thought, then the concepts children form on the basis of their nonlinguistic experiences would seem to provide an ideal basis for language learning.

Research on semantic universals was particularly central to Slobin's seminal work on the acquisition of the "grammaticized" portion of language—inflections, case endings, prepositions and postpositions, connectives, negative markers, and other closed-class forms. Drawing on Talmy (1983, 1985), Slobin (1985) proposed that the meanings of closed-class forms are constrained across languages in ways that children are highly sensitive to. After surveying crosslinguistic evidence on the meanings children initially associate with such forms, he concluded that children approach language acquisition with a prestructured "semantic space" in which meanings and clusters of meanings constitute a "privileged set of grammaticizable notions" onto which grammatical forms are initially mapped. The particular forms that are mapped vary of course across languages, but the basic meanings are constant. A similar conclusion was reached by Bickerton (1981) in his work on the meanings that become grammaticized when new languages undergo a process of creolization.

Few theorists have supposed, of course, that grammatical development can be adequately described only as a process of discovering the mapping between preestablished concepts and linguistic forms. Even researchers generally sympathetic to the Cognition Hypothesis pointed to aspects of language that are difficult to reduce to matters of meaning (e.g., Cromer, 1974). More fundamentally, many investigators argued that the fit between meaning and grammar is too imperfect for children to be able to arrive at an adult knowledge of syntax starting only with meanings and general-purpose learning mechanisms that analyze the distribution of linguistic forms (e.g., Pinker, 1984). Children must be helped—just as Chomsky had claimed—by inborn knowledge of grammatical categories and relationships.

The appeal to innate grammatical knowledge did not, however, supplant the need to invoke nonlinguistic cognition: concepts established independently of language were now recruited to solve a new problem. Assume that children do come with inborn knowledge of the abstract properties of nouns, verbs, subjects, direct objects, and so on. To benefit from this knowledge, they have to be able to identify a given segment in the speech they hear as an instantiation of one or another of these constructs. How do they do this? If children have foreknowledge not only of syntactic categories and relations but also of canonical mappings between syntax and meaning, they could use the meaning expressed by a form as a guide to its likely syntactic status ("Semantic Bootstrapping," Pinker, 1984; see also Grimshaw, 1981). For instance, they could assume that words specifying concrete objects are nouns and words specifying actions are verbs; similarly, the word in a sentence that names the agent of an action is likely to be the sentence subject and the word naming an object acted on the direct object. In this scenario, children's nonlinguistic concepts and categories play just as important a role in language acquisition as in the Cognition Hypothesis. The difference is in whether the concepts are seen as serving directly as building blocks for the child's early grammar, or indirectly as cues to already known syntactic categories.

Since the 1970s the appeal to prelinguistic concepts has been basic to research not only on morphological and grammatical development but also on early lexical development. In an influential early study of the "cognitive" era, Nelson (1974, p. 268) argued that prior researchers were mistaken in assuming that "the child learns meaning from his encounters with the language rather than from encounters with the physical and social world." It is posing the question backward, urged Nelson, to ask "How does the child form a concept to fit the word?" The right approach, in her view, was to ask "How does the child match words to his concepts?" (see also Huttenlocher, 1974, p. 356 for a similar view). Much of the contemporary work on early lexical development asks "How do language learners determine the intended referent of a novel word?" ("Quine's problem"; cf. Quine, 1960). Although at first glance this may seem like a return to the formulation of the question that Nelson rejected, proposed solutions (e.g., P. Bloom, in press; Gleitman, 1990; Markman, 1990; Tomasello, 1995) take for granted what Nelson was arguing to establish: that the needed referent concept itself—for example, 'ball,' 'throw,' 'give,' 'see'—is already part of the child's cognitive repertoire. That is, learners are seen as needing to identify the referent concept from among the set of possibilities compatible with the context, not to construct the concept in the first place.

In summary, although students of language acquisition have had different opinions about many issues since the 1970s, they have agreed widely on the view that language learners are highly structured and constrained in their cognitive development and that they rely on nonlinguistically established concepts and categories to help them acquire grammar and lexicon. For the study of language development, the legacy of the cognitive revolution has been the pervasive assumption that the meanings associated with the basic vocabulary and grammatical structure of a language arise in language learners independently of the linguistic input.[1]

THE CHALLENGE OF CROSSLINGUISTIC VARIATION IN SEMANTIC STRUCTURE

After a particular intellectual framework has been firmly in place for a while, problems that were swept aside in the initial enthusiasm begin to reassert themselves, at first tentatively and then more insistently. And there is indeed a major difficulty in the vision of language acquisition I have just sketched—a problem that is stimulating a rethinking of the role of nonlinguistic cognition in language development. What is this problem? Put simply, it is the conflation of semantics with cognition: the assumption that the semantic categories of a language can be equated directly with the concepts that human beings everywhere formulate spontaneously in the course of their nonlinguistic cognitive development.

This equation would be plausible if languages everywhere partitioned conceptual content in just the same way. And indeed the identification of semantics with cognition arose, as I mentioned earlier, in an intellectual climate of stress on semantic universality. It is undoubtedly true that the patterning of meaning in language is constrained, perhaps even strongly constrained. But "constrained" does not mean uniform. In virtually every conceptual domain, languages display a striking range of crosscutting options for structuring and combining the categories of meanings with which words, grammatical morphemes, and construction patterns are associated.

Semantic variation commanded considerable interest earlier in the 20th century, as attested especially in work on North American Native American languages by linguists and anthropologists such as Boas, Sapir, and Whorf. But attention to differences in the structuring of meaning was associated with the controversial idea that patterns of language determine patterns of thought (the Whorfian hypothesis; cf. Whorf, 1956). Attempts to test this hypothesis in the 1950s and 1960s yielded mixed or negative results. As enthusiasm for cognitive and linguistic universalism bloomed in the 1970s, the Whorfian hypothesis was widely dismissed, and the differences in semantic structure that had given rise to it were downplayed or forgotten.

---

[1]In reviewing the development of the cognitivist position I have necessarily simplified somewhat. Even those who strongly rely on the view that meanings are established first have sometimes acknowledged problems for this view (e.g., Gleitman, 1990, fn. 1), and crosslinguistic challenges of the kind I will discuss in the next section have been foreshadowed in earlier studies, for example, Bowerman (1985), Gentner (1982), Pinker (1989), and Schlesinger (1977).

In the rejection of the Whorfian hypothesis, the baby was thrown out with the bath water. Whether or not the semantic categories of a language influence the way its speakers think, we must still account for how children acquire them—how they master language-specific ways of organizing meaning. The equation of semantic development with nonlinguistic cognitive development has led to neglect of a whole chapter in the story of language acquisition: how children end up controlling the semantic patterns of their own language, as distinct from those of other languages.

Significant variation in semantic structuring has been documented for a variety of conceptual domains, including, for example, notions of agency and causality, temporality, modality, animacy, criteria for individuating entities, and criteria for determining what will be treated as an "event." In this chapter, I focus on the domain of space. Space may seem like a surprising content area with which to explore crosslinguistic semantic variation and its effects on children. The ability to perceive and mentally represent spatial relationships is fundamental to human life, and it is supported and constrained not only by vision and other biological systems but also by universal physiological and environmental factors like upright posture, front–back asymmetry, and the workings of gravity (H. Clark, 1973). In linguistics, spatial concepts are often taken as basic because they provide structuring principles not only for spatial language per se, but also for other semantic domains like time, state change, and causality (e.g., Talmy, 1976; Jackendoff, 1976; E. Clark, in press).

Children clearly know a great deal about spatial relations before they begin to talk about them. Piaget and Inhelder (1956) showed this early on for toddlers, and it has been demonstrated since in ever more sophisticated ways for ever younger infants (e.g., Antell & Caron, 1985; Baillargeon, 1995; Behl-Chadha & Eimas, 1995; Needham & Baillargeon, 1993; Quinn, 1994; Sitskoorn & Smitsman, 1995; Spelke, Breinlinger, Macomber, & Jacobson, 1992; see Bowerman, 1996a for a review). Consistent with these findings, space has long served as a paradigm case for the claim that language maps to children's nonlinguistic concepts, and with good reason. Consider findings like these:

1. Both within and across languages, children acquire locative markers (prepositions, postpositions, case endings) in a relatively consistent order: first morphemes for notions of containment (*in*), contiguity and support (*on*), and occlusion (*under*); then for proximity (*next to, beside, between*); and finally for projective relationships (*in front of, behind*; Johnston, 1985; Johnston & Slobin, 1979; Sinha, Thorseng, Hayashi, & Plunkett, 1994). This sequence is consistent with the order of emergence of spatial concepts as established through nonlinguistic testing by Piaget and Inhelder (1956). This has suggested that cognitive development is the pacesetter for spatial semantic

development (Johnston & Slobin, 1979): as new concepts mature, children look for linguistic forms to express them with.

2. Early spatial words often generalize rapidly from familiar to novel situations. For example, by as early as the one-word stage, forms like *in, out, up, down, off,* and *open* are extended to a wide variety of events that are similar in trajectory of movement or salient outcome state, abstracted across entities of different kinds (McCune-Nicolich, 1981; Smiley & Huttenlocher, 1995). Rapid generalization has suggested to researchers that the child's use of the words is guided not by concepts that are in the process of being formulated, perhaps under guidance from language, but by concepts that are already in place when the words are acquired.

3. Children often use spatial words somewhat idiosyncratically from the adult point of view. For example, children learning English tend to apply the verb *open* too broadly, using it not only for actions on doors, boxes, and drawers, but also for separating two Frisbees, taking a piece out of a jigsaw puzzle, and pulling the stem off an apple (Bowerman, 1978; see also E. Clark, 1993). Conversely, English-speaking toddlers initially restrict words like *up, down, in,* and *on* to situations in which an object moves (e.g., [put the] *ball in*), and extend them only later to situations of static position ([There's a] *ball in* [there]; Smiley & Huttenlocher, 1995). Overextensions, underextensions, and other deviations from adult usage have been taken to show that children initially link spatial words to their own spontaneously generated spatial concepts (Bowerman, 1978, 1980; E. Clark, in press; Griffiths & Atkinson, 1978; Johnston, 1985; Smiley & Huttenlocher, 1995).

The conviction that first spatial words express nonlinguistic spatial concepts has rested not only on empirical findings but also, more implicitly, on the sense shared by native speakers of a language that the meanings of everyday vocabulary items reflect the obvious way to conceptualize things. The first spatial words in English and closely related languages are particles like *in, out, on, off, up, down,* and *back* and verbs like *fall, come, go, give, open,* and *break*. It is easy for researchers who speak these languages to assume that the meanings of such words reflect an inevitable conceptual parsing of space into such seemingly basic concepts as *containment, support, verticality,* and motion *toward* or *away from* the speaker. But none of the semantic categories associated with these words is, in fact, universal.[2]

---

[2]For crosslinguistic differences in the categorization of 'in - out' and 'on - off' - type relations see Bowerman (1989, 1996a, 1996b); Bowerman & Choi (in press); Brugman (1984); Choi & Bowerman (1991); and P. Brown (1994); for 'up - down' and 'fall' relations, see P. Brown (in press); Choi & Bowerman (1991); and de León (in press); for 'give' see Margetts (1998), Newman (1998), and Talmy (1982, 1985; cf. Bowerman 1994, p. 39 for implications of Talmy' analysis for acquisition); for 'come - go' see Wilkins & Hill 1995; for 'open' see Bowerman (1996a); and for 'break' see Pye (1996).

Consider, for example, the linguistic classification of the following actions: (a) putting a block into a pan, (b) putting a small book into a fitted case, (c) putting a Lego piece on a stack of Legos, (d) putting a ring on a finger, (e) putting a cup on a table, (f) putting a hat on someone's head, and (g) putting a towel on a towel rack. In events (a) and (b), the moving object (the Figure) ends up contained by the reference-point object (the Ground; these terms are Talmy's, 1985). English speakers describe such actions with a verb-particle construction that includes the particle *in*, for example, *put in*. In (c) through (g), the Figure ends up in contact with and supported by an external surface of the Ground; events of this kind are typically called *(put) on*. This way of grouping and distinguishing the events is shown in Fig. 9.1.

In Dutch, as in English, the main work of encoding spatial relationships is carried out by prepositions/particles. One of these forms—*in* 'in'—picks out the same two containment situations distinguished in English (a, b; see Fig. 9.2). But Dutch makes a finer breakdown among the contact-and-support relationships: actions (c), (d), and (e) are typically described with *op* 'on1,' action (f) with *om* 'around,' and action (g) with *aan* 'on2.'

Om 'around' has a meaning similar to English *around*, so in itself this category is familiar, but its application is more insistent: in many situations where English speakers prefer *on*, stressing the contact-and-support aspect of the situation over the encirclement aspect, Dutch speakers routinely select *om*, for example, "put your safety belt *om*," "put the ring *om* your finger," or "put the diaper *om* the baby."

The difference between *op* 'on1' and *aan* 'on2' is more exotic to English speakers (see Bowerman, 1996b for analysis). When used for concrete spatial situations, *aan* applies to relations in which the Figure is construed as acted on by an external force—most typically gravity—that would pull it away from the Ground if it were not held in place, for example, by attachment at a fixed point. *Aan* is thus the preposition of choice for situations of less attachment by hanging (e.g., 'picture *aan* wall,' 'coat on hook') and by screws, string, and the like ('side-view mirror *aan* car,' 'handle *aan* cupboard door,' 'kite *aan* string,' 'dog *aan* leash'). *Op*, in contrast, picks out relations in which the Figure is construed as "at rest"—not pulled away from the Ground by any salient external force. This conceptualization applies most obviously to things supported from below ('cup *op* table,' 'child *op* stool'), but also to living creatures who seem to rest as naturally on a vertical or underneath surface as we do on the floor ('spider *op* wall,' 'fly *op* ceiling')[3] and to lightweight, relatively flat

---

[3]A contrast can be made between, for example, 'spider *op* wall' and 'spider *aan* wall': the former indicates that the spider is living and stays in contact with the wall in the way that is natural for spiders, whereas the latter suggests that the spider is dead and so could be expected to drop off the wall, but somehow remains stuck in place.

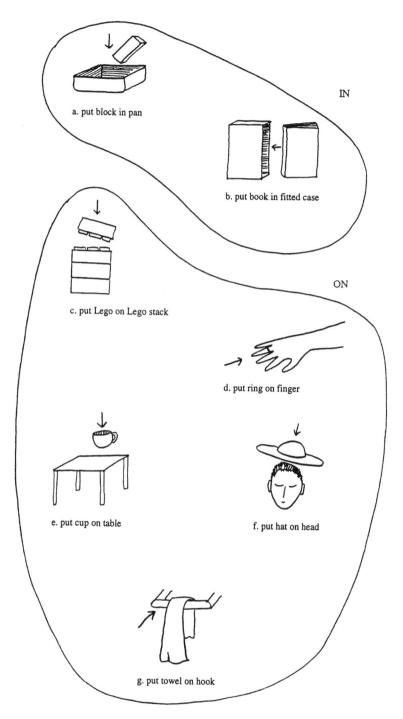

IN

a. put block in pan

b. put book in fitted case

ON

c. put Lego on Lego stack

d. put ring on finger

e. put cup on table

f. put hat on head

g. put towel on hook

FIG. 9.1.   Classification of some actions in English.

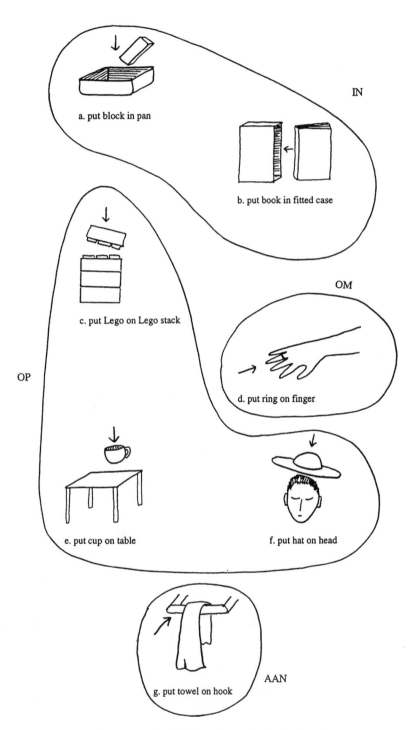

IN

a. put block in pan

b. put book in fitted case

OM

c. put Lego on Lego stack

d. put ring on finger

OP

e. put cup on table

f. put hat on head

g. put towel on hook

AAN

FIG. 9.2.   Classification of some actions in Dutch.

Figures that stay in place by adhesion or surface tension ('bandaid *op* leg,' 'raindrops *op* window,' 'dust *op* wall').

In Korean, the classification is again different. Korean has no forms comparable to the spatial prepositions/particles of English and Dutch; most of the work of expressing spontaneous or caused motion along a path is done by verbs.[4] The semantic categories associated with path verbs often differ strikingly from the path categories of English, especially for caused motions of putting something somewhere (Choi & Bowerman, 1991). This is illustrated for the current set of actions in Fig. 9.3.

Notice first that the containment category—so fundamental in English and Dutch—is absent. Instead there is a new, crosscutting category that treats one of the containment actions—(b) 'put book in fitted case'—as similar to two of the support actions ((c) 'put Lego on Lego stack' and (d) 'put ring on finger'), and different from the other containment action ((a) 'put block in pan'). This category is labeled by the high-frequency verb *kkita*. What do the actions called *kkita* have in common? They all involve the joining of three-dimensional objects whose shapes are complementary and fit together snugly. English has no word for this topological spatial concept.[5] Other examples include putting an earplug *in* an ear, glasses *in* a glasses case, and one nesting cup *in* another; putting a tight-fitting lid *on* a pan, a cap *on* a pen, a ring *on* the pole of a stacking toy; putting two paper cups or two Lego blocks *together*, and even buttoning a button, snapping a snap, and closing a latching cupboard door.

The four other manipulations shown in Fig. 9.3 fall into distinct semantic categories of Korean. Action (a) is described with *nehta*, which applies most prototypically to putting something into a loosely fitting container, but also to putting an object loosely around another object, such as a loosely fitting ring on a pole. Action (e) is encoded by *nohta* 'put loosely down on a surface'; (f) by *ssuta* 'put clothing or related item on the head or face' (e.g., hat, glasses, mask; put up umbrella). Other common cloth-

---

[4]In Talmy's (1985, 1991) typological classification of the characteristic way in which languages express path meanings, Korean is a "verb-framed" language, that is, a language that expresses path primarily through verbs (Choi & Bowerman, 1991). In contrast, English and Dutch are "satellite-framed" languages—languages that express path primarily through particles, prefixes, and so forth. English does have some verbs that express path—for example, *enter, exit, ascend, descend, insert*, and *extract*—but these were borrowed from French, a verb-framed language, and belong to a somewhat higher register than everyday expressions such as *go in / out / up / down*, and *put in, take out / off*.

[5]For example, *fit* is too general because it is not sensitive to the criteria that the shapes be complementary before the action is carried out (cf. "Does this belt fit?") and that they fit in a three-dimensional sort of way ("This bandaid is too small, it won't fit over the wound."). *Interlock* or *mesh* come a bit closer, but these suggest the engagement of more than one projecting part from each object, so it seems absurd to use them for putting, for example, a book in a case or a cap on a pen.

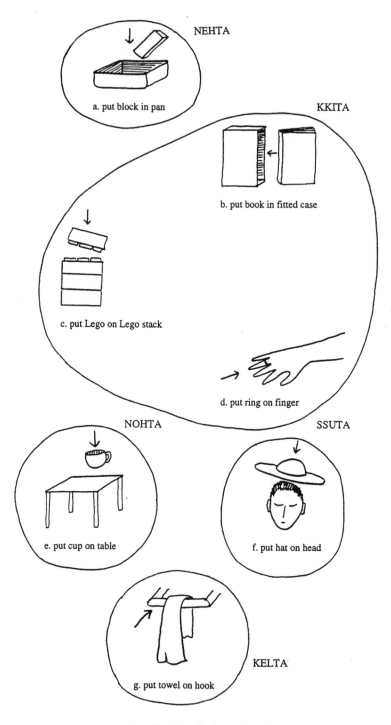

NEHTA

a. put block in pan

KKITA

b. put book in fitted case

c. put Lego on Lego stack

d. put ring on finger

NOHTA

e. put cup on table

SSUTA

f. put hat on head

KELTA

g. put towel on hook

FIG. 9.3.   Classification of some actions in Korean.

ing verbs include *ipta* 'put clothing on the trunk' and *sinta* 'put clothing on the feet'. Finally, (g) is specified by *kelta* 'attach with hook, peg, or the like' (e.g., hanging a Christmas tree ornament on a tree; hooking two train cars together).

As these examples suggest, spatial situations are characterized by a multitude of properties that can be used to distinguish them from or class them together with other situations. In learning to talk about space, children must learn to attend to different things to decide what spatial relationship is at stake. For the English and Dutch speaker, what is relevant for talking about putting a book into a fitted case is that the book comes to be contained, but for the Korean speaker, it is that the book and the case have snugly fitting complementary shapes. The Dutch speaker must assess the force dynamics of how a Figure stays in contact with an external surface of a Ground to select a preposition (cf. 'picture *aan* wall' but 'fly *op* wall'), whereas for the English speaker this is irrelevant—*on* works fine across a wide range of contact-and-support situations.[6]

Crosslinguistic variation in semantic categorization raises questions for the view that children's early uses of spatial morphemes are guided directly by their nonlinguistic conceptualizations of spatial situations. Which of all the various overlapping conceptualizations that could be applied to any given situation will children home in on spontaneously? Notice that reliance on containment and support—conceptualizations that seem so obvious to English speakers—would lead to rapid and correct generalization for children learning English, but to many errors for children learning, for example, Korean. But children do of course make errors. Recall Slobin's (1985) conclusion, based on crosslinguistic analyses of children's under- and overextensions of grammatical morphemes, that all children initially rely on the same set of meanings. According to this view, learners are at first insensitive to the way meanings are structured in the language they hear. It is their own meanings that they first try to express—sensitivity to language-specific categories develops only gradually. This is a testable hypothesis, so let us see whether it is correct for space.

---

[6]In still another scenario, children learning Tzeltal and Tzotzil, Mayan languages of Mexico, must learn to select among different verbs to specify the location of objects of different shapes and orientations (P. Brown, 1994; de León, in press). For instance, in Tzeltal, *pachal* 'to be located' is said of a bowl-shaped object in upright position (e.g., 'bowl *pachal* at table'; but also of things located *inside* such an object 'apple *pachal* at bowl'). *Waxal* works similarly, but for a narrow-mouthed container in upright position (e.g., bottle on table), or its contents (e.g., water in bottle). *Pakal* is said of an inverted object lying with its flat surface down, *wolol* of a small sphere, *k'olol* of a large sphere, *lechel* of a smallish flat thing, *chepel* of things sitting bulging in a bag, and so on.

LEARNING TO CATEGORIZE SPACE
FOR LANGUAGE

Together with colleagues, I have investigated the early development of spatial semantic categories in children learning English, Korean, Dutch, and Tzotzil Mayan. I first summarize results of an elicited production study in which the youngest subjects were 2 to 2½ years old, and then move to still earlier developmental stages—first to the emergence of spatial words in spontaneous speech and then to a comprehension study with children who often did not yet actually produce the critical words.

Joining and Separating Objects in Elicited Speech

Exploiting crosslinguistic differences of the sort just discussed, Soonja Choi and I examined how speakers of English, Korean, and Dutch describe actions that involve joining and separating objects (Bowerman, 1996a; Choi, 1997). In a play-like situation, we elicited descriptions of a wide range of actions from ten adults for each language, and ten children in each of three age groups from 2;0 (years; months) to 3;6. The actions included putting things into tight and loose containers (e.g., piece into puzzle, Legos into pan) and taking them out, putting objects down on surfaces, attaching and detaching things in various ways (e.g., Band-Aid, train cars joined with hooks or magnets, suction cup, rubber band, lid on pan, Legos, Pop-beads), opening and closing things (e.g., suitcase, box), hanging things up and taking them down (towel on hook), buttoning and unbuttoning, and donning and doffing various clothing items.

Speakers were tested individually. We encouraged them to talk about each action by presenting the relevant objects—for example, a ring poised over a pole—and almost but not quite performing the action to be described, pausing to say things like "What should I do? Tell me what to do." This technique worked well: even in the youngest age group, 87% of the responses were attempts to label the intended action.[7]

To explore and compare speakers' classification systems, we constructed for each speaker a similarity matrix that represents all the actions taken pairwise. If the speaker used the same expression for both members of a given pair (e.g., *[put] in* for putting both a piece into a puzzle and a Lego into a pan), the corresponding cell of the matrix was assigned a score of

---

[7]The responses of children learning English and Dutch typically consisted of a particle, sometimes accompanied—especially among the older children—by a verb, for example, *(put it) on!* The responses of the children learning Korean were usually verbs, for example, *kki-e* (stem of *kkita* 'interlock complementary shapes' - MODAL).

1; if he or she used different expressions (e.g., *kkita* for putting a piece into a puzzle and *nehta* for putting a Lego into a pan), the cell was assigned a 0.[8] Similarity matrices—which are more familiar from studies in which subjects are explicitly asked to sort items—can be used to assess the overall degree of similarity in the classification patterns of different respondents independent of the actual words they used, and the structure in the matrices can be further explored with techniques like multidimensional scaling and cluster analysis.[9]

Our most basic question was straightforward: do young children classify more like same-age children learning other languages or adult speakers of their own language? If children proceed by mapping their first spatial words to a small set of putatively universal nonlinguistic concepts like containment and support, as these become available through cognitive development, they should initially classify very similarly to each other, even though the actual words they use will of course differ, depending on the language being learned. But if early word use is based on learners' analyses of the spatial categories of the input language, they should classify more like adult speakers of their own language.

To assess overall degree of similarity among different groups of speakers, we treated each cell in the similarity matrix as a variable and correlated every individual with every other individual. A high correlation between two speakers indicates high agreement in which actions they treated as similar (i.e., described with the same words, regardless of what words these were) or as different (described with different words). With paired t tests, we then compared the average correlations among speakers of different groups.

The outcome was clear: even the children of the youngest age group grouped and distinguished the actions significantly more like adult speakers of their own language than like same-age children learning the other two languages. There was no evidence for a uniform starting set of spatial categories across children learning different languages. Some of the differences we found between the youngest speakers of English and Korean (2;0 to 2;5 years) are shown in Figs. 9.4 and 9.5. These figures indicate how the two sets of children classified a subset of the "joining" actions— those actions for which at least 4 of the 10 speakers of at least one of the languages used the same word (the actual number is indicated next to the action), and there was no other equally frequent response (for more detail, see Figures 3 and 4 in Bowerman, 1996a).

---

[8]In some analyses we graded similarity more finely; for example, the score assigned to *put in* versus *push in* would fall between 0 and 1, reflecting a partial but not complete correspondence in the speaker's responses.

[9]In analyzing these data, Choi and I were joined in our collaboration by Jim Boster.

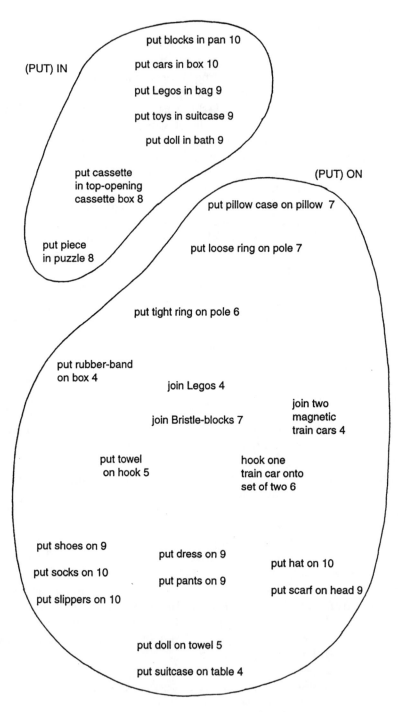

FIG. 9.4.   Classification of some joining actions by children age 2;0 to 2;5 learning English.

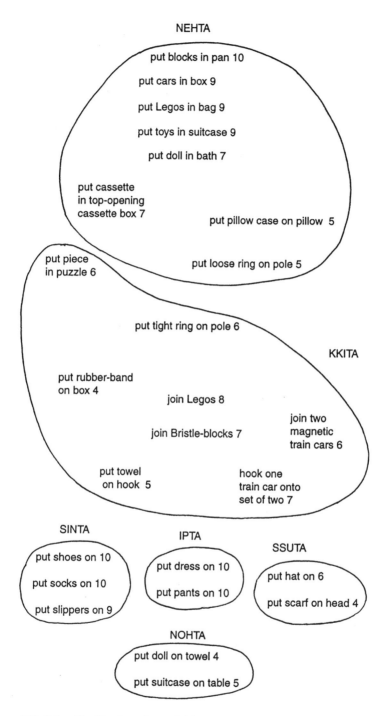

FIG. 9.5. Classification of some joining actions by children age 2;0 to 2;5 learning Korean.

Spatial Categories in Early Spontaneous Speech

The study just described shows that at least by 2;0 to 2;5 years, children learning different languages classify spatial situations differently for purposes of talking about them. There is no evidence, for example, that all children initially draw directly on concepts of containment or support. But although these children are young, they are beyond the very first phase of language acquisition. Perhaps we must look to still younger children to find evidence for a uniform way of classifying space. To explore earlier stages, Choi and I charted the emergence and early use of spatial words in longitudinal spontaneous speech samples collected from English- and Korean-speaking children between the ages of about 1 and 3 years (Choi & Bowerman, 1991).

In some ways both sets of children were very similar: they first began to use spatial words at about 14 to 16 months, and by 20 months or earlier they used these words productively, extending them to novel situations and sometimes making errors. The kinds of situations they talked about were also similar. But language-related differences, including those illustrated in Figs. 9.4 and 9.5, were strongly present from the beginning.

For example, the English-speaking toddlers distinguished systematically between containment and surface contact/support regardless of fit, saying *in* for putting, e.g., a book into a fitted case (snug) and a toy into a bag (loose) and *out* for the reverse of these actions; and *on* for snapping a rein back onto the side of a rocking-horse's mouth and joining Lego pieces (snug), for climbing on a stool and putting on clothing (both snug and loose), and *off* for the reverse of these actions. The Korean children, in contrast, ignored the containment-support distinction in favor of a "snug-loose" distinction. For snugly fitted relations, they said *kkita* 'interlock complementary shapes' and its opposite, *ppayta* 'separate interlocked shapes' (e.g., putting a peg doll into a perfectly fitting niche in a toy chair and taking it out; putting one Lego piece on another and taking it off). For loose relations they used a variety of words, including *nehta* 'put loosely in or around' and its opposite *kkenayta* 'take out / off . . .' (e.g., blocks into and out of a pan, a loose ring on and off a pole), *nohta* 'put down on surface,' and the clothing verbs *ssuta* 'put clothing on head,' *ipta* 'put clothing on trunk,' *sinta* 'put clothing on feet,' and *pesta* 'remove clothing item.'

The two sets of children also talked differently about vertical motion. In the speech of children learning English, the words *up* and *down* are among the first spatial words to appear—sometimes by as early as 12 to 14 months (e.g., Greenfield & Smith, 1976; Nelson, 1974) and typically by 16 to 17 months (L. Bloom, 1973; Gopnik, 1980). The words are at first often restricted to movements of the child's own body, although within that context they are used for many different kinds of movement, including posture changes like standing up and sitting or lying down, spontaneous motions like going up and down stairs and climbing on and off furniture or laps, and caused motions like being picked up and put down, being put into a high chair and taken down. Soon the words are also extended to movements of many other kinds of objects, including the spontaneous motions of other animate beings and caused motions like picking objects up off the floor, moving objects to a higher surface, moving them lower, or putting them down on the floor. Researchers have often interpreted the rapid extension of *up* and *down* as evidence for the operation of core concepts of vertical movement (Nelson, 1974; L. Bloom, 1973; McCune-Nicolich, 1981).

The English-speaking children in Choi's and my study also said *up* and *down* across a wide range of situations by 18 months or earlier, depending on the child and the word. Our Korean-speaking children, in contrast, used no uniform expressions for events involving motion *up* or *down*, and their various words for such events came in slowly over a long period of time. The earliest such words (17–20 months) included *anta* 'hold/carry in arms' and *epta* 'hold/carry on back' as requests to be picked up, and *ancta* 'assume a sitting posture' (up or down), *nwupta* 'lie down,' and *ileseta* 'stand up' for posture changes. Somewhat later (21–22 months), expressions like *ollita* 'cause to ascend' and *naylita* 'cause to descend' began to be applied to caused motions of putting an object (e.g., book, child) on a raised surface or taking it down. Becoming productive still later were the intransitive expressions *olla kata* 'ascend go' (= go up) and *naylye kata* 'descend go' (= go down), used for spontaneous vertical motions like climbing up on a couch, getting down from a step or a high chair, and going up and down stairs.[10]

A special case of vertical motion is falling. Like other learners of English, our English-speaking children said *fall* or *fall down* early and often for a broad range of uncontrolled motions downward, for example, when they themselves tripped and fell, when a toy toppled over, or when an object fell off a table or chair. Korean-speaking children, in contrast, distinguished, as Korean requires, between falls from a higher to a lower place (e.g., pencil falls from table, magnet falls from refrigerator: *ttelecita*) and falls onto the same surface (e.g., child falls on floor, tower is knocked over: *nemecita*).

Children learning Tzotzil, a Mayan language spoken in the Chiapas highlands of Mexico, encode still other spatial semantic categories in their

---

[10]As these examples illustrate, the English- and Korean-speaking children also differed in their treatment of caused versus spontaneous motion along a path. The English speakers used some path particles for both caused and spontaneous motion by 14 to 16 months and many by 20 months, for example, *down* both when pushing a cat's head downward and when climbing down from a doll's crib (17 months). The Korean speakers, in contrast, distinguished scrupulously between caused and spontaneous motion, using only transitive verbs for the former and—somewhat later to emerge—intransitive verbs for the later; for example, *naylita* 'cause to descend' for taking an object down from a counter and *naylye kata* 'descend go' for getting down from a counter. (See Choi & Bowerman, 1991, for discussion.)

early spontaneous speech (Bowerman, de León, & Choi, 1995; de León, 1999, in press). Like learners of Korean, these children initially express spatial meanings with verbs. One of their earliest productive spatial words—comparable in frequency and productivity to *in* in English and *kkita* 'interlock complementary shapes' in Korean—is *xoj*. In adult speech this verb specifies actions that cause an elongated object to end up encircled by a ring- or tube-shaped object (there is no comparable word in either English or Korean). Children use it appropriately to specify, for example, putting a ring *on* a pole or a pole *through* a ring, a coil of rope *over* a peg, and an arm, leg, or head *into* a sleeve, pant-leg, or opening in a shawl.

Tzotzil toddlers are also quick to master several different verbs that distinguish language-specific categories of position: *nuj* 'be located face down/upside down,' *kot* 'be located standing on all fours,' *pak* 'be located on the ground,' and *kaj* 'be located on a high surface.' They use no all-purpose words for vertical motion, but—like Korean children—distinguish between various posture changes, being picked up and carried on different body parts, and falling in different ways, for example, *p'aj* 'fall straight down from height,' *lom* 'topple over,' of a vertical figure like a tree or lamp post, *jach'* 'animate being in motion slips and falls on base (e.g., mud, ice)' (de León, in press).

Although the children approximated the semantic spatial categories of the input language remarkably well, they did make certain kinds of errors. For instance, the English speakers sometimes overextended *in* to 'between' situations like putting a ping-pong ball in the space between the knees and looking for coins between the cushions on a couch. The Korean children sometimes used *kkita* for snug fit events in which the joined objects did not have complementary shapes before the action was performed, as the verb requires, but only afterward (e.g., plunging a fork into an apple). Such errors are important because—along with correct use for novel referents—they show that children's good conformity to the semantic classes of the input language cannot be dismissed as due simply to learning what to say in specific situations, but rather is guided by productive principles of categorization (see Choi & Bowerman, 1991, for discussion of this issue). But the errors did not converge on a uniform set of spatial concepts such as containment or support. Rather, they pointed to learners' problems in identifying the boundary conditions of categories that, at least in broad outline, were already language specific.

Still Earlier Evidence for Language-Specific Categories?

The evidence just reviewed suggests that there is no period during which children's use of spatial words is guided directly by a universally shared set of spatial conceptualizations. Already from earliest productivity, spatial words are associated with language-specific categories of events. But when, then, does this sensitivity develop? Presumably it must already begin to emerge sometime during the period from about 9 months to 2 years of age, when children understand far more words than they can produce (Benedict, 1979; Goldin-Meadow, Seligman, & Gelman, 1976; Huttenlocher, 1974).

Most studies of very early comprehension have used rather minimal evidence to credit children with understanding a word; for example, children are asked to look at or pick up an object referred to by a noun (e.g., *doll*) or point to or perform an instance of an action specified by a verb (e.g., *dance*). With rare exceptions (e.g., Huttenlocher, Smiley, & Charney, 1983), researchers have not worried in detail about the structure of the category the child associates with the word. And crosslinguistic work on category structure in early comprehension is virtually nonexistent. To address this gap, Choi, McDonough, Bowerman, and Mandler (1999) designed a preferential looking study to compare young children's comprehension of the category structure of two overlapping language-specific categories: *(put) in* for learners of English and *kkita* 'interlock complementary shapes' for learners of Korean.

The basic preferential looking technique was pioneered for use in studies of language development by Golinkoff, Hirsh-Pasek, Cauley, and Gordon (1987) and further adapted by Naigles (1990).[11] The child sits on a parent's lap in front of two TV monitors, mounted side by side. The monitors show different scenes. These are first introduced one by one, while an audio from a loudspeaker between the monitors encourages the child in general terms to examine them. Then the two scenes are shown simultaneously, along with an audio input that "matches" (describes) only one of the scenes. If children understand the auditory input, they gaze longer overall at the matching scene.

Our crosslinguistic experiment was composed of four pairs of videotaped actions of putting objects somewhere.[12] For two of the pairs, the matching scene was the same in both languages: the Figure ended up both contained by and tightly fitted with the Ground (e.g., 'putting books into a tightly fitted case'), so the action qualified as an instance of both *put in* and *kkita* (in this pair the other scene was 'putting books on top of each other'). These two pairs were termed *conflated pairs*, because the properties of containment and

---

[11]We modeled our lab on that of Letty Naigles, whom we thank for her generous sharing of software and expertise.

[12]Each action was performed three times in succession. To avoid unnecessary distractions only the actor's hands and arms were shown, and within each pair of scenes care was taken to equate colors and the rhythm with which the actions were performed, and other factors that might influence the relative salience of the two scenes. For half the children the side on which the matching screen was shown was left, right, right, left across the four pairs, and for the other half it was right, left, left, right.

tight-fit/interlocking—critical for *in* and *kkita*, respectively—were combined in the same scene. In the two other pairs (*split pairs*), these two properties were split and assigned to different scenes, so the matching scene was different for the two languages. For example, one of the split pairs showed 'putting plastic rings into a basket' (containment, the match for English) versus 'putting rings on tapered plastic poles' (tight fit, the match for Korean). The target word intended to direct the child's attention was embedded in a carrier sentence such as "Where's she putting it *IN*?" for English or "Eti-ey *KKI-e*?" (roughly, "Where's (she) tight-fitting it?") for Korean.

Thirty children between 18 and 23 months were tested, 20 learning English and 10 learning Korean. Only 6 of the English learners and 2 of the Korean learners were producing the target word for their language, according to parental report, so the majority did not yet use the word. If the English-speaking children understood *in*, they should look longer at scenes showing putting an object into a container, regardless of whether the container fit tightly or loosely. And if the Korean-speaking children understood *kkita*, they should look longer at scenes showing putting an object into a tight-fitting relation, regardless of whether the fit involved containment or surface attachment. So on the conflated pairs the two groups should look at the same scene (e.g., 'putting books into fitted cases'), but for different reasons—the English-speaking group because it depicts containment and the Korean-speaking group because it depicts tight fit. Which property children were attending to on the conflated pairs is revealed by where they looked on the split pairs.

The predictions were borne out. Under the influence of the target word, the children from both groups looked significantly longer overall at the matching scenes for their language than at the nonmatching scenes.[13] Between 18 and 23 months, then, children learning English and Korean already assign language-specific semantic categories to their target words: English learners know that containment is relevant for *in* but degree of fit is not, whereas Korean learners know that fit is relevant for *kkita* but containment is not. When both properties are present in a situation at once, the target word directs the learners' attention to the property of the situation that is relevant to its semantic classification in the language being learned.

Recall that most of the children were not yet producing the target word for their language. Evidence for sensitivity to language-specific spatial cat-

---

[13]To control for the possibility that the children's gaze behavior was guided not by the target word they heard but by a nonlinguistic preference for one scene over the other, we compared whether the children's preference for the matching scene over the nonmatching scene was significantly greater on trials when they heard the target word (test trials) than when they did not (control trial). On the control trials the children showed no overall preference for either the matching or nonmatching scene, so we can conclude that their significant preference for the matching scenes on the test trials was indeed due to the presence of the target word.

egories in comprehension, before production begins, allows us to make sense of two observations that otherwise seem to conflict. On the one hand, children often generalize spatial words rapidly to a wide range of referents in their production—a finding that, as noted earlier, has been interpreted to mean that the words are being used to express meanings that originate in nonlinguistic cognition. On the other hand, children's spatial words pick out language-specific categories from the beginning of productive use, which suggests that the meanings are influenced by the input language. If children are able to get a sense of the contours of semantic categories in comprehension, before production begins, we need not be suprised by generalization in production that is both rapid and language specific.

DISCUSSION

Previous work had suggested that early spatial semantic development follows a universal course, with children mapping morphemes like *in, on, up,* and *down* to such presumably basic concepts of space as containment, support, and vertical motion as these become available through nonlinguistic cognitive development. The crosslinguistic studies reviewed here concur with these studies in some respects, but disagree critically in others.

It is true that terms like *containment, support,* and *vertical motion* capture kinds of spatial configurations and events that are highly salient to language learners—for instance, children talk about object placements involving containers and surfaces long before those involving relationships "in front of" or "behind." This initial focus on certain kinds of relations is presumably due to children's cognitive biases. But within these bounds, cognition appears to constrain children's early word meanings less than has often been supposed: the specific meanings learners associate with their early spatial words vary strikingly as a function of the input language. For instance, in the speech of young learners of English, *in* and *on* are indeed associated with a fundamental distinction between containment and surface contact/support. But the speech of toddlers learning Korean is insensitive to this distinction: what is critical in their spatial semantics is a crosscutting distinction between interlocking relations (*kkita*), loose containment-or-encircling relations (*nehta*), and various other kinds of surface-contact relations.

Early steps in acquiring the meanings of spatial words are, then, less uniform than has often been supposed. There is no reason, of course, to suppose that this is true only for space. There is significant crosslinguistic variation in the acquisition of other domains as well, including modality (Choi, 1991, 1996), temporality (Behrens, in press), and object reference (Imai & Gentner, 1997). Nonlinguistic cognitive development provides a critical foundation on which children can build to work out the meanings needed for the local language, but it does not strongly channel them to a universal starting set of meanings. Rather, early meanings vary in alignment with differences in the semantic structure of the adult languages being learned. The existence of this language-conditioned semantic variation means that semantic development can no longer be viewed as a process of simply mapping forms onto concepts that have arisen nonlinguistically and that the child now wants to express. The relationship between linguistic and cognitive development is more complex than this.

The mechanisms underlying this relationship are still far from clear. One possibility is that spatial words are mapped directly to nonlinguistic concepts, just as the Cognition Hypothesis posited, but that the toddler's repertoire comprises many more such concepts than has previously been envisioned (Mandler, 1992). And these concepts would overlap and crosscut each other in complex ways; for example, every child would develop concepts suitable for mapping to English *in* and *on*, to Korean *kkita* 'interlock complementary three-dimensional shapes' and *nehta* 'put loosely in or around,' and to Tzotzil Mayan *xoj* 'bring about a ring-around-pole-shaped configuration'—all words used appropriately at a very young age, often for similar referents. The language learner's task on encountering a new word—for example, *(put) in* or *kkita* in the context of play with nesting cups—would be to determine which of the candidate concepts is the one the word denotes. A wrong guess might be corrected later if the child sees that it does not adequately account for adult uses of the word.

There is some evidence for this scenario: in particular, learners sometimes seem to fleetingly associate a word or bound morpheme with a meaning that is wrong for the language being learned, but that is commonly used in other languages (Bowerman, 1980; Clark, 1976, in press). Such wrong hypotheses might be particularly likely when the language the child is learning categorizes the erred-on domain in a crosslinguistically unusual way. (The child might have a tendency first to try those concepts that, across languages, are more often relevant; Bowerman, 1985, 1993.) An experimental study comparing spatial prepositions in early English versus Dutch found support for this proposal (Bowerman, 1993; Bowerman & Gentner, in preparation; Gentner, 1996). The Dutch categorization of surface contact and support situations (described briefly on p. 208) is crosslinguistically rare, whereas the English classification is common (Bowerman & Pederson, 1992, in preparation; see Bowerman & Choi, in press, for a summary). Children learning Dutch indeed have more trouble with their system than those learning English, and their errors reflect a crosslinguistically more common classification pattern.

But do we do full justice to children's early semantic abilities if we assume that learners are capable *only* of sorting through preexisting concepts to find a plausible match to a word? Or might they also have a more creative skill: the ability to flexibly construct *new* semantic categories (i.e., meanings that do not correspond directly to any preexisting concepts) by observing how forms are distributed across contexts in fluent speech?[14]

There is indeed evidence for such an ability. Consider words that can be applied to actions of separating objects. Children often make errors with such words—recall, for instance (p. 207), overextensions of the verb *open*. Children's anomolous extension patterns in this domain have often been interpreted as direct reflections of nonlinguistic concepts (Bowerman, 1978; McCune & Vihman, 1997). But detailed crosslinguistic comparisons of these patterns show that category contours differ in ways that are closely related to statistical and other properties of the linguistic input, such as the frequency with which given words are used, the consistency of their range of application, the presence or absence of polysemy, and the number of words that populate a given corner of semantic space (see Bowerman, 1996a; Bowerman & Choi, in press, for examples and discussion).

Such findings suggest that even very young children can build categories on the basis of the way words are used in the input. Factors that are likely to influence this process are suggested by "usage-based" approaches to language that stress the dynamic properties of linguistic knowledge—for example, the effect of type vs. token frequency on the ability to induce and restructure schemas, and the role of competition among forms (Bybee, 1985, 1991; MacWhinney, 1987). Such an approach lends itself well to computational modeling of category induction (see Regier, 1997, for a computational model of some of the English vs. Dutch learning patterns documented for "separation" by Bowerman and Choi). And it also provides a way to understand how children could draw on form–meaning mappings they have already acquired to project language-appropriate meanings for new forms, and so get quickly into the typological semantic patterns of their language ("typological bootstrapping"—Slobin, in press; see Choi & Bowerman, 1991; Brown, in press; de León, in press, for specific proposals).

It is unlikely that all early words are learned in the same way—for some words a fairly direct mapping of a preexisting meaning may be sufficient, while others may require the construction and fine-tuning of a new concept under guidance of language (Gentner, 1982; Gentner & Boroditsky,

---

[14]To build categories they must draw of course on the perceptual and conceptual sensitivities provided by nonlinguistic cognition, but we can consider a category "new" either if these sensitivities have been combined in a new way or if the child's attention has been drawn to a way of grouping and distinguishing referents that was previously only implicit or potential. Whether such categories, once formed, are used only for producing and comprehending language— "thinking for speaking" (Slobin, 1996)—or have deeper consequences for thought goes beyond the scope of this chapter, but see Gopnik (in press), Levinson (in press), and Lucy and Gaskins (in press) for new perspectives on this perennially controversial Whorfian issue.

in press). A detailed picture of how children's cognitive sensitivies are applied to the discovery of semantic structure will require intensive further study. But it is clear that in sharpening and testing our hypotheses about this process, we have much to gain from comparisons of children learning different languages.

REFERENCES

Allan, K. (1979). Classifiers. *Language, 53*, 285–311.

Antell, S. E. G., & Caron, A. J. (1985). Neonatal perception of spatial relationships. *Infant Behavior and Development, 8*, 15–23.

Baillargeon, R. (1995). A model of physical reasoning in infancy. In C. Rovee-Collier & L. P. Lipsitt (Eds.), *Advances in infancy research* (Vol. 9, pp. 305–371). Norwood, NJ: Ablex.

Behl-Chadha, G., & Eimas, P. D. (1995). Infant categorization of left-right spatial relations. *British Journal of Developmental Psychology, 13*, 69–79.

Behrens, H. (in press). Cognitive-conceptual development and the acquisition of grammatical morphemes: The development of time concepts and verb tense. In M. Bowerman & S. C. Levinson (Eds.), *Language acquisition and conceptual development*. Cambridge, England: Cambridge University Press.

Benedict, H. (1979). Early lexical development: Comprehension and production. *Journal of Child Language, 7*, 183–200.

Berlin, B., & Kay, P. (1969). *Basic color terms*. Berkeley: University of California Press.

Bickerton, D. (1981). *Roots of language*. Ann Arbor, MI: Karoma Publishers.

Bloom, L. (1970). *Language development: Form and function in emerging grammars*. Cambridge, MA: MIT Press.

Bloom, L. (1973). *One word at a time: The use of single word utterances before syntax*. The Hague: Mouton.

Bloom, P. (in press). Roots of word learning. In M. Bowerman & S. C. Levinson (Eds.), *Language acquisition and conceptual development*. Cambridge, England: Cambridge University Press.

Blount, B. G. (1969). *Acquisition of language by Luo children*. Unpublished doctoral dissertation, University of California, Berkeley.

Bowerman, M. (1973). *Early syntactic development: A cross-linguistic study with special reference to Finnish*. Cambridge, England: Cambridge University Press.

Bowerman, M. (1976). Semantic factors in the acquisition of rules for word use and sentence construction. In D. Morehead & A. Morehead (Eds.), *Directions in normal and deficient child language* (pp. 99–179). Baltimore: University Park Press.

Bowerman, M. (1978). The acquisition of word meaning: An investigation into some current conflicts. In N. Waterson & C. Snow (Eds.), *The development of communication* (pp. 263–287). New York: Wiley.

Bowerman, M. (1980). The structure and origin of semantic categories in the language-learning child. In M. L. Foster & S. H. Brandes (Eds.), *Symbol as sense: New approaches to the analysis of meaning* (pp. 277–299). New York: Academic Press.

Bowerman, M. (1985). What shapes children's grammars? In D. I. Slobin (Ed.), *The crosslinguistic study of language acquisition: Vol. 2. Theoretical issues* (pp. 1257–1319). Hillsdale, NJ: Lawrence Erlbaum Associates.

Bowerman, M. (1989). Learning a semantic system: What role do cognitive dispositions play? In M. L. Rice & R. L. Schiefelbusch (Eds.), *The teachability of language* (pp. 133–168). Baltimore: Paul H. Brookes.

Bowerman, M. (1993). Typological perspectives on language acquisition: Do crosslinguistic patterns predict development? In E. V. Clark (Ed.), *The proceedings of the twenty-fifth annual Child Language Research Forum* (pp. 7–15). Stanford, CA: Center for the Study of Language and Information.

Bowerman, M. (1994). From universal to language-specific in early grammatical development. *Philosophical Transactions of the Royal Society of London B, 346,* 37–45.

Bowerman, M. (1996a). Learning how to structure space for language: A crosslinguistic perspective. In P. Bloom, M. Peterson, L. Nadel, & M. Garrett (Eds.), *Language and space* (pp. 385–436). Cambridge, MA: MIT Press.

Bowerman, M. (1996b). The origins of children's spatial semantic categories: Cognitive vs. linguistic determinants. In J. J. Gumperz & S. C. Levinson (Eds.), *Rethinking linguistic relativity* (pp. 145–176). Cambridge, England: Cambridge University Press.

Bowerman, M., & Choi, S. (in press). Shaping meanings for language: Universal and language specific in the acquisition of spatial semantic categories. In M. Bowerman & S. C. Levinson (Eds.), *Language acquisition and conceptual development.* Cambridge, England: Cambridge University Press.

Bowerman, M., & Gentner, D. (in preparation). *Are some ways to partition space more natural than others? Learning to categorize 'in' and 'on' relations in Dutch and English.*

Bowerman, M., de León, L., & Choi, S. (1995). Verbs, particles, and spatial semantics: Learning to talk about spatial actions in typologically different languages. In E. V. Clark (Ed.), *Proceedings of the twenty-seventh Annual Child Language Research Forum* (pp. 101–110). Stanford, CA: Center for the Study of Language and Information.

Bowerman, M., & Pederson, E. (1992, December). *Cross-linguistic perspectives on topological spatial relationships.* Paper presented at the annual meeting of the American Anthropological Association, San Francisco.

Bowerman, M., & Pederson, E. (in preparation). *Cross-linguistic perspectives on topological spatial relationships.*

Braine, M. D. S. (1976). First word combinations. *Monographs of the Society for Research in Child Development, 41*(1, Serial No. 164).

Brown, P. (1994). The INs and ONs of Tzeltal locative expressions: The semantics of static descriptions of location. *Linguistics, 32,* 743–90.

Brown, P. (in press). Learning to talk about motion UP and DOWN in Tzeltal: Is there a language-specific bias for verb learning? In M. Bowerman & S. C. Levinson (Eds.), *Language acquisition and conceptual development.* Cambridge, England: Cambridge University Press.

Brown, R. (1973). *A first language: The early stages.* Cambridge, MA: Harvard University Press.

Brugman, C. (1983). *Metaphor in the elaboration of grammatical categories in Mixtec.* Unpublished manuscript, University of California, Berkeley.

Bybee, J. L. (1985). *Morphology: A study of the relation between meaning and form.* Amsterdam: John Benjamins.

Bybee, J. L. (1991). Natural morphology: The organization of paradigms and language acquisition. In T. Huebner & C. A. Ferguson (Eds.), *Crosscurrents in second language and linguistic theories* (pp. 67–91). Amsterdam: John Benjamins.

Choi, S. (1991). Early acquisition of epistemic meanings in Korean: A study of sentence-ending suffixes in the spontaneous speech of three children. *First Language, 11,* 93–119.

Choi, S. (1996, July). *Development of modality in Korean and a crosslinguistic comparison with Turkish.* Paper presented at the Seventh International Congress for the Study of Child Language, Istanbul.

Choi, S. (1997). Language-specific input and early semantic development: Evidence from children learning Korean. In D. I. Slobin (Ed.), *The crosslinguistic study of language acquisition: Vol. 5. Expanding the contexts* (pp. 41–133). Mahwah, NJ: Lawrence Erlbaum Associates.

Choi, S., & Bowerman, M. (1991). Learning to express motion events in English and Korean: The influence of language-specific lexicalization patterns. *Cognition, 41,* 83–121.

Choi, S., McDonough, L., Bowerman, M., & Mandler, J. (1999). Early sensitivity to language-specific spatial categories in English and Korean. *Cognitive Development, 14*, 241–268.

Chomsky, N. (1959). [Review of the book *Verbal Behavior* by B. F. Skinner]. *Language, 35*, 26–58.

Chomsky, N. (1965). *Aspects of the theory of syntax*. Cambridge, MA: MIT Press.

Clark, E. V. (1976). Universal categories: On the semantics of classifiers and children's early word meanings. In A. Juilland (Ed.), *Linguistic studies offered to Joseph Greenberg on the occasion of his sixtieth birthday: Vol. 3. Syntax* (pp. 449–462). Saratoga, CA: Anna Libri.

Clark, E. V. (1993). *The lexicon in acquisition*. Cambridge, England: Cambridge University Press.

Clark, E. V. (in press). Emergent categories in first language acquisition. In M. Bowerman & S. C. Levinson (Eds.), *Language acquisition and conceptual development*. Cambridge, England: Cambridge University Press.

Clark, H. H. (1973). Space, time, semantics, and the child. In T. E. Moore (Ed.), *Cognitive development and the acquisition of language* (pp. 27–63). New York: Academic Press.

Cromer, R. F. (1974). The development of language and cognition: The cognition hypothesis. In B. Foss (Ed.), *New perspectives in child development* (pp. 184–252). Harmondsworth, Middlesex, England: Penguin.

de León, L. (1999). Verbs in Tzotzil early syntactic development. *International Journal of Bilingualism, 3*, 219–240.

de León, L. (in press). Finding the richest path: Language and cognition in the acquisition of verticality in Tzotzil (Mayan). In M. Bowerman & S. C. Levinson (Eds.), *Language acquisition and conceptual development*. Cambridge, England: Cambridge University Press.

Gentner, D. (1982). Why nouns are learned before verbs: Linguistic relativity versus natural partitioning. In S. A. Kuczaj II (Ed.), *Language development: Vol. 2. Language, thought, and culture* (pp. 301–334). Hillsdale, NJ: Lawrence Erlbaum Associates.

Gentner, D. (1996, July). *Crosslinguistic differences in the lexicalization of spatial relations, and effects on acquisition*. Paper presented at the Seventh International Congress for the Study of Child Language, Istanbul.

Gentner, D., & Boroditsky, L. (in press). Individuation, relativity, and early word learning. In M. Bowerman & S. C. Levinson (Eds.), *Language acquisition and conceptual development*. Cambridge, England: Cambridge University Press.

Gleitman, L. (1990). The structural sources of verb meanings. *Language Acquisition, 1*, 3–55.

Goldin-Meadow, S., Seligman, M. E. P., & Gelman, R. (1976). Language in the two-year-old. *Cognition, 4*, 189–202.

Golinkoff, R. M., Hirsh-Pasek, K., Cauley, K. M., & Gordon, L. (1987). The eyes have it: Lexical and syntactic comprehension in a new paradigm. *Journal of Child Language, 14*, 23–45.

Gopnik, A. (1980). *The development of non-nominal expressions in 12-24 month old children*. Unpublished doctoral dissertation, Oxford University.

Gopnik, A. (in press). Theories, language, and culture: Whorf without wincing. In M. Bowerman & S. C. Levinson (Eds.), *Language acquisition and conceptual development*. Cambridge, England: Cambridge University Press.

Greenfield, P., & Smith, J. (1976). *The structure of communication in early language development*. New York: Academic Press.

Griffiths, P., & Atkinson, M. (1978). A 'door' to verbs. In N. Waterson & C. Snow (Eds.), *The development of communication* (pp. 311–319). New York: Wiley.

Grimshaw, J. (1981). Form, function, and the language acquisition device. In C. L. Baker & J. J. McCarthy (Eds.), *The logical problem of language acquisition* (pp. 165–182). Cambridge, MA: MIT Press.

Huttenlocher, J. (1974). The origins of language comprehension. In R. L. Solso (Ed.), *Theories in cognitive psychology: The Loyola symposium* (pp. 331–368). Potomac, MD: Lawrence Erlbaum Associates.

Huttenlocher, J., Smiley, P., & Charney, R. (1983). Emergence of action categories in the child: Evidence from verb meanings. *Psychological Review, 90,* 72–93.
Imai, M., & Gentner, D. (1997). A crosslinguistic study of early word meaning: Universal ontology and linguistic influence. *Cognition, 62,* 169–200.
Jackendoff, R. (1976). Toward an explanatory semantic representation. *Linguistic Inquiry, 7,* 89–150.
Johnston, J. R. (1985). Cognitive prerequisites: The evidence from children learning English. In D. I. Slobin (Ed.), *The crosslinguistic study of language acquisition: Vol. 2. Theoretical issues* (pp. 961–1004). Hillsdale, NJ: Lawrence Erlbaum Associates.
Johnston, J. R., & Slobin, D. I. (1979). The development of locative expressions in English, Italian, Serbo-Croatian and Turkish. *Journal of Child Language, 6,* 529–545.
Kernan, K. T. (1969). *The acquisition of language by Samoan children.* Unpublished doctoral dissertation, University of California, Berkeley.
Levinson, S. C. (in press). Covariation between spatial language and cognition, and its implications for language learning. In M. Bowerman & S. C. Levinson (Eds.), *Language acquisition and conceptual development.* Cambridge, England: Cambridge University Press.
Lucy, J. A., & Gaskins, S. (in press). Grammatical categories and the development of classification preferences: A comparative approach. In M. Bowerman & S. C. Levinson (Eds.), *Language acquisition and conceptual development.* Cambridge, England: Cambridge University Press.
MacWhinney, B. (1987). The competition model. In B. MacWhinney (Ed.), *Mechanisms of language acquisition* (pp. 249–308). Hillsdale, NJ: Lawrence Erlbaum Associates.
Mandler, J. (1992). How to build a baby: II. Conceptual primitives. *Psychological Review, 99,* 587–604.
Margetts, A. (1998, June). *'Give' verbs in Saliba.* Paper presented at the Workshop on Crosslinguistic Perspectives on Argument Structure: Implications for Learnability, Nijmegen, The Netherlands.
Markman, E. (1990). Constraints children place on word meanings. *Cognitive Science, 14,* 55–77.
McCune, L., & Vihman, M. (1997). *The transition to reference in infancy.* ms.
McCune-Nicolich, L. (1981). The cognitive bases of relational words in the single-word period. *Journal of Child Language, 8,* 15–34.
Naigles, L. (1990). Children use syntax to learn verb meanings. *Journal of Child Language, 17,* 357–374.
Needham, A., & Baillargeon, R. (1993). Intuitions about support in 4.5-month-old infants. *Cognition, 47,* 121–148.
Nelson, K. (1974). Concept, word, and sentence: Interrelations in acquisition and development. *Psychological Review, 81,* 267–285.
Newman, J. (Ed.). (1998). *The linguistics of giving.* Amsterdam: John Benjamins.
Piaget, J. (1954). *The construction of reality in the child.* New York: Basic Books.
Piaget, J., & Inhelder, B. (1956). *The child's conception of space.* London: Routledge & Kegan Paul.
Pinker, S. (1984). *Language learnability and language development.* Cambridge, MA: Harvard University Press.
Pinker, S. (1989). *Learnability and cognition: The acquisition of argument structure.* Cambridge, MA: MIT Press.
Pye, C. (1996). K'iche' Maya verbs of breaking and cutting. *Kansas Working Papers in Linguistics, 21,* 87–98.
Quine, W. V. (1960). *Word and object.* Cambridge, MA: MIT Press.
Quinn, P. C. (1994). The categorization of above and below spatial relations by young infants. *Child Development, 65,* 58–69.
Regier, T. (1997). Constraints on the learning of spatial terms: A computational investigation. In R. L. Goldstone, P. G. Schyns, & D. L. Medin (Eds.), *Psychology of learning and motivation* (Vol. 36, pp. 171–217). San Diego, CA: Academic Press.

Schlesinger, I. M. (1971). Production of utterances and language acquisition. In D. I. Slobin
(Ed.), *The ontogenesis of grammar* (pp. 63–101). New York: Academic Press.
Schlesinger, I. M. (1977). The role of cognitive development and linguistic input in language
acquisition. *Journal of Child Language, 4,* 153–169.
Sinha, C., Thorseng, L. A., Hayashi, M., & Plunkett, K. (1994). Comparative spatial seman-
tics and language acquisition: Evidence from Danish, English, and Japanese. *Journal of
Semantics, 11,* 253–287.
Sitskoorn, M. M., & Smitsman, A. W. (1995). Infants' perception of dynamic relations
between objects: Passing through or support? *Developmental Psychology, 31,* 437–447.
Slobin, D. I. (1966). The acquisition of Russian as a native language. In F. Smith & G. A.
Miller (Eds.), *The genesis of language: A psycholinguistic approach* (pp. 129–148). Cambridge,
MA: MIT Press.
Slobin, D. I. (1970). Universals of grammatical development in children. In G. B. Flores
D'Arcais & W. J. M. Levelt (Eds.), *Advances in psycholinguistics* (pp. 174–186). Amsterdam:
North-Holland.
Slobin, D. I. (1973). Cognitive prerequisites for the development of grammar. In C. A. Fer-
guson & D. I. Slobin (Eds.), *Studies of child language development* (pp. 175–208). New York:
Holt, Rinehart & Winston.
Slobin, D. I. (1985). Crosslinguistic evidence for the Language-Making Capacity. In D. I.
Slobin (Ed.), *The crosslinguistic study of language acquisition: Vol. 2. Theoretical issues* (pp.
1157–1256). Hillsdale, NJ: Lawrence Erlbaum Associates.
Slobin, D. I. (1996). Learning to think for speaking: Native language, cognition, and rhetor-
ical style. In J. J. Gumperz & S. C. Levinson (Eds.), *Rethinking linguistic relativity* (pp.
70–86). Cambridge, England: Cambridge University Press.
Slobin, D. I. (in press). Form/function relations: How do children find out what they are? In
M. Bowerman & S. C. Levinson (Eds.), *Language acquisition and conceptual development.*
Cambridge, England: Cambridge University Press.
Smiley, P., & Huttenlocher, J. (1995). Conceptual development and the child's early words
for events, objects, and persons. In M. Tomasello & W. Merriman (Eds.), *Beyond names for
things: Young children's acquisition of verbs* (pp. 21–61). Hillsdale, NJ: Lawrence Erlbaum
Associates.
Spelke, E. S., Breinlinger, K., Macomber, J., & Jacobson, K. (1992). Origins of knowledge.
Psychological Review, 99, 605–632.
Talmy, L. (1976). Semantic causative types. In M. Shibatani (Ed.), *Syntax and semantics: Vol. 6.
The grammar of causative constructions* (pp. 43–116). New York: Academic Press.
Talmy, L. (1982). Borrowing semantic space: Yiddish verb prefixes between Germanic and
Slavic. *Berkeley Linguistics Society, 8,* 231–250.
Talmy, L. (1983). How language structures space. In H. Pick & L. Acredolo (Eds.), *Spatial ori-
entation: Theory, research, and application* (pp. 225–282). New York: Plenum.
Talmy, L. (1985). Lexicalization patterns: Semantic structure in lexical form. In T. Shopen
(Ed.), *Language typology and syntactic description: Vol. 3. Grammatical categories and the lexicon*
(pp. 57–149). Cambridge, England: Cambridge University Press.
Talmy, L. (1991). Path to realization: A typology of event conflation. *Berkeley Linguistics Soci-
ety, 17,* 480–519.
Tomasello, M. (1995). Pragmatic contexts for early verb learning. In M. Tomasello & W. Mer-
riman (Eds.), *Beyond names for things: Young children's acquisition of verbs* (pp. 115–146).
Hillsdale, NJ: Lawrence Erlbaum Associates.
Whorf, B. L. (1956). *Language, thought, and reality* (J. B. Carroll, Ed.). Cambridge, MA: MIT
Press.
Wilkins, D. P., & Hill, D. (1995). When GO means COME: Questioning the basicness of basic
motion verbs. *Cognitive Linguistics, 6,* 209–259.

Chapter 10

Culture and Universals: Integrating Social and Cognitive Development

Patricia M. Greenfield
University of California, Los Angeles

In this chapter, I use a small-scale, homogenous society to introduce a large theory of development. After introducing the theory, I then proceed to show the broad applicability of the theory by applying it to our own large-scale, heterogeneous society. The theory links culture and biological maturation to explain development. Although encompassing a critique of the great developmental theories of Piaget and Vygotsky, it is not intended to replace them. Instead, it provides a broader framework for selected components of their theories.

PIAGET, VYGOTSKY, DEVELOPMENT, AND CULTURE

Reinterpreting Piaget: Age-Dependent Sensitive Periods for Cultural Learning

Beginning in the 1960s, cultural and cross-cultural developmentalists severely criticized Piaget for taking culture-specific sequences as universal (e.g., Greenfield, 1966; Cole & Scribner, 1974). By considering Piagetian theory from a cross-cultural perspective, I aim in this chapter to restore balance concerning Piaget's theoretical role in cultural psychology. I introduce the central idea that Piagetian stage theory has an important universal element as a theory of *innate potentials* and *age-dependent sensitive periods* for *cultural learning*.

The notion of age-dependent sensitive periods does lead to two important points of difference with Piaget and Inhelder (1969). The first is that, whereas they emphasize minimal ages for certain developments, the notion of age-dependent sensitive periods also implies constraints on the upper age for actualizing these same cognitive capacities. The really important difference, however, has to do with the issue of specificity/generality of stages. The sensitive period idea is that the original capacity for a particular kind of development can be general, but that the way in which it is actualized through cultural learning makes it more specific. The analogy is to language: human beings start out with a general capacity for language, but they learn specific ones. After they have learned a particular language, they, to some extent, lose their capacity to learn different ones. I make the case for this principle by using the example of concrete operations. The principle contrasts in a fundamental way with the Piagetian notion of domain-general stages.

By analogy with language, the sensitive period model of development leads to the hypothesis that, after culture-specific actualizations of a cognitive stage take place through experience during the optimal maturational window, other alternative actualizations become more difficult to acquire, even by the same experience later in development. This theoretical formulation leads to a definition of stages that is less general than Piaget and Inhelder posited. In my view, the sphere of application for a given stage becomes limited by the particular experiences that have actualized the maturational potential of that stage.

On the other hand, the concepts of innate potentials and age-dependent sensitive periods also have much in common with the view of Piaget and Inhelder (1969) on the role of maturation in development: "Where we do have some data, we see that maturation consists essentially of opening up new possibilities and thus constitutes a necessary but not in itself a sufficient condition for the appearance of certain behavior patterns" (p. 154). These maturationally given possibilities provide the potential for particular sorts of active construction to take place. In other words, the concept of age-dependent sensitive periods is in no way a statement of maturational reductionism. I would also agree with Piaget and Inhelder's important point that "Organic maturation is undoubtedly a necessary factor and plays an indispensable role in the unvarying order of succession of the order of the stages of the child's development" (Piaget & Inhelder, pp. 154–155).

Piaget and Inhelder (1969; Piaget, 1972) noted that acquisitions become more variable in their time of acquisition the further they are removed from their sensorimotor origins. I agree with this but would also go two steps further: (a) acquisitions become more variable (and therefore more culture specific) not only in their timing but also in their form the further they are removed from their sensorimotor origins; and (b) as the forms of stage behavior become more variable and culture specific in the course of movement from sensorimotor to concrete operational to formal operations, so too do the forms of experience that are required to actualize each stage.

The notion of stages as sensitive periods for cultural learning does entail a major modificaton of the theory: no longer is the presence of a stage measured by its cross-domain applicability; stages are now by definition domain specific. Extrapolating from Piaget (1972), I believe that the culture and experience specificity of formal operations is greater than for the other stages. However, I would also assert that the principle of specificity still applies to concrete and even sensorimotor operations, although in progressively lesser degrees. My examples later in this chapter relate to the transition from pre-operational to concrete operational thought.

The Content of Cultural Learning: The Western Scientist as a Culture-Specific Developmental Outcome

The Piagetian concept of maturation contributes to a biologically grounded universal stage theory. However, because of the role of cultural learning in actualizing universal stages, Piagetian theory is also an *ethnotheory*, or a formalization of Western ethnotheories of development, that is, a folk theory of development. In using the term *ethnotheory*, I am asserting that scientists and lay people alike have some common cultural assumptions that enter implicitly and without awareness into the very foundation of both scientific and lay theories of development.

In the 1970s, I introduced the idea of Piagetian theory as a theory of the development of the Western scientist rather than of the universal individual (Greenfield, 1974/1976). I have since realized that Piaget himself asserted that understanding the basis for Western scientific thought was his most fundamental concern (Piaget, 1977). One can infer from this statement that Piaget saw his theory and research on child cognitive development as a way of understanding the developmental pathway to mature scientific thought. Alternative endpoints could have been selected. The ethnotheoretic aspect of Piagetian theory occurs in that aspect of the human condition Piaget selected as the endpoint of development (Greenfield, 1974/1976), not in the sequence of stages leading to that endpoint.

Piagetian theory, like the Western scientist, emphasizes the development of knowledge of the physical world apart from social goals. This corresponds to an ethnotheory of development in which cognitive knowledge is valued for its own sake, apart from the social uses to which it is put. This ethnotheory is typical of European-derived cultures (Mundy-Castle, 1974).

Needed: A Developmental Theory That Can Include
Cultures That Subordinate the Cognitive to the Social

Other cultures, however, have a different ethnotheory concerning the relationship between the cognitive and the social. They treat cognitive and
social development as tightly integrated, with cognitive development subordinate to social development (Wober, 1974; Dasen, 1984). Such cultures
see cognition not as a value in itself, but as a means to social ends. This is a
view that is not encompassed in Piagetian theory. Even in Piaget's treatment
of social cognition (notably, the work on moral judgment, Piaget, 1965b),
the social is very much subordinated to the cognitive. The point here again
concerns what is selected as the endpoint of development.

My assertion is that there are cultural differences in what constitutes the
ideal, mature human being and that the nature of the ideal in Western
European culture involves a scientific rationality that is superordinate to
or independent of social relationships and social feelings. Because this
ideal endpoint is taken for granted as the only possibility, it then automatically becomes what needs to be accounted for in a developmental theory that is created within this type of culture.

But what about Vygotsky? This is a subject to which I now turn. Vygotsky (1962, 1978) does, of course, have a sociocultural theory; it is the basis
for the sociocultural component of the framework I am going to present.
In Vygotsky's theory, the most important means to development is social
interaction. For Piaget, the most important means is the child's experi-
mentation with the physical world. Undoubtedly, one could link this difference in emphasis between Piaget and Vygotsky to cultural differences of
the time. It does not seem coincidental that a greater emphasis on child
development as a function of the sociocultural environment of the child
arose in a communist country. This difference in learning mechanisms will
be taken up in a moment.

However, for present purposes, I emphasize the commonalities
between Piaget and Vygotsky that stem from the fact that both were
steeped in the epistemology and culture of Western Europe. Both Vygotsky and Piaget have selected the same endpoint of development to
explain and, not coincidentally, it is a cognitive one. In other words, even
for Vygotsky, social interaction functions as a means to cognitive development. Development itself is defined cognitively, in terms of language and
conceptual thought.

What is needed in our field is a formal theory of development that is
broad enough to be fair to cultures in which the ethnotheory of development treats cognitive development as a means to social development,
rather than vice versa. A first step would be to develop a theory of development for this alternative ideal endpoint: the person who has used his

or her cognitive capacities to become wise in social relations and to achieve social goals. However, if we were to take that route, we would simply have a second ethnotheory of development in a different sort of culture from our own. What is really needed is a theory that includes mechanisms for the differentiation of these two major developmental pathways. This is critical to the development of a truly universal theory, not merely one that claims universality on the basis of unwitting culture-specific assumptions.

Mechanisms of Cultural Learning: Vygotsky and Piaget

Both Vygotsky and Piaget present models of learning as well as of development. Vygotsky (1978) has an explicit model of socially guided learning. Piaget has an implicit model of discovery learning (Piaget, 1965a/ 1977). I hope to show that, as theories of environmental learning, both the implicit theory of Piaget and the explicit theory of Vygotsky are more tied to specific sociohistorical circumstances than either theorist realized. I demonstrate that each model of learning describes adaptive responses to particular ecological circumstances. The notion is that both types of learning process are part of the universal armoire of developmental processes, but that each is selectively emphasized as a means of transmitting knowledge under different sociohistorical circumstances. Sociohistorical circumstances are seen, in turn, as having a strong economic foundation. The model that is dominant at a particular place or time does have implications for the learning processes of the individual learner, as I hope to demonstrate. Where guided learning is dominant, my hypothesis is that the learner comes to rely more on guidance as a means to acquire new knowledge and will tend to excel at learning and applying culturally normative modes of thought, action, and feeling. Where discovery learning is dominant, my hypothesis is that the learner becomes practiced at discovering new knowledge and will tend to develop individual creativity.

A THEORETICAL FRAMEWORK
FOR DEVELOPMENT

My goal in this chapter is to present an outline of a theory of development that:

1. Captures the relationship between biological maturation and culture-specific learning.
2. Provides insight into the relationship between social and cognitive development by exploring its cross-cultural variability.

3. Shows how mechanisms of learning and apprenticeship (and not merely the content of what is learned) are adaptations to particular sociohistorical circumstances and therefore vary over time and place.
4. Explains real-world phenomena.

Components of the Theory

The theoretical framework has the following four principal components:

- *Maturational component* : Age-dependent sensitive periods for cultural learning (Fairbanks, 2000; Fischer, 1987; Newport, 1988). Part (although not all) of this component is encompassed by Piagetian stages.
- *Sociocultural component:* The maturational component is actualized through communicative and linguistic interaction with other members of the sociocultural milieu (e.g., Heath, 1983; Ochs & Schieffelin, 1984) often mediated by activities and cultural practices (e.g., Scribner & Cole, 1981; Saxe, 1991; Rogoff, Baker-Sennett, Lacasa, & Goldsmith, 1995); tools (both concrete and symbolic; e.g., Bruner, 1964; Bruner & Olson, 1973; Greenfield, 1993); and values (e.g., Rabain, 1979; Shweder & Bourne, 1982; Greenfield, 1994).
- *Ecological component*: The sociocultural component is adapted to an ecological niche (e.g., Weisner, 1984; Whiting & Whiting, 1975; LeVine, 1977; Super & Harkness, 1997).
- *Historical component* (Scribner, 1985; Vygotsky & Luria, 1993): The ecological niche changes over time (Greenfield, 1999a, 1999b).

Each component has been studied individually and has a long history in the field, as the sample citations indicate. The news, both theoretical and empirical, lies in the specification of their interactions. These interactions are specified in the very definitions of the components, each of which directly interacts with the next one down in the hierarchy:

1. Culture is integrated with maturation: What matures are abilities to acquire different elements of culture through the sociocultural component of the model.
2. The sociocultural component is adapted to the ecological conditions.
3. Ecology changes over time.

An interdisciplinary approach, drawing on methods and concepts from psychology, anthropology, and sociology, is required to test the model.

APPLICATION IN A SMALL-SCALE, HOMOGENOUS
SOCIETY: ZINACANTAN, CHIAPAS, MEXICO

Because the contextual components of the theory are so complex, the model can most easily be explored in a relatively small, relatively self-contained community over an extended period of ecological change. With my colleagues Carla Childs, Ashley Maynard, and Leslie Devereaux, I have been studying socialization in just such a community: Nabenchauk, a Zinacantec Maya village in Chiapas, Mexico. Our period of study goes from 1969 to 1995.

Interaction of the Maturational and Sociocultural Components

The focus here is on the interaction of universal age-dependent sensitive periods with cultural practices. The activity domain selected for this analysis is weaving, the most complex technology in traditional Zinacantec life. (See Fig. 10.1 for a statue of the ancient Maya backstrap loom, still used in Nabenchauk in 1997.) I begin with a physical component of weaving in order to provide a very concrete illustration of the interaction between maturational sensitivity and cultural experience. I then use Piagetian stage concepts to move to a cognitive example, where the analysis is more abstract and inferential.

The physical example has to do with the uses of the body in learning to weave (Maynard, Greenfield, & Childs, 1999). Note in Figs. 10.2 and 10.5 that, while a post forms one side of the loom frame, the weaver's body in a kneeling position forms the other end. My focus is on the physical skill of kneeling.

Kneeling is a universal biologically given capacity all human beings are born with. However, it can be maintained only by experience. This is demonstrated by Molleson's (1996) research in physical anthropology. By relating differential bone development in male and female skeletons to known gender differences in work activity at the same archeological site, Molleson shows that culturally defined experience in kneeling for many hours from a young age shapes bone development (e.g., flattens the two first metatarsal bones of both feet), so that the capacity to kneel for long periods of time is maintained into adulthood.

Zinacantec cultural practices provide just such experience for girls. Girls grow up watching their mothers and other older females sitting in a kneeling position with their legs under them during weaving and many other daily activities, such as making tortillas (Fig. 10.3) and changing a baby (Fig. 10.4). Cultural values come into play too; weaving, preparing tortillas, and child care are all highly valued activities that define women's work. Girls learn to maintain the kneeling position through cultural activities. Start-

FIG. 10.1. Pottery figure of ancient Maya backstrap loom, Jaina, Campeche, A.D. 700–900. Photo courtesy of the Instituto Nacional de Antropologia e Historia.

ing at a young age, they kneel for many hours in a variety of situations and tasks, including play weaving at a toy loom, a traditional activity shown in Fig. 10.5, and newer activities such as creating designs for embroidered blouses, shown in Fig. 10.6.

The experience of my collaborator Ashley Maynard confirmed Molleson's conclusion that, without kneeling experience, the capacity

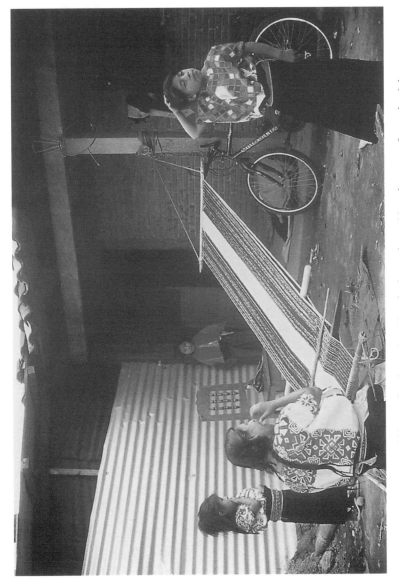

FIG. 10.2.   Girl seated at the ancient Maya backstrap loom. Note that a post forms the right side of the loom frame while the weaver's body in a kneeling position forms the left end. Nabenchauk, 1995. Photo courtesy of Ashley Maynard.

FIG. 10.3.   Adult women kneeling to prepare tortillas. Nabenchauk, 1991. Photo courtesy of Lauren Greenfield.

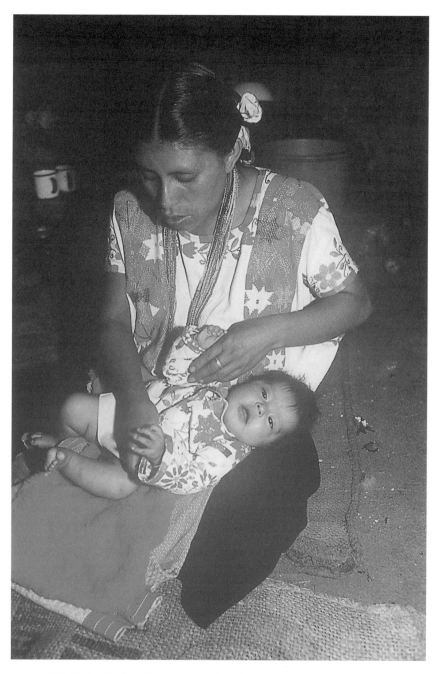

FIG. 10.4.   Mother (Maruch Perez) kneeling to change her baby. Nabenchauk, 1991. Photo courtesy of Lauren Greenfield.

241

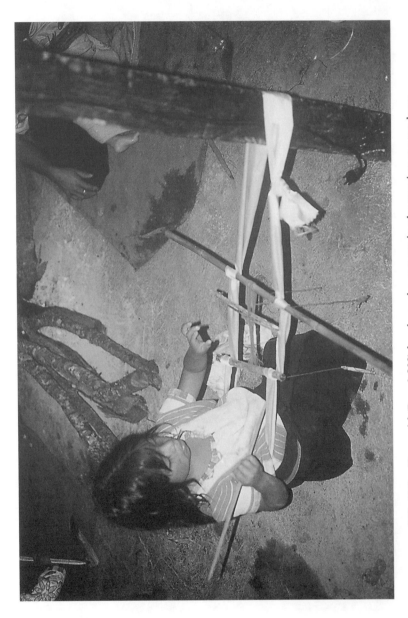

FIG. 10.5. Young girl (Rosy 1-209) kneels, as she engages in play weaving at a toy loom. Nabenchauk, 1993. (The numerals are to identify families from our larger, two-generation study of weaving apprenticeship, e.g., Greenfield, 1999b; Greenfield & Childs, 1996.) Photo by Patricia Greenfield.

FIG. 10.6. Girls (Loxa and Maruch 1-201) use the traditional kneeling position, even in newer activities such as drawing designs to embroider on their blouses. Nabenchauk, 1991. Photo courtesy of Lauren Greenfield.

to maintain a kneeling position for long periods of time can be lost with age (Maynard et al., 1999); Ashley was taught at age 23 to weave in Nabenchauk as part of an ethnographic study of weaving apprenticeship (Maynard, 1995). Unlike Zinacantec girls, she had not had extended and repeated kneeling experience at a young age, and, indeed, she encountered problems in learning to weave because she was not able to kneel for long periods of time. Kneeling was very painful for her and she resorted to sitting cross-legged, much to the derision of the Zinacantec teachers and other women who observed her weaving (Maynard et al., 1999). The absence of culturally mandated kneeling experience at a younger age had caused her to lose her ability to kneel for the long periods required by weaving. Her experience showed that there is a sensitive period during which this experience must take place.

Here I have used kneeling to demonstrate the interaction of biological sensitive periods with cultural practices. I now turn to more cognitive aspects of weaving, using Piagetian stage concepts. My thesis is that the timing of the transition from preoperations to concrete operations is a sensitive period, a developmental window, that is actualized differently in different cultures.

Developmentally Gradated Tools.   My theme here is that cultures have sets of artifacts and practices that respect and stimulate sensitive periods for cognitive and neural development. I argue that the developmental timing and order in which girls are exposed to various weaving tools show implicit knowledge of and respect for cognitive development. Specifically, these tools show implicit knowledge of the progression from the preoperational to the concrete operational stage and the timing of this progression. Vygotsky noted how much cognitive history is contained in cultural artifacts and that these artifacts function, in turn, as tools for the stimulation of current cognitive development (Scribner, 1985). I would like to take this line of thinking a step further: Not only cognitive history but also cognitive development can be contained in cultural artifacts. To provide evidence for this point, I analyze the cognitive requirements of a developmentally gradated set of Zinacantec weaving artifacts: the toy loom, the warping frame, and the real loom.

Play weaving on the toy loom, illustrated in Fig. 10.5, is widespread in Nabenchauk. It begins at age 3 or 4, in Piaget's preoperational period. It is used several years earlier than the real loom and warping frame; the latter is not used before age 6, the beginning of the concrete operational period. Preparing the real loom to weave on a warping frame is a concrete operational task, as I demonstrate later. Because the toy loom is just slightly different from the real loom, it does not require concrete operational thinking to set up. The difference lies in the ropes between the two end sticks, one rope on each side (Fig. 10.7). By holding together the two end sticks (shown at the top and bottom of the loom in Fig. 10.7), these ropes permit the warp or frame threads (the white threads in Fig. 10.7) to be wound directly on the loom. Figure 10.5 shows how the end sticks that constitute the loom are connected by a loop of ribbon (functionally equivalent to the rope in Fig. 10.7) that goes around the weaver's back (hence the name *backstrap*) to the post; the tension necessary to keep the loom from collapsing is provided by the weaver, who leans back against the strap. Note that, unlike the real loom (Fig. 10.8), the top and bottom end sticks are connected by the ribbon looped around them. The real loom (shown in Fig. 10.8) does not have the side ropes (Fig. 10.7) or ribbons (Fig. 10.5) holding the loom frame (top and bottom end sticks) together. Note that only the warp threads (multicolored in Fig. 10.8) hold the two end sticks together. However, these threads cannot be wound directly on the loom (the two end sticks) because if the warp threads were not there, the loom would collapse; the loom has nothing to hold the two end sticks together before the winding of the warp threads begins.

Therefore, a real loom must have the warp prewound on a separate apparatus, the *komen*, or warping frame, shown (with a warp already wound on it) in Fig. 10.9. My thesis is that winding the warp on a *komen* intrinsically involves concrete operational thinking. This is the case because winding on the *komen* requires mental transformation, the essence of concrete operations (e.g., Piaget, 1963/1977). The form of the warp threads wound on the *komen* (Fig. 10.9) is quite different from the form of the threads on the final loom (Fig. 10.8). Complex topological transformation is required to understand the connection between how one winds the warp and how the warp looks and functions on the loom. Let me illustrate this point with a sequence of photographs.

Figure 10.10a shows a *komen* or warping frame, ready to begin winding. In Fig. 10.10b, a girl has begun to wind the threads on the warping frame; in Fig. 10.10c she has gotten a bit farther. Figure 10.10d shows a close-up of the resulting configuration of threads. Compare this image with Fig. 10.8. Figure 10.8 shows how the warp might turn out (with additional winding and more colors) after being transferred to the loom. Note the difference in the configuration of threads between Fig. 10.10d where warp threads are still on the warping frame, and Fig. 10.8, where the warp threads have been transferred to the loom. Threads on the left side of the stick in the warping frame of Fig. 10.10d go to one end of the loom (e.g., top end stick in Fig. 10.8), while threads on the right side of the stick in the warping frame of Fig. 10.10d go to the other end of the loom (e.g., bottom endstick in Fig. 10.8).

This sequence illustrates an important cognitive point: that a complex series of mental transfomations is required for a weaver to understand the connection between how the threads are wound on the warping frame and

FIG. 10.7.   Toy loom. The side ropes that hold the two frame sticks together while the warp (white threads) is being wound are visible. Photo courtesy of Lauren Greenfield.

FIG. 10.8. Real loom. Note the absence of the side ropes; therefore, the warp threads hold the loom together. However, they cannot be wound directly onto the loom because the loom does not exist as connected sticks before the warp is wound.

FIG. 10.9. *Komen* or warping frame with warp threads already wound on it. Nabenchauk, 1991. Photo by Patricia Greenfield.

FIG. 10.10a.   The *komen* or warping frame, ready to begin. Nabenchauk, 1995. Photo by Patricia Greenfield.

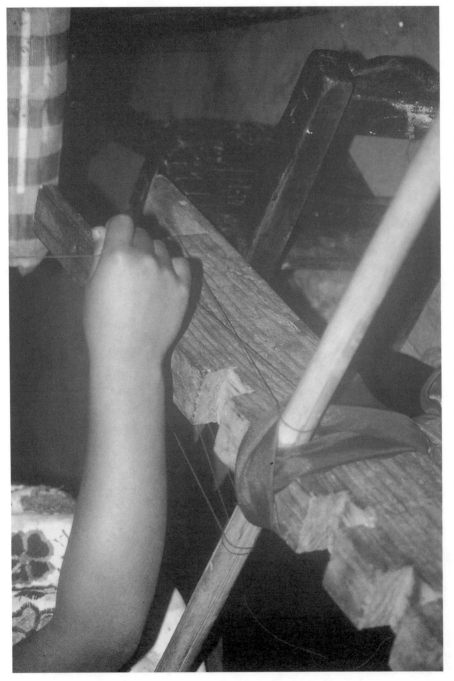

FIG. 10.10b. A girl has begun to wind on the frame. Nabenchauk, 1995. Photo by Patricia Greenfield.

FIG. 10.10c.   Girl has wound a few more threads. Nabenchauk, 1995.
Photo by Patricia Greenfield.

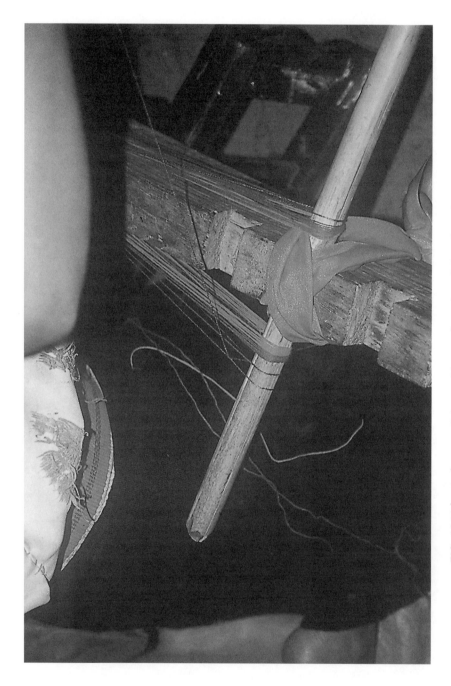

FIG. 10.10d. A close-up of the resulting configuration of threads. Nabenchauk, 1995. Photo by Patrica Greenfield.

how they end up in the configuration shown on the loom in Fig. 10.8. Because mental transformations characterize the Piagetian stage of concrete operations, winding a warp on the warping frame in order to set up a backstrap loom is a culture-specific concrete operational task.

I now compare the cognitive level required to set up a real loom with that required to set up a toy loom. Whereas to set up a real loom demands the mental transformations of concrete operations, mental transformations are not required for the toy loom. Because of the extra supporting rope or ribbon on the sides (Figs. 10.5 and 10.7), the warp can be wound directly on the loom. The sequence in Figs. 10.11a and 10.11b illustrates this central point. In Fig. 10.11a, a young girl has just started winding the warp directly on the loom, which is already set up. The top and bottom end sticks (left and right in the photo) are being held in place by white string connecting the sticks; one of the two side strings is shown clearly at the top of Figs. 10.11a and 10.11b.

In Fig. 10.11b, the young girl continues winding the warp between the endsticks, seen in the photograph. In Figs. 10.11a and 10.11b, the warp threads are being wound into their final position between two endsticks, similar, for example, to the way warp threads are stretched between endsticks on the looms shown in Figs. 10.7 and 10.8. Unlike winding the warp on a warping frame, there is no mental transformation required to go from the winding process to the set up loom.

The important conclusion from this analysis is that Piagetian theory is part of the Zinacantecs' implicit ethnotheory of development. Whereas Zinacantec girls start on the toy loom from age 3, they do not set up a real loom before age 6 at the earliest, the beginning of the normal age range of concrete operations. So, most interestingly, Piagetian theory is implicitly (but not explicitly) built into the developmental progression of Zinacantec weaving tools. If one thinks of Piagetian stages as age-dependent sensitive periods, then learning how to set up a real loom using a warping frame can be seen as an activity that actualizes concrete operations in a culture-specific form.

Cognitive Stages as Age-Dependent Sensitive Periods. What is the evidence for Piagetian stages as age-dependent sensitive periods and how does play weaving fit into this picture? I should like to draw upon a new theory of primate play by Fairbanks (2000) and propose that it applies both to human play in general and to play weaving in particular. Fairbanks (2000) has developed a theory of monkey play that posits the role of play in stimulating neuromuscular pathways that underlie particular adult monkey skills. She contrasts her theory with the theory that play functions as direct practice of an adult behavioral skill. She observes that because the height of each monkey-play form occurs years before the adult behavior, it would not

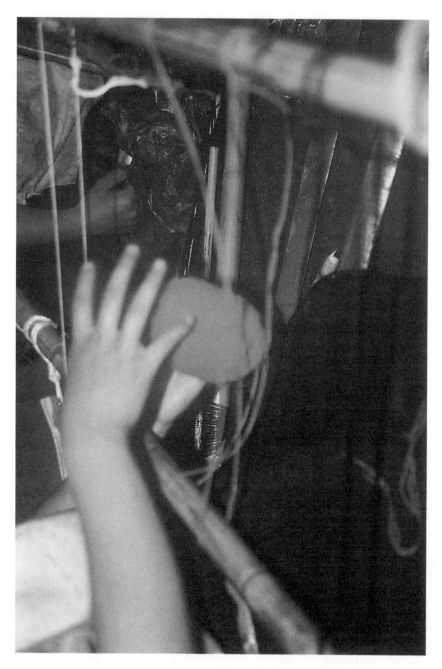

FIG. 10.11a. A young girl has just started winding the warp of her toy loom. Nabenchauk, 1995. Photo by Patricia Greenfield.

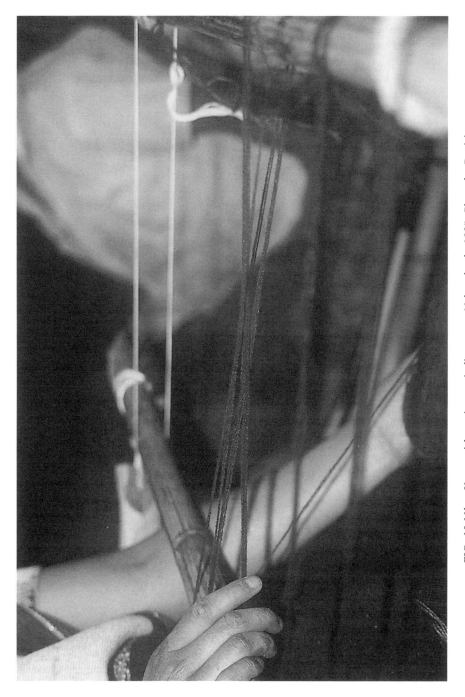

FIG. 10.11b. Young girl continues winding warp. Nabenchauk, 1995. Photo by Patricia Greenfield.

be very useful as practice for the adult behavior. However, the playful form is most frequent just at the time the relevant neural substrate for that particular activity is developing. For example, play fighting in monkeys reaches its maximum just as the neural circuitry for adult aggression is developing, but years before aggression is required in adult monkey social life.

Could this analysis apply to human play in general and to play weaving in particular? There are several parallels with Fairbanks' theory and data. First, there is the behavioral parallel: just as play fighting occurs in monkeys several years before the real thing, so does play weaving on the toy loom occur several years before weaving utilitarian items on the real loom. Second, Thatcher (1994) presented electroencephalogram evidence for spurts in neural development. These spurts are periods of neural instability that serve as developmental transition points in the nervous system. One of these transition points or spurts is at age 4 (Fischer & Rose, 1994), in the age range when play weaving begins.

My theoretical interpretation of these transition points in neural development is that they are sensitive periods—developmental windows—when stimulation, often in the form of culture-specific practices, actualizes maturationally specific neural circuits. It follows from this that play weaving could stimulate neural and neuromuscular pathways that provide a foundation for the later cognitive development required to weave on a real loom.

Fischer and Rose (1994) identified a second spurt in neural development that occurs between 6 and 10 years of age. This is precisely the period in which weaving on a real loom begins for most Zinacantec girls. It is also Piaget's period of concrete operations, which, as I have tried to illustrate, are indeed required for setting up a real loom. Hence, this spurt of neural development could provide a developmental window for the culture-specific actualization of concrete operations.

The Role of Values. One aspect of values relevant to this theory is the ethnotheory of development to which Zinacantecs connect weaving. First, they are in agreement that development is important: a girl will weave when she has enough soul (implies can listen to instruction, follow instruction, do what is needed and tolerate frustration), and this takes time to develop (Devereaux, personal communication, 1991). However, there is something different here, different both from our ethnotheories of development and from our formal theories of development (specifically those of Piaget and Vygotsky). According to the ethnographic research of Devereaux, Zinacantecs do not value weaving as a technical skill; rather, they value weaving for its social aspects: "the social interactional aspects of the learning process," the social utility of what is woven, and the enhancement of a girl's marriageability by being a good weaver.

To compare this with our ethnotheories and theories of development, the Zinacantecs do not have separate theories of cognitive and social development. For them, cognitive development is embedded in and subordinate to social interaction and the development of social activity. So, for example, one mother told us that her mildly retarded child (my diagnosis) would not be able to learn to weave. However, she explained, this was fine because the daughter had another useful job, putting thread on spools. It was not important to her that this job was cognitively much simpler than weaving. What mattered was that it made a contribution to the family. My point is the following: Cognitive development may follow a common pattern across cultures, but the value attached to it does not.

This subordination of cognitive skills to social relationships and goals is part of a system of values that emphasizes social interdependence in the definition of the self (Greenfield, 1994; Markus & Kitayama, 1991); this system of values is often called *collectivism* (Triandis, 1989). The emphasis on an individual's knowledge and technical expertise for its own sake is part of a system of values that emphasizes independence and autonomy (Greenfield, 1994; Markus & Kitayama, 1991; Mundy-Castle, 1974). Consistent with this value system, we, in the United States, for example, might value backstrap loom weaving if we thought it stimulated the development of concrete operational thought. However, this is not at all the way the Zinacantecs think about weaving. Instead, Zinacantecs are more interested in the social function than in the purely cognitive aspects of weaving. Zinacantec culture contrasts with ours in this respect.

Weaving Apprenticeship in Sociocultural Context. Let me illustrate the weaving apprenticeship practices in 1970, the year we did our first video study (Childs & Greenfield, 1980). In the course of the apprenticeship process, maturational readiness for Piagetian stages was met with Vygotskian scaffolding (Greenfield, 1984; Wood, Bruner, & Ross, 1976). Help in completing the novice's weaving task was provided by an expert, usually the mother. The interindividual activity theorized by Vygotsky (1978) is beautifully exemplified by a controlled, historical case study of two generations in a single family. This case illustrates the interaction of maturational readiness with the process of sociocultural construction.

Katal, age 9, was taped as she learned to weave in 1970. Throughout our videotaping of her weaving apprenticeship, Katal's mother, Xunka', serving as her teacher, was actively engaged in a process of scaffolding (Fig. 10.12). Xunka' was constantly anticipating her daughter's need for guidance and helping her to complete a weaving the daughter could not do on her own. For example, at one point during the taping, the mother entered the scene without being summoned, the teacher initiating help on her own. In anoth-

FIG. 10.12.   Video frame of Katal's mother, Xunka', helping Katal 1 to
weave. Nabenchauk, 1970. Video by Patricia Greenfield.

er typical instance of weaving scaffolding, Fig. 10.13 shows four hands on the
loom; two belong to the learner, two to the teacher. This image symbolizes
a paradigmatic interindividual process and demonstrates the interdependence of learner and teacher in weaving apprenticeship in 1970
(Greenfield, 1999).

We also noted that this highly scaffolded process of apprenticeship left
little room for error. In fact, errors were to be avoided because weaving
materials were costly and difficult to obtain. This is one aspect of the ecological component to which the socializing process of apprenticeship is
adapted.

Correlatively, this highly scaffolded process of apprenticeship left little
room for discovery. This was a quality well suited for the maintenance of
weaving tradition in a society in which learning to weave meant learning
to weave a closed stock of about four traditional patterns. Because the
teacher was the mother, a member of the older generation, this example
of weaving apprenticeship also illustrates the flow of authority from elder
to younger members (Greenfield & Childs, 1996). The collectivistic values
of interdependence and respect for the authority of elders were implicit
(although not explicit) in Zinacantec weaving apprenticeship.

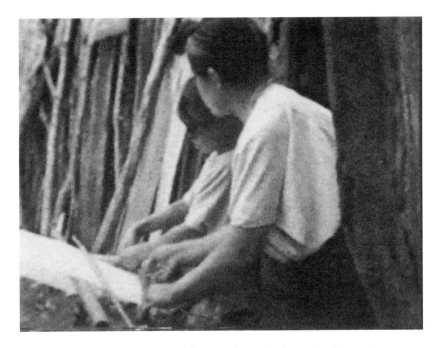

FIG. 10.13.   Video frame of four hands on the loom, Katal 1 and her
mother. Nabenchauk, 1970. Video by Patricia Greenfield.

Ecological Component: The Sociocultural Component
Is Adapted to an Ecological Niche

Reverence for stable tradition was related to the functionality of authority
in agrarian societies, where the older generation controlled land, the
essential means of subsistence and production (Collier, 1990). There was
an absolute view of the world. For example, when I asked why a group of
Zinacantecs were dressed like us rather than like them, the answer in
Tzotzil was, "They don't know how to dress." Innovation was a negative.
To be different was to gather opprobrium. This was a value interpretation.
However, note that it is primarily in a situation of value conflict, such as
the flouting of the Zinacantec dress code, that values move from the
implicit to the explicit level. Weaving was part of a collectivistic value system that emphasized interdependence in social relations, as well as
respect for authority and cognitive skills in the service of social goals. This
value system was well adapted to life in a subsistence, agriculturally based
economy, in which the younger generation depended on the elders' land
and in which cooperative exchanges of labor were required for the production of food and clothing.

Historical Component: The Ecological Niche Changes Over Time

In the decades from 1970 to the 1990s, there have been significant economic changes in the culture of Nabenchauk. Zinacantecs have moved from an agrarian, subsistence culture to a commercial society, from family- and community-held land to individually owned trucks and vans. Commerce promotes individualistic practices because nuclear family members are regularly moving in every direction independently of each other. For instance, a child may go to a nearby market to sell fruit with a neighbor, or a father may drive 18 hours one way to pick up some commodity to be sold. Members of a nuclear family operate more and more independently of each other as their involvement with commerce increases.

Even weaving has been commercialized. Woven textiles are sold both to outsiders (see Fig. 10.14) and to other Zinacantecs. In Fig. 10.14, woven and embroidered *servilletas* (napkins) are for sale to tourists and others who stop to buy; the *servilletas*, seen hanging in the background, are an item specially developed to sell to outsiders.

This type of entrepreneurship is part of a pattern of innovation and individualism. Innovation is seen in the change from a small closed stock of traditional woven patterns to a constant process of pattern innovation; each woven artifact is now unique, a mode of individual expression. For example, instead of a situation in which all males wear the same poncho (Fig. 10.15), we found an infinite variety of designs, giving a larger role to individual creativity and uniqueness (see Figs. 10.16a, 10.16b, and 10.16c). Although the style and background pattern of red and white stripes has stayed the same, the woven and embroidered decoration is distinct for each poncho, and this decoration is getting increasingly elaborate; this can be seen by comparing Fig. 10.16a (poncho from 1991) with Fig. 10.16b and Fig. 10.16c (ponchos from 1995); (Greenfield, 1999a, 1999b; Greenfield & Childs, 1996). Thus, the developmental outcome in terms of artistic expression has changed. Artistic expression has become more individualized.

This societal level of historical change also brought with it a change in the cultural practices concerned with weaving apprenticeship. This was revealed by our study of the next generation. Recall the case of Katal, who was learning to weave under her mother's tutelage in 1970 (Figs. 10.12 and 10.13). She grew up and had children of her own. In 1991, one of them, Loxa, was about the same age her mother had been in 1970, and we were able to study how she learned to weave. As with her mother, we again made a videotape of her weaving apprenticeship. Figure 10.17 presents a frame from the tape that is typical in many respects. Comparing Figs. 10.12 and 10.13 (mother learning to weave in 1970) with Fig. 10.17 (daughter learning to weave at same age in 1991), some differences are striking. Note that

FIG. 10.14. Woven and embroidered *servilletas* (used as tortilla covers, place mats, or hand towels) are for sale at a roadside stand. A Zinacantec woman makes a sale to an outsider, as her young daughter looks on. Nabenchauk, 1991. Photo courtesy of Lauren Greenfield.

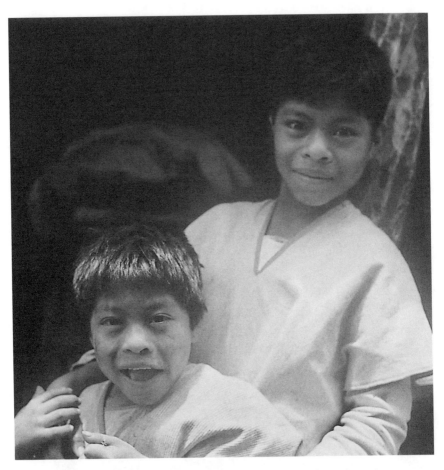

FIG. 10.15.   Pavlu brothers; both are wearing virtually identical ponchos.
Nabenchauk, 1970. Photo courtesy of Sheldon Greenfield.

in contrast to the previous generation (Fig. 10.12 and 10.13), Loxa's mother is not present in the frame. Instead, mother has assigned Loxa's older sister, Xunka', to serve as teacher. This change in the generation of the weaving teacher is related to the historical increase in innovation; that is,
weaving innovation is concentrated in teenage girls.

   In addition, the learner has become much more independent. Unlike
her mother's teacher, Loxa's teacher does not anticipate her need for
help. Note that the older sister is paying no visual attention to the weaving learner in Fig. 10.17; she is also much farther away from the learner
than the teacher in Fig. 10.12 and 10.13. The learner must take the initiative to summon her teacher when help is required. The scaffolding

FIG. 10.16a, b, and c.   Three distinctly different ponchos from the 1990s.
FIG. 10.16a.   Poncho from Nabenchauk, 1991. Photo courtesy of Lauren
Greenfield.

process is directed by learner rather than teacher. There has been a movement from interdependence to independence of learner and teacher. In
fact, the movement has been toward the independent discovery learning
favored by Piaget (1965a) and away from the scaffolded guidance
described by Wood, Bruner, and Ross (1976), based on Vygotsky's (1978)
theory (R. Gelman, personal communication, 1991).

     This method is adapted to a situation where errors are less costly, and
innovation and discovery are valued. Earlier, I noted that innovation in
woven patterns had come to be valued. In fact, errors had become less
costly too. There had been a switch from the more expensive (to buy) cotton and the more expensive (to produce) wool to the cheaper acrylic, a

FIG. 10.16b.   Poncho from Nabenchauk, 1995. Photo by Patricia Greenfield.

petroleum-based product of the 1980s oil boom in Mexico. In addition, the development of a transport business and the local commerce that followed made the materials (thread) easier to get. Whereas in 1970, cotton thread had to be purchased retail in the city of San Cristóbal, acrylic thread could now be purchased wholesale in San Cristóbal and resold retail in Nabenchauk. In other words, as materials became more plentiful, easier to get, and cheaper, errors became less costly over the same historical period in which apprenticeship changed (cf. Rogoff, 1991).

Theoretical Conclusion and Summary.   A general theoretical conclusion follows. In circumstances where the goal of apprenticeship is to maintain tradition and avoid error, the Vygotskian model of socially guided

FIG. 10.16c.   Poncho from Nabenchauk, 1995. Photo by Patricia Green-field.

learning is dominant; in circumstances where innovation is desired and errors are not too costly, the Piagetian model of independent discovery learning is dominant.

Note that there is still a process of sociocultural construction of weaving skill by which the maturational potential of a 9-year-old for concrete operations is actualized in backstrap loom weaving. But the nature of the sociocultural process has been transformed in this particular family.

FIG. 10.17.   Video frame of Katal 1's daughter, Loxa 1-201, learning to weave in 1991. Loxa is about the same age as her mother was when she was videotaped learning to weave in 1970. Nabenchauk, 1991. Video by Patricia Greenfield.

Testing Generality and Integrating Levels of the Theoretical Model: Structural Equation Modeling

Was the observed historical change general? If so, was the change in fact mediated by the hypothesized change in ecological conditions? We used interview and demographic census data, plus structural equation modeling, to answer these questions (Greenfield, Maynard, & Childs, in press). Such a model also takes account of within-culture individual differences in a way that a paradigmatic case study cannot.

Figure 10.18 presents a structural equation model (Bentler, 1989) that represents our results well. Several levels and aspects of the theoretical model are represented in this model and their interaction is represented quantitatively. The causality goes from the more distal and abstract to more proximal levels of influence, ending with the apprenticeship process. For this reason, structural equation modeling is well suited to test this type of multilevel theory. The model is based on 72 subjects from two generations, those girls observed learning to weave in 1970 and those observed learning to weave in 1991 or 1993.

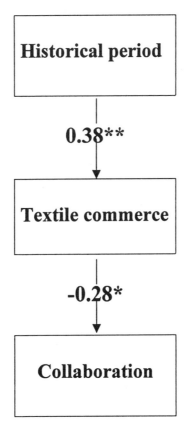

FIG. 10.18.   Structural equation model of the role of historical change and economic development in weaving apprenticeship. $**p < .01$, $*p < .05$, (Greenfield, Maynard, & Childs, in press).

Historical Level.   Top of the model: Was the girl a learner in 1970 or in the 1990s?

Ecological Level.   Next level down: How involved was the girl and her mother in textile commerce? This involvement was measured by a textile commerce scale that assessed the involvement of a girl and her mother in various aspects of textile commerce (Greenfield, Maynard, & Childs, in press). Sample scale items included selling *servilletas*, as in Fig. 10.14, and weaving on order for another Zinacantec.

Sociocultural Level.   How much collaborative activity on the weaving was there between teacher and learner? More, as in Figs. 10.12 and 10.13, or less, as in Fig. 10.17? We took collaborative activity as an index of interdependence.

Looking at Fig. 10.18, first note that each level, starting at the top, has a causal influence on the one below. Thus, historical period has a causal influence on weaving commerce; there is less commerce in the earlier period. Weaving commerce is, as hypothesized, a mediator between historical period and style of weaving apprenticeship. Note the excellent fit of the model to the data (Comparative Fit Index = 1.00, the maximum value) and the fact that each individual link is statistically significant.

A structural equation model allows individual differences to be part of a cultural model. Let me point out, for example, that there are individual differences in the ecological level. Note that historical period is not sufficient to predict apprenticeship. Individual variation in the ecological level not predicted entirely by historical period is also important. As the three levels of the model in Fig. 10.18 show, the relationship between historical period and apprenticeship is mediated by commerce. This is because commercial activity is not totally correlated with historical change; historical movement to a commercial way of life has been uneven within the population of Nabenchauk as a whole and even within the sample. This individual variability (and uneven social change) is captured by the weaving commerce scale. It is reflected in individual differences at the next level.

On the sociocultural level, textile commerce is causally related to teacher–learner collaboration in weaving apprenticeship (bottom arrow in Fig. 10.18). The more involved a girl and her mother are in textile commerce, the more frequently the teacher and learner work together, as in Figs. 10.12 and 10.13. This causal relationship is represented by the lowest arrow in the model shown in Fig. 10.18.

Uneven Social Change and Value Conflict: Interaction Between the Sociocultural and Ecological Components

In a situation of uneven social change, some people have changed considerably toward the new more individualistic cultural practices; others have changed much less. In this situation, one might expect some conflict between the two models of learning and apprenticeship. I now want to present some ethnographic evidence for conflicting mental models of the apprenticeship process. In the conflict, we see how underlying values are made explicit in the interpretive process of verbal discourse.

A little girl, Rosy, age 7, had spontaneously set up a toy loom. A teenage girl next door saw Rosy working, decided what she was doing was not good, and came over and undid everything. In Fig. 10.19, the teenage neighbor is in the middle of taking out Rosy's warp (frame threads). At this point it is important to present ethnographic evidence for conflicting mental models of the apprenticeship process. Clearly, the teenage neighbor felt that Rosy should not make her own mistakes. Of Rosy's warp, she

FIG. 10.19.   Teenage neighbor taking out Rosy's warp threads because she thinks Rosy 1-209 has done an inadequate job. Nabenchauk, 1995. Photo by Patricia Greenfield.

made the evaluative comment "bad." Rosy's mother had another model in mind: independent learning. "Let her do it by herself," said Rosy's mother, Maruch. "She doesn't know how," replied the self-appointed teenage teacher. This reply reflected the older model of scaffolded, relatively errorless learning, in sharp contrast to the mother's model. Later, Rosy's mother elaborated her model even more explicitly. She told me that it was better for Rosy to learn by herself, as her older sister had done. She had neither helped nor talked to Rosy's older sister, said the mother.

It is interesting that Rosy's family was much more heavily involved in commerce than was the neighbor's family, so the conflicting models also represented the two ecologies identified in the structural equation model (Fig. 10.18). Later, I asked Rosy about her own model of learning: Did she want to weave by herself or with help? She replied, "By myself." Upon further questioning, she added that it was "worse" to have the girl help. So Rosy, like her mother but unlike her self-styled teacher, had in mind the newer model of more independent apprenticeship.

EXTENSION OF THE THEORETICAL FRAMEWORK TO A MULTICULTURAL SOCIETY

We see learning to weave as but one example of two contrasting models of development mentioned earlier. These models, which I call the interdependence script and the independence script (Greenfield, 1994), are very basic and generative. Each model is a value framework that guides development, socialization, and behavior across many domains and in many cultures. Just as the model can explain cultural variability in Nabenchauk, it can explain cultural variability in Los Angeles. Here I focus on the sociocultural level of values.

Because change has been quite gradual in Nabenchauk and the Zinacantecs have kept changes pretty much under their own control in an intact community, this conflict between two models of socialization is relatively recent. The Zinacantecs are just beginning their journey on the path to individualism. However, the path is much more abrupt and disruptive for the many immigrants who come from rural Mexico to the United States. Although they have been much more integrated into the modern Mexican commercial economy, more touched by formal education, and less collectivistic than the Zinacantecs, they carry with them an ancestral value system that, relative to urban Los Angeles, is considerably more collectivistic. As research has shown, these immigrants, many from rural backgrounds, come to the United States with an interdependent script of socialization and development (Delgado-Gaitan, 1994; Greenfield, 1994; Tapia Uribe, LeVine, & LeVine, 1994). They meet a highly commercial, individualistic society that has a developmental script based on independence and autonomy (Greenfield, Raeff, & Quiroz, 1998; Raeff, Greenfield, & Quiroz, 2000). This culture conflict is expressed in many ways. For example, relative to the dominant culture, these immigrants experience parallel struggles to those of Rosy—between a model that stresses helpfulness and one that stresses doing it yourself. Here is an example:

> We arrived to start a study in an elementary school in West Los Angeles serving low-income Latino families. There had just been a major conflagration in the school involving the federally funded school breakfast program. The problem, as seen by the school, was that immigrant Latino mothers were accompanying their children to school, having breakfast with them, and helping their school age children to eat. When the school locked the families out of the schoolyard at breakfast, there was a major blow-up. (Quiroz & Greenfield, 1996)

One of the problems, as seen by the school personnel, was that these mothers were literally spoon-feeding their school-age kids instead of letting them eat by themselves. Such behavior was seen as leading to dependency rather than to the self-sufficiency advocated by the schools. On the other hand, helping the children eat their food also reflected Latino cultural values: being helpful toward one another is a highly desirable trait. Part of this conflict between the two value systems sets independence over and above helpfulness.

How general was this conflict over school breakfasts? Would it be correct to say that it reflected two contrasting cultural models of development? With Catherine Raeff and Blanca Quiroz, I conducted experimental research to investigate these questions (Raeff, Greenfield, & Quiroz, 2000). We administered a set of scenarios concerning social dilemmas at home and at school in two different schools. Each dilemma could be solved in a number of different ways, some consonant with an individualistic model of development and socialization, some consonant with a collectivistic model. Parents, teachers, and children were tested in two schools. Here I focus on one school in which the families were Latino immigrants. I have selected a sample dilemma that relates to the school breakfast issue; in this dilemma, which takes place at school, the issue is whether to help or not:

> It is the end of the school day, and the class is cleaning up. Denise isn't feeling well, and she asks Jasmine to help her with her job for the day which is cleaning the blackboard. Jasmine isn't sure that she will have time to do both jobs. What do you think the teacher should do? (Raeff, Greenfield, & Quiroz, 2000)

Figure 10.20 shows the results. Just as the school was unified in the opinion that mothers should not help their school-age children to eat, the majority of teachers (Fig. 10.20) were in agreement that Jasmine should not have to help Denise. Most frequently they thought a third person should be found to do the job (see Fig. 10.20). The point, often, was to get someone who would volunteer, that is, do the job by choice. They did not want to infringe on Jasmine's autonomy in achieving completion of her own job. Latino immigrant parents, in sharp contrast, were quite unified in their view that Jasmine should help Denise (Fig. 10.20). This response paralleled their desire to help their children eat breakfast.

This pattern of results shows a strong conflict between helpfulness and independent autonomy, with Latino parents supporting helpfulness and teachers (representing dominant societal culture) going for preserving Denise's autonomy. The Latino children (like Rosy) are often in between, constructing their own values out of two disparate and conflicting value systems. Here, for example, they are in between parents and teachers on helpfulness (Fig. 10.20).

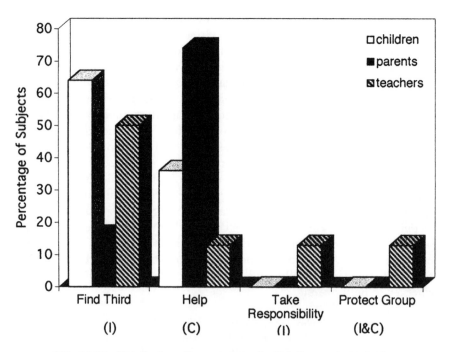

FIG. 10.20.   Distribution of responses to the "jobs" scenario by Latino immigrant parents, their children, and teachers. Figure courtesy of Catherine Raeff.

As we saw for the Zinacantecs, another aspect of the collectivistic world view is an ethnotheory of development in which cognitive skills are in the service of social goals. In the Latino immigrant ethnotheory, cognitive development is subordinated to social relations—just as it is for the Zinacantecs. This can lead to other kinds of cross-cultural value conflicts and misunderstandings in the individualistic schools. Here is an example:

> During one of our observations of a Los Angeles prekindergarten class made up of mostly Hispanic children, the teacher was showing a real chicken egg that would soon hatch. While teaching the physical properties of the egg, she asked children to describe eggs by thinking about the times they had cooked and eaten them. One child tried three times to talk about how she cooked eggs with her grandmother, but the teacher disregarded these comments in favor of a child who explained that the insides of eggs are white and yellow. (Greenfield, Raeff, & Quiroz, 1996, p. 44)

From the Latino point of view, the first child's answer was typical of the associations encouraged in her home culture of interdependence. That is, objects are most meaningful when they mediate social interactions. The child therefore acted on this value of interpersonal relations in answering the teacher's question. The teacher, however, did not recognize this effort on the part of the child and considered the social descriptions of the time they had eaten eggs as irrelevant; only physical descriptions of these occasions seemed to be valued (Greenfield, Raeff, & Quiroz, 1996). Here, the ethnotheory of development that places knowledge of the physical world as a means to social relationships is not valued or understood. Cognitive development expressed in relation to a social context is devalued.

CONCLUSION

I have tried to present a model that features a new idea: age-dependent sensitive periods for cultural learning. Because of the actualization of these biologically grounded developmental windows by the sociocultural component, the implication is that the same cognitive stage will take different forms in different cultures. Just as we would not expect concrete operational children in the United States to set up a backstrap loom, we might not expect concrete operational children in Nabenchauk to solve a problem in cross-classification (and in fact in an experiment I tried, concrete operational children could not do this; Greenfield, 1973).

My theoretical model also explains development as an interaction among various levels: the maturational, the sociocultural, the ecological, and the historical. Thus, biological concepts are integrated with sociocultural ones. I have tried to illustrate the complex interactions among the various levels by using findings from a relatively simple, homogeneous society, a Maya community in Chiapas, Mexico. I have selected a part of the model, the level of symbolic value interpretations, to test in Los Angeles, where we have found the same opposition between two different ethnotheories or models of development, a more collectivistic model stressing helpfulness and a more individualistic one stressing autonomy.

Integrating Theories of Social and Cognitive Development

In the West, there is a split between theories of social and cognitive development. This reflects a split in Western goals for development and a split in Western ethnotheories of development. In many cultures, such a split between the cognitive and the social is not the norm; cognitive skills are seen as a means to social goals. I propose that our formal theories are only as universal as the ethnotheories they presuppose. Therefore, we need a formal theory of development that does not presuppose the dominance of cognitive development nor the split between the social and the cognitive. In conclusion, we need a universal theory that transcends culture-specific ethnotheories of development. This requires a higher order theory that integrates different ethnotheories as alternative paths in a more universal theory of development.

ACKNOWLEDGMENTS

This chapter was originally presented at the Annual Symposium of the Jean Piaget Society, Santa Monica, CA, June, 1997. The research on which it is based was supported by the Spencer Foundation; the Wenner-Gren Foundation for Anthropological Research; the Fogarty International Center of National Institute of Health (Steven Lopez, Principal Investigator); El Colegio de la Frontera Sur, San Cristobal de las Casas, Chiapas, Mexico; the University of California at Los Angeles Urban Education Studies Center; the Harvard Chiapas Project (directed by Evon Z. Vogt); the Harvard Center for Cognitive Studies (codirected by Jerome Bruner); the Milton Fund of Harvard University; and the Radcliffe Institute. I would like to express my appreciation to our participants in Chiapas and Los Angeles and to my collaborators Carla Childs, Ashley Maynard, Leslie Devereaux, Catherine Raeff, and Blanca Quiroz. Thanks to my lab group for their useful and important feedback on earlier versions.

REFERENCES

Bentler, P. M. (1989). *EQS structural equations program manual*. Los Angeles: BMDP Statistical Software.

Bruner, J. S. (1964). On the course of cognitive growth. *American Psychologist, 19*, 1–15.

Bruner, J. S. (1977–1978). Symbols and texts as the tools of intellect. *Interchange, 8*(4), 1–15.

Bruner, J. S., & Olson, D. R. (1973). Learning through experience and learning through media. In G. Gerbner, L. P. Gross, & W. H. Melody (Eds.), *Communications technology and public policy*. New York: Wiley.

Childs, C. P., & Greenfield, P. M. (1980). Informal modes of learning and teaching: The case of Zinacanteco weaving. In N. Warren (Ed.), *Studies in cross-cultural psychology* (Vol. 2, pp. 269–316). London: Academic Press.

Cole, M., & Scribner, S. (1974). *Culture and thought: A psychological introduction*. New York: Wiley.

Collier, G. A. (1990). Seeking food and seeking money: Changing productive relations in a Highland Mexican community (Discussion Paper 11). United Nations Research Institute for Social Development, Geneva.

Dasen, P. R. (1984). The cross-cultural study of intelligence: Piaget and the Baolé. In P. S. Fry (Ed.), *Changing conceptions of intelligence and intellectual functioning: Current theory and research* (pp. 107–134). Amsterdam: North-Holland.

Delgado-Gaitan, C. (1994). Socializing young children in Mexican-American families: An intergenerational perspective. In P. M. Greenfield & R. R. Cocking (Eds.), *Cross-cultural roots of minority child development* (pp. 55–86). Hillsdale, NJ: Lawrence Erlbaum Associates.

Fairbanks, L. A. (2000). Behavioral development of nonhuman primates and the evolution of human behavioral ontogeny. In S. Parker, J. Langer, & M. Mackinney (Eds.), *Biology, brain, and behavior: The evolution of human development* (pp. 131–158). Santa Fe, NM: SAR Press.

Fischer, K. W. (1987). Relations between brain and cognitive development. *Child Development, 58*, 623–632.

Fischer, K. W., & Rose, S. P. (1994). Dynamic development of coordination of components in brain and behavior: A framework for theory. In G. Dawson & K. W. Fischer (Eds.), *Human behavior and the developing brain* (pp. 3–66). New York: Guilford.

Greenfield, P. M. (1966). On culture and conservation. In J. S. Bruner, R. R. Olver, & P. M. Greenfield, *Studies in cognitive growth* (pp. 225–256). New York: Wiley.

Greenfield, P. M. (1973). Comparing categorization in natural and artificial contexts: A developmental study among the Zinacantecos of Mexico. *Journal of Social Psychology, 93*, 157–171.

Greenfield, P. M. (1974). Cross-cultural research and Piagetian theory: Paradox and progress. In K. F. Riegel & J. A. Meacham (Eds.) (1976). *The developing individual in a changing world* (Vol. 1: Historical and cultural issues, pp. 322–333). The Hague: Mouton.

Greenfield, P. M. (1984). A theory of the teacher in the learning activities of everyday life. In B. Rogoff & J. Lave (Eds.), *Everyday cognition: Its development in social context* (pp. 117–138). Cambridge, MA: Harvard University Press.

Greenfield, P. M. (1993). Representational competence in shared symbol systems: Electronic media from radio to video games. In R. R. Cocking & K. A. Renninger (Eds.), *The development and meaning of psychological distance* (pp. 161–183). Hillsdale, NJ: Lawrence Erlbaum Associates.

Greenfield, P. M. (1994). Independence and interdependence as developmental scripts: Implications for theory, research, and practice. In P. M. Greenfield & R. R. Cocking (Eds.), *Cross cultural roots of minority child development* (pp. 1–37). Hillsdale, NJ: Lawrence Erlbaum Associates.

Greenfield, P. M. (1999a). Cultural change and human development. In E. Turiel (Ed.), *Culture, evolution, and development* (pp. 38–59). *New Directions in Child Development.* San Francisco: Jossey-Bass.

Greenfield, P. M. (1999b). Historical change and cognitive change: A two-decade follow-up study in Zinacantan, a Maya community in Chiapas, Mexico. *Mind, Culture, and Activity, 6,* 92–108.

Greenfield, P. M., & Childs, C. (1996, November). Learning to weave in Zinacantan: A two-decade follow-up study of historical and cognitive change. In I. Zambrano & E. Z. Vogt (Chairs), *Microcosms of the social world: Formal and informal education in the Maya area of Chiapas.* Symposium presented at the American Anthropological Association, San Francisco.

Greenfield, P. M., Maynard, A., & Childs, C. P. (in press). History, culture, learning, and development. *Cross-Cultural Research.*

Greenfield, P. M., Raeff, C., & Quiroz, B. (1996). Cultural values in learning and education. In B. Williams (Ed.), *Closing the achievement gap: A vision for changing beliefs and practices* (pp. 37–55). Alexandria, VA: Association for Supervision and Curriculum Development.

Greenfield, P. M., Raeff, C., & Quiroz, B. (1998). Cross-cultural conflict in the social construction of the child. *Aztlán, 23,* 115–125.

Heath, S. B. (1993). *Ways with words: Language, life, and work in communities and classrooms.* New York: Cambridge University Press.

LeVine, R. A. (1977). Child rearing as cultural adaptation. In P. H. Leiderman, S. R. Tulkin, & A. Rosenfeld (Eds.), *Culture and infancy: Variations in the human experience* (pp. 15–27). New York: Academic Press.

Markus, H. R., & Kitayama, S. (1991). Culture and the self: Implications for cognition, emotion, and motivation. *Psychological Review, 98,* 224–253.

Maynard, A. E. (1995). *The Zinacantec model of teaching and learning.* Master's thesis, Department of Psychology, University of California, Los Angeles.

Maynard, A., Greenfield, P. M., & Childs, C. P. (1999). Culture, history, biology, and body: Native and non-native acquisition of technological skill. *Ethos,* 379–402.

Molleson, T. (1996, March). The physical anthropology of role specialization from Neolithc times. In *Culture and the uses of the body.* In G. Lewis & F. Sigaut (Chairs). Symposium conducted at the meeting of the Fondation Fyssen Colloquium, St. Germain-en-Laye, France.

Mundy-Castle, A. C. (1974). Social and technological intelligence in Western and non-Western cultures. *Universitas, 4,* 46–52.

Newport, E. L. (1988). Constraints on learning and their role in language acquisition: Studies of the acquisition of American Sign Language. *Language Sciences, 10,* 147–152.

Ochs, E., & Schieffelin, B. B. (1984). Language acquisition and socialization: Three developmental stories and their implications. In R. Shweder & R. LeVine (Eds.), *Culture theory: Essays on mind, self, and emotion* (pp. 276–320). Cambridge, England: Cambridge University Press.

Piaget, J. (1963/1977). Intellectual operations and their development. In H. E. Gruber & J. J. Vonèche (Eds.), *The essential Piaget: An interpretive reference and guide* (pp. 342–358). New York: Basic Books. (Original work published in 1963)

Piaget, J. (1965a/1977). Developments in pedagogy. In H. E. Gruber & J. J. Vonèche (Eds.), *The essential Piaget: An interpretive reference and guide* (pp. 696–719). New York: Basic Books. (Original work published in 1965)

Piaget, J. (1965b). *The moral judgment of the child.* New York: The Free Press.

Piaget, J. (1972). Intellectual evolution from adolescence to adulthood. *Human Development, 15,* 1–12.

Piaget, J., & Inhelder, B. (1969). *The psychology of the child.* New York: Basic Books.

Piaget, J. (1977). Foreword. In H. E. Gruber & J. J. Vonèche (Eds.), *The essential Piaget: An interpretive reference and guide* (pp. xi–xii). New York: Basic Books.

Quiroz, B., & Greenfield, P. M. (1996). Cross-cultural value conflict: removing a barrier to Latino school achievement. Unpublished manuscript, Department of Psychology, UCLA.

Rabain, J. (1979). L'enfant du lignage [Child of the lineage]. Paris: Payot.

Raeff, C., Greenfield, P. M., & Quiroz, B. (2000). Developing interpersonal relationships in the cultural contexts of individualism and collectivism. In S. Harkness, C. Raeff, & C. R. Super (Eds.), The social construction of the child: The nature of variability. New Directions in Child Development (pp. 59–74). San Francisco: Jossey-Bass.

Rogoff, B. (1991). Apprenticeship in thinking. New York: Oxford University Press.

Rogoff, B., Baker-Sennett, J., Lacasa, P., & Goldsmith, D. (1995). Development through participation in sociocultural activity. In J. Goodnow, P. Miller, & F. Kessel (Eds.), Cultural practices as contexts for development (pp. 45–65). San Francisco: Jossey-Bass.

Saxe, G. B. (1991). Culture and cognitive development: Studies in mathematical understanding. Hillsdale, NJ: Lawrence Erlbaum Associates.

Scribner, S. (1985). Vygotsky's uses of history. In J. V. Wertsch (Ed.), Culture, communication, and cognition: Vygotskian perspectives (pp. 119–145). Cambridge, England: Cambridge University Press.

Scribner, S., & Cole, M. (1981). The psychology of literacy. Cambridge, MA: Harvard University Press.

Shweder, R. A., & Bourne, E. J. (1982). Does the concept of the person vary cross-culturally? In R. A. Shweder & R. A. Levine (Eds.), Culture theory: Essays on mind, self, and emotion (pp. 158–199). New York: Cambridge University Press.

Super, C. M., & Harkness, S. (1997). The cultural structuring of child development. In J. W. Berry, P. R. Dasen, & T. S. Saraswathi (Eds.), Handbook of cross-cultural psychology: Vol. 2. Basic processes and human development (2nd ed., pp. 1–39). Boston: Allyn & Bacon.

Tapia Uribe, F. M., LeVine, R. A., & LeVine, S. E. (1994). Maternal behavior in a Mexican community: The changing environments of children. In P. M. Greenfield & R. R. Cocking (Eds.), Cross-cultural roots of minority child development (pp. 41–54). Hillsdale, NJ: Lawrence Erlbaum Associates.

Thatcher, R. W. (1994). Cyclical cortical reorganization: Origins of human cognitive development. In G. Dawson & K. W. Fischer (Eds.), Human behavior and the developing brain (pp. 232–266). New York: Guilford.

Triandis, H. C. (1989). Cross-cultural studies of individualism and collectivism. Nebraska Symposium on Motivation, 37, 41–133.

Vygotsky, L. S. (1962). Thought and language. Cambridge, MA: MIT Press.

Vygotsky, L. S. (1978). Mind in society: The development of higher psychological processes. Cambridge, MA: Harvard University Press.

Vygotsky, L. S., & Luria, A. R. (1993). Studies on the history of behavior: Ape, primitive, and child (V. I. Golod & J. E. Knox, Trans.). Hillsdale, NJ: Lawrence Erlbaum Associates. (Original work published 1930)

Weisner, T. (1984). A cross-cultural perspective: Ecocultural niches of middle childhood. In A. Collins (Ed.), The elementary school years: Understanding development during middle childhood (pp. 335–369). Washington, DC: National Academy Press.

Whiting, B. B., & Whiting, J. W. M. (1975). The children of six cultures: A psychocultural analysis. Cambridge, MA: Harvard University Press.

Wober, M. (1974). Towards an understanding of the Kiganda concept of intelligence. In J. W. Berry & P. R. Dasen (Eds.), Culture and cognition (pp. 261–280). London: Methuen.

Wood, D., Bruner, J. S., & Ross, G. (1976). The role of tutoring in problem solving. Journal of Child Psychology and Psychiatry, 17, 89–100.

Author Index

Subject Index